MAKE-BELIEVE MEDIA
The Politics of Entertainment

Michael Parenti

MAKE-BELIEVE MEDIA
The Politics of Entertainment

ST. MARTIN'S PRESS
NEW YORK

Senior editor: Don Reisman
Managing editor: Patricia Mansfield
Project editor: Elise Bauman
Production supervisor: Alan Fischer
Text design: Leon Bolognese and Associates
Photo researcher: Inge King
Cover design: Tom McKeveny

Manufactured in the United States of America.
65432
fedcb

For information, write:
St. Martin's Press, Inc.
175 Fifth Avenue
New York, NY 10010

ISBN: 0-312-05894-2
    0-312-05603-6 (pbk.)

Library of Congress Cataloging-in-Publication Data

Parenti, Michael, 1933–
    Make-believe media: politics of film and television / Michael
Parenti
    p.   cm.
    ISBN 0-312-05894-2: $19.95
    1. Motion pictures—Political aspects—United States.
2. Television and politics—United States. 3. Television
broadcasting—United States—Influence. 4. Social values.
I. Title.
PN1995.9.P6P37   1991
302.23'4—dc20   90-29154
                                                        CIP

ACKNOWLEDGMENTS

Excerpt from "Cruel & Unusual: Negative Images of Arabs in American Popular Culture," by Laurence Michalak, from *ADC Issues,* January 1984. © ADC Research Institute 1988. Reprinted by permission.
"Red-Bashing on Madison Avenue," by Michael Olmert, from *The New York Times,* December 22, 1985. © 1985 by The New York Times Company. Reprinted by permission.

Acknowledgments and copyrights are continued at the back of the book on page 231, which constitutes an extension of the copyright page.

 The text of this book has been printed on recycled paper.

Preface

Make-Believe Media tells how movies and television have propagated images and themes that support militarism, imperialism, racism, sexism, authoritarianism, and other undemocratic values. I discuss many films and television programs. Do I select only the ones that paint the entertainment media in the worst possible light? If anything, I give disproportionately greater attention to the relatively few quality films and programs of progressive hue. While only a small fraction of the immense number of films that boost militaristic, anti-labor, and other conservative themes are treated herein, proportionately more of the progressive ones are touched upon. Thus, the selection is skewed toward the more enlightened productions.

For almost every criticism I make of the "make-believe media," one could find some exceptions. I do not claim that the political biases criticized on the pages ahead are the only ones in the entertainment media, but they are the predominant ones.

Some readers will maintain that one or another topic has not been given sufficient treatment. There is no separate chapter on women, for instance. But I do deal with the way women are treated or mistreated by the media within the context of almost every chapter in this book. There is no mention of gays and lesbians or the elderly, and only scant mention of the media's stereotypic treatment of Latinos, Asians, Arabs, Native American Indians, and various other social groups and themes. All I can do is plead for a division of labor. There was no way I could do justice to every important subject and keep this volume to a manageable size. The interested reader should consult the references provided at the end of the book that deal with the areas I have not treated.

Even for the subjects I do cover, I make no claim that the treatment is definitive. Many films and programs have gone unmentioned, including no doubt some that the reader loves or loves to hate.

My hope is that readers will find this critical treatment of the entertainment media to be entertaining as well as informative. There is nothing wrong with mindless relaxation in front of a screen now and then. What is wrong is when it becomes the national pastime, a way of life, preempting our experiences and providing us with a prefabricated understanding of what the world is supposed to be. And this it does for too many people.

So I hope this book leaves at least some individuals better attuned to what is false, contrived, and politically distorted about our entertainment media. Perhaps a better awareness of such things will cause us to waste fewer hours of our precious lives in front of both the big and little screens, allowing us more time for reading, conversing, relating to our friends and families, criticizing social injustice, and becoming active citizens of our society and the agents of our own lives.

Acknowledgments

I wish to thank Shelley Moskowitz, Linda Valentino, Kathy Lipscomb, and Jane Hallaran for the important assistance they rendered. Eric Smooden of American University has my appreciation for his valuable criticisms as do Steve Barkin, University of Maryland–College Park, and Timothy Cook, Harvard University.

Once again the staff at St. Martin's Press has proven most helpful in the production of this book, especially my editor Don Reisman, who is the best editor an author might hope for, and my project editor, Elise Bauman. My thanks also to Hollywood producer Edward Lewis, who provided me with some helpful information.

Michael Parenti

Contents

MAKE-BELIEVE MEDIA
The Politics of Entertainment

1

Political Entertainment

Make-believe. The term connotes the playful fantasies of our childhood, a pleasant way of pretending. But in the world created by movies and television, make-believe takes on a more serious meaning. In some way or other, many people come to believe the fictional things they see on the big and little screens. The entertainment media are the make-believe media; they make us believe.

Today, very little of our make-believe is drawn from children's games, storytelling, folktales, and fables, very little from dramas and dreams of our own making. Instead we have the multibillion-dollar industries of Hollywood and television to fill our minds with prefabricated images and themes. Nor are these just idle distractions. I will argue that such images often have real ideological content. Worse still, they discourage any critical perception of the great and sometimes awful realities of our lives and sociopolitical system, implanting safe and superficial pictures in our heads. Even if supposedly apolitical in its intent, the entertainment industry is political in its impact.

How can we speak of Hollywood films and television shows as being "purely" entertainment when they regularly propagate certain political themes and carefully avoid others? To borrow Robert Cirino's phrase: "We're being more than entertained."[1] Hollywood and television are permeated with class, racial, gender, and other political biases. George Gerbner argues that all media carry a "hidden curriculum" of values and explanations about how things happen.[2] The sociologist Hal Himmelstein believes that through its settings, music, words, and stories, television has become "one of our society's principal repositories of ideology."[3] A leading communications critic, Herbert Schiller, writes that "one central myth dominates the world of fabricated fantasy; the idea that [media] entertainment and recreation are value-free, have no

1

point of view, and exist outside . . . the social process."[4] Another critic, Erik Barnouw, concludes: "Popular entertainment is basically propaganda for the status quo."[5]

In accord with those observations, I will try to demonstrate in the chapters ahead that over the years, films and television programs have propagated images and ideologies that are supportive of imperialism, phobic anticommunism, capitalism, racism, sexism, militarism, authoritarian violence, vigilantism, and anti–working-class attitudes. More specifically, media dramas teach us that:

- Individual effort is preferable to collective action.

- Free enterprise is the best economic system in the world.

- Private monetary gain is a central and worthy objective of life.

- Affluent professionals are more interesting than blue-collar or ordinary service workers.

- All Americans are equal, but some (the underprivileged) must prove themselves worthy of equality.

- Women and ethnic minorities are not really as capable, effective, or interesting as White males.

- The police and everyone else should be given a freer hand in combatting the large criminal element in the United States, using generous applications of force and violence without too much attention to constitutional rights.

- The ills of society are caused by individual malefactors and not by anything in the socioeconomic system.

- There are some unworthy persons in our established institutions, but they usually are dealt with and eventually are deprived of their positions of responsibility.

- U.S. military force is directed only toward laudable goals, although individuals in the military may sometimes abuse their power.

- Western industrial and military might, especially that of the United States, has been a civilizing force for the benefit of "backward" peoples throughout the Third World.

- The United States and the entire West have long been threatened from abroad by foreign aggressors, such as Russians, Communist terrorists, and swarthy hordes of savages, and at home by un-American subversives and conspirators. These threats can be eradi-

cated by a vigilant counterintelligence and by sufficient doses of
force and violence.

The Hollywood director Samuel Goldwyn once said that if you
want to send a message use Western Union. Hollywood is strictly an
entertainment business and not a purveyor of social messages or political causes, he maintained. In fact, Hollywood, like television, is very
much in the business of sending political messages. Certainly not the
kind of reformist or dissident messages that Goldwyn objected to, but
ones—like those listed above—with which he felt comfortable, so comfortable that he did not think they had political content.

What the media actually give us is something that is neither purely
entertainment nor purely political. It is a hybrid that might be called
"political entertainment." The entertainment format makes political
propagation all the more insidious. Beliefs are less likely to be preached
than assumed. Woven into the story line and into the characterizations,
they are perceived as entertainment rather than as political judgments
about the world. When racial subjugation is transmuted into an amusing Sambo and imperialist violence into an adventuresome Rambo,
racism and imperialism are more likely to be accepted by viewers, who
think they are merely being entertained. "Beliefs, attitudes, and values
are more palatable and credible to an audience when they are molded
and reinforced by characters and program plots than when they are
preached by a newscaster or speaker for a particular cause."[6] To quote
Schiller:

> For manipulation to be most effective, evidence of its presence
> should be nonexistent. When the manipulated believe things are the
> way they are naturally and inevitably, manipulation is successful. In
> short, manipulation requires a false reality that is a continuous de-
> nial of its existence.
>
> It is essential, therefore, that people who are manipulated be-
> lieve in the neutrality of their key social institutions. They must be-
> lieve that government, the media, education, and science are beyond
> the clash of conflicting social interests.[7]

Seeing Is Believing

People are affected by social forces sometimes far removed from their
immediate perceptions. They perceive only a relatively small portion of
the influences that play upon them. In modern mass society, people rely

to a great extent on distant imagemakers for cues about a vast world. In both their entertainment and news shows, the media invent a reality much their own.[8] Our notion of what a politician, a detective, a corporate executive, a farmer, an African, or a Mexican-American is like; what rural or inner-city life should be; our anticipations about romantic experience and sexual attractiveness, crime and foreign enemies, dictators and revolutionaries, bureaucrats and protestors, police and prostitutes, workers and Communists, are all heavily colored by our exposure to the media.

Many of us have never met an Arab, but few of us lack some picture in our minds of what an Arab is supposed to be like. This image will be more a stereotype than a reality, and if drawn largely from the mass media, it is likely to be a rather defamatory stereotype.[9] As Walter Lippmann noted, stereotypic thinking "precedes reason," and "as a form of perception [it] imposes a certain character on the data of our senses."[10] When we respond to a real-life situation with the exclamation, "Just like in the movies," we are expressing recognition and even satisfaction that our media-created mental frames find corroboration in the real world.

The media images in our heads influence how we appraise a host of social realities, including our government's domestic and foreign policies. If we have "learned" from motion pictures and television dramas that our nation is forever threatened by hostile alien forces, then we are apt to support increased military spending and CIA interventions. If we have "learned" that inner-city denizens are violent criminals, then we are more apt to support authoritarian police measures and cuts in human services to the inner city. Remarking on the prevalence of media-induced stereotypes of African-Americans, Ellen Holly put it well:

> When I express concern for [the image of Black people] in the media, don't imagine for one moment that anything as shallow as a racial ego posture is involved. The way we are perceived by this society affects the most basic areas of our lives. When you apply for a job the interviewer in personnel reacts to you not only in terms of who you are but also in terms of who he *thinks* you are. There are countless images floating around in his head and many of them are traceable to the media. You may sit in front of him as a neatly dressed, intelligent female who would do an efficient job, but if he has been fed one stereotype too many he may look and see not you but Flip Wilson's "Geraldine" goofing on the job, painting her fingernails and calling up her boyfriend to chat on company time. If so, for all your qualifications, you're not the one who is going to get the job. . . .

Again and again I have seen Black actors turned down for parts because they were told that they did not look the way a Black person should or sound the way a Black person should. What is this business of should? What kind of box are we being put into? I have seen Black writers told that the Black characters they put down on a page were not believable because they were too intelligent.[11]

Audiences usually do some perceptual editing when watching a movie or TV program, projecting their own viewpoint upon the performance. But this editing is itself partly conditioned by the previously internalized images fed to audiences by the same media they are now

Media Influence Is Sometimes for the Better

Those who doubt that the media can influence actual behavior might want to ponder this report by Diana Maychick, which appeared in the New York Post on February 9, 1983. It describes audience behavior during Gandhi, a movie that portrayed the courage, sacrifice, and nonviolent collective action of India's patriots under Mohandas Gandhi's leadership.

At the Ziegfeld Theater [in New York City], Gandhi, starring Ben Kingsley, is taming the thousand plus crowds who daily fill the 1140 plush red velour seats at 12, 4, and 8 P.M. Once the three-hour epic is half over, the audience remembers the value of courtesy.

"They come here anxious and impatient about seats. Outside, we have to monitor the line. [People wait for approximately 45 minutes to an hour]," said Ziegfeld manager Manual Soto. "But once the movie begins, something happens. The people calm down. . . . And during intermission, they're like different people from the usual rude New Yorkers," Soto said about the effect of Gandhi, which has grossed $11.6 million nationwide.

At intermission, moviegoers wait patiently on lines for candy, for the telephone, and for the bathrooms.

"I've never seen anything like it," says Nadege Guillame, a concession stand employee. Protocol is evident on popcorn lines; patrons voluntarily speed up the process by forming sublines composed of those who prefer small containers, large ones, and extra butter.

"You don't have to push to get ahead. That's what this movie is all about," said George Vardas on a recent Saturday.

"It's the weirdest thing," says Ziegfeld ticket-taker Lionel Stevens. "We don't have any problems with crowd control. This Gandhi must've been something else."

viewing. In other words, rather than being rationally critical of the images and ideologies of the entertainment media, our minds—after prolonged exposure to earlier programs and films—sometimes become active accomplices in our own indoctrination.

We are probably far more affected by what we see than we realize. Jeffrey Schrank notes that 90 percent of the nation's adult viewers consider themselves to be "personally immune" to the appeals of TV advertisements, yet these viewers account for about 90 percent of all sales of advertised products.[12] While we might think it is always other people (less intelligent than ourselves) who are being manipulated by sales appeals and entertainment shows, the truth might be something else.

Another investigator, Jerry Mander, argues that media images are "irresistible," since our brains absorb them regardless of how we might consciously regard such images. Children believe that what they are seeing in the make-believe media is real. They have no innate capacity to distinguish between real and unreal images. Only as they grow older, after repeated assurances from their elders, do they begin to understand that the stories and characters on the big and little screens do not exist

Media Influence Is Sometimes for the Worse

The former United States president Ronald Reagan has credited the movie *Mr. Smith Goes to Washington* as the one that most affected his life and led to his quest for the nation's highest office.

"I began to realize, through the power of that motion picture, that one man can make a difference," said Mr. Reagan. He made his statements as part of the all-star video gala to celebrate the opening of the Disney–MGM Studio's Theme Park in Florida.

World leaders, including the British prime minister, Mrs. Margaret Thatcher, and the Polish Solidarity leader, Lech Walesa, along with celebrities such as Jimmy Stewart and Mickey Rooney, will be discussing the films that made deep impressions on them.

Stewart starred in *Mr. Smith Goes to Washington,* playing a man who fought corruption in the Senate. The 1939 film became one of the most beloved of director Frank Capra's optimistic fables.

"When Jimmy Stewart walked the halls of the Capitol building, I walked with him," said Mr. Reagan. "When he stood in awe of that great man at the Lincoln Memorial, I bowed my head, too."

NZPA-AP report in *The Press* (Christchurch, New Zealand), April 6, 1989.

in real life. In other words, their ability to reject media images as unreal has to be learned.[13] The problem does not end there, however. Even as adults, when we *consciously* know that a particular movie or television program is fictional, we still "believe" it to some extent; that is, we still accumulate impressions that lead to beliefs about the real world. When drawing upon the images in our heads, we do not keep our store of media imagery distinct and separate from our store of real-world imagery. "The mind doesn't work that way," Mander concludes.[14]

It has been argued that the claims made about media influence can be unduly alarmist; it is not all a matter of our helpless brains being electronically pickled by the sinister media. Indeed, things can be overstated, but that is no excuse for dismissing the important impact the media do have. Consider some of the more troubling instances such as the "copycat" or "trigger" effects, when media exposure sparks imitative responses from viewers. One sociologist reports that suicides (along with auto fatalities and airplane accidents) increase significantly for a brief period immediately after news reports about suicide.[15] Probably the most dramatic instance of copycat behavior was the rash of self-killings following the news that Marilyn Monroe had taken her life. Other incidents are worth pondering:

- After *The Deer Hunter* began playing in theaters in 1979, at least twenty-five viewers around the country reenacted the movie's Russian roulette scene and blew their brains out.

- NBC showed the film *The Doomsday Flight,* about a man who tries to extract a ransom from an airline after planting a bomb on one of its planes. Within a week, a dozen bomb threats were reported by the major airlines, a dramatic increase over the previous month.

- A woman in Boston's Roxbury district was doused with gasoline and burned to death shortly after the telecasting of the film *Fuzz,* which portrayed a similar act.

- A fourteen-year-old whiz kid in Syracuse committed a series of robberies fashioned after techniques he saw on "Mission Impossible." He was apprehended only after a friend informed the police.

- In Los Angeles, a maid caught a seven-year-old boy sprinkling ground glass into his family's dinner. He said he wanted to see if it would work as it did on television.[16]

For some viewers, it is less a matter of consciously imitating the media and more an inability to distinguish between the real world and make-believe. Some years ago it was reported that an actor who played a villainous character on "Secret Storm" was shot by an irate viewer. Eileen Fulton, who played the much-hated Lisa on "As the World Turns," was assaulted by an angry viewer who called her "a terrible woman."[17]

A half-century ago Orson Welles caused panic across the nation with his radio dramatization of an invasion from Mars. Thousands of people mistook the program for an actual newscast. Presumably, audiences have become more media-sophisticated since then. Yet such panic reactions are not unknown today. In 1983, for instance, NBC ran a made-for-television film *Special Bulletin* about peace activists who take hostages on a boat outside Charleston, South Carolina, and demand the dismantling of nuclear warheads. In the ensuing confrontation, the nuclear device on the boat—which the protestors are using as a threat—accidentally detonates, destroying Charleston and its environs. The movie was done with grainy film and a handheld camera to give it a documentary effect. However, the word "dramatization" was also flashed across a corner of the screen every few minutes. Obviously, the show's producers anticipated that many viewers might have difficulties telling fact from fiction. Indeed, despite the precaution of the repeatedly flashed message, the network was swamped with calls from concerned people who thought the explosion had really taken place. Perhaps many viewers simply did not know the meaning of "dramatization" or were so convinced by the documentary quality of the film as to place no significance on the word.

The more time people spend watching television and movies, the more their impressions of the world seem to resemble those of the make-believe media. Gerbner and Gross found that heavy TV users, having been fed abundant helpings of television crime and violence, are more likely to overestimate the amount of crime and violence that exists in real life. They are also more apt to overestimate the number of police in the United States and the percentage of persons with professional jobs. (Professionals and police are overrepresented on TV as opposed to other service and blue-collar employees.) "While television may not directly cause the results that have turned up in our studies, it certainly can confirm or encourage certain views of the world."[18]

Consider how media's advertisements influence consumption patterns. Bombarded by junk-food television commercials over the years, Americans, especially younger ones, changed their eating habits dramatically. Compared to the pre-TV days of the 1940s, per capita consumption of vegetables, fruits, and dairy products was down 20 to 25 percent by the mid-1970s, while consumption of cakes, pastry, soft drinks, and other snacks was up 70 to 80 percent.[19] Television advertising campaigns transformed "soda pop" from something consumed at ball games and picnics to a beverage drunk daily with almost every meal and between meals, complete with "family-size" bottles. In 1961, after years of television ads, annual soft-drink consumption was up to 128 bottles per capita. By 1981, following a still more intense media blitz, it rose to 412.3 bottles per person.[20] This represented not only a dramatic increase in quantity, but a transformation in the social definition of the product itself—from an occasional indulgence to a national drink.

Along with commercials, entertainment shows influence consumption patterns. A salesman at Continental Gun Shop in Miami reported: "Everybody comes in and bugs me about that Bren 10mm semi[automatic] that guy uses in 'Miami Vice.' " The Bren sold like hotcakes at $885 each.[21] Manufacturers have become aware of the "product placement" opportunities in motion pictures: Jerry Lewis selling Dunkin' Donuts in *Hardly Working* (1981), Kevin Kline flashing his Nike shoes in *The Big Chill* (1983), Melanie Griffith drinking Coors beer in *Working Girl* (1988), to name a few. The producers of *E.T., The Extra-Terrestrial* (1982) received promotional help from Hershey Foods in exchange for featuring Reese's Pieces in the film. Sales of that candy product then shot up 70 percent.[22]

Regarding personal styles, people often take their cues from entertainment figures. One need only recall the Beatles imitators, the Madonna imitators, and the "Miami Vice" imitators (a day's growth of beard for that sexy, rugged look). There was the Calvin Klein jeans craze, the Cabbage Patch doll craze, the Michael Jackson craze, and other such hypes that were induced mostly by mass media. A study conducted by the National Institute of Mental Health finds that most adults and children treat television dramas and other fictional shows as valid guides for dealing with actual life situations, including family relations, friendships, and social, cultural, and political issues.[23] In sum, people are influenced by the media in the way they dress, talk, interrelate, spend their money, define social problems, identify with prominent personalities, and in the kinds of ideological images they embrace.

Preempting Life

The chapters ahead will concentrate on Hollywood films and entertainment television. The distinctions between the two media are breaking down. Successful films become the seminal vehicles for TV series or are themselves eventually rerun on the small screen or made accessible as video cassettes for home viewing. Many Hollywood films are specifically made for TV and never reach a theater. At the same time, television situation comedies, or "sitcoms," have had their baneful effect on the scenarios and humor found in Hollywood films.

Still, there is a difference in the manner of consumption between the two media. Imagine spending six or seven hours a day at a movie theater when you were a 12-year-old. Your elders would not have permitted it. Yet children half that age spend six or more hours a day watching TV.[24] Seeing a movie still requires an admission fee and a special effort to get to the theater. Television, however, is woven into the domestic scene—almost like a member of the family. In fact, no member of the family is likely to hold our attention for three or four hours at a time the way the tube does. "Television does more than inform and entertain us—its ubiquitous presence helps us regulate our lives. The progression of news-time, prime-time, bedtime . . . is a pattern which defines the evening for vast numbers of Americans."[25] For many people, especially those who live alone or who are lonely, television is a home companion, used for company and background sounds. Such users turn on their sets almost the moment they come home. Even if not constantly monopolizing their time, the television is rarely idle, becoming something of an electronic hearth.

There are more television sets in American homes than bathrooms or telephones. Some 97 percent of all households have a TV, and more than 30 percent have two or more. On any one evening, eighty-five million people are in front of the little screen, with as many as thirty-five million fixed on the same program. In 1969, the average household spent about 41 hours a week viewing television. By the mid-1980s it was about 52 hours a week. In households with three or more people, the television is on 61 hours a week.[26]

Access to cable and to a greater number of regular channels may have contributed to the increase in viewing. Also, with the growing use of remote-control channel changers or "zappers," the empowered viewer spends more time in front of the tube. The philosopher Bertrand Russell once pointed out that, as transportation becomes more accessible and rapid, people spend *more* time traveling, not less. The same might be true about television viewing. Armed with their zappers, viewers have quicker access to the entire range of programs; they can skip effortlessly from channel to channel, fleeing from advertisements, foraging for morsels from ten or more channels simultaneously, and doing this for hours—experiencing more distraction and using less concentration than when they watched one show at a time.

In England Too, the TV Pied Piper

In the pre-television era, playgrounds, streets and greens were alive with children playing a multitude of games and singing rhymes, sometimes unchanged for centuries, carrying out traditional customs and doing all the activities forming our "children's culture" . . . . Seasonal games like conkers or marbles, top spinning, hoops, skipping to rhymes, local customs such as "mischief nights," jingles, hopscotch and countless other activities formed the rich fabric of children's culture. . . . Weeks after Edward VIII's abdication, children all over the country were singing, "Hark the herald angels sing, Mrs. Simpson's pinched our King!" This age-old children's culture is semi-underground, and not for the usual adult.

Nowadays, although children's culture may still thrive on some school playgrounds in certain areas, one can be in a park or on a street at a time when it would once have been bubbling with children playing; now there are but few children, and even fewer who play the old games. Where have all the children gone on a Saturday morning, a Sunday afternoon or after school? The television, like the Pied Piper of Hamelin drawing all the children into the mountain cave, has taken many of our modern children away from their hobbies, play, games, streets and greens for at least twenty hours a week. Only the few odd ones out who watch little or no television continue to play. . . .

Martin Large, *Who's Bringing Them Up? Television and Child Department* (Gloucester, England: M.H.C. Large, 1980), p. 35.

The most pervasive effect of television—aside from its actual content—may be its very existence, its readily available, commanding, and often addictive presence in everybody's home, its ability to reduce hundreds of millions of citizens to passive spectators for major portions of their lives.[27] Television minimizes personal interactions within families and communities. One writer only half-jokingly claims: "I watched television, mainly as a way of getting to know my husband and children. . . ."[28] An associate of mine, who spent years in western agricultural regions, relates how a farmer once told her: "Folks used to get together a lot. Now with television, we see less of each other."

With the advent of Hollywood—even more with the advent of television—a single information source can transmit images and viewpoints directly into millions of minds, making it difficult for people to separate the real from the unreal, pacifying and immobilizing them, fragmenting their perceptions, blunting their imaginations and their critical judgments, shortening their attention spans, and diminishing their taste for intelligent public and private discourse.

Americans are not the only targets of this communication universe. One survey found that in Colombia people spend an average of seven hours a day watching TV and only six hours sleeping.[29] In many other countries viewing averages range equally high. The mass media's influence is global, with the lion's share going to U.S. productions. American television programs are watched in just about every country in the world. Likewise, Hollywood films occupy more than half the world's big-screen time. The U.S. motion-picture industry virtually monopolizes international cinema distribution.[30] Much of what is said in the pages ahead, then, applies not only to the United States but to a large part of the world.

Those who produce images for mass consumption exercise enormous power, but they are not omnipotent, for they are not entirely free from public pressure. The viewing audience is something more than just a passive victim. There are times when popular agitation, new developments in democratic consciousness, and changes in public taste have forced the make-believe media to modify or discard images. I will note some of these instances in the pages ahead. But the public is not able to exercise much democratic control over image manipulation unless it is aware of the manipulation. The first step, then, is to develop a critical perspective. When it comes to the media, criticism is a form of self-defense. So let us begin defending ourselves.

2

Swarthy Hordes and Other Aliens

For centuries the land, labor, and resources of peoples in Asia, Africa, and Latin America have been forcibly expropriated by European and North American colonizers. To justify the violence and pillage that have long been a necessary part of these undertakings, defenders of colonialism and neocolonialism have either denied that such crimes ever occurred or have portrayed the victimized populations as the victimizers. Thus, for generations it was taught that darker-skinned peoples were prone to savagery and violence, were incapable of self-governance, and were in need of the White man's uplifting rule. For centuries such images of Third World peoples have been propagated in Western society. In North America, racism was embraced by the early Puritan settlers who slaughtered Native American Indians in order to consign their souls to what the Puritans felt was their proper place in hell, thus clearing the land for incorporation by the Puritan leaders and the settlers who followed.[1]

Colonialist atrocities were going on for many centuries before the invention of cinematography and television. The racist images of Third World peoples found in the entertainment media, therefore, cannot be seen as the cause of the atrocities. But in their relatively short history, the media have done their part in making Western imperialism seem like an okay thing.

The Wagon Circle

Over the decades, first the motion-picture industry and then television have produced a wide variety of action-adventure films that contain the same basic scenario. The enemies are Indians on the American plains or

13

Africans and Asians in the jungle or alien monsters from outer space or Communist terrorists from Russia or ethnic criminals in the inner city. The homeland, the safe place, is American White Anglo-Protestant, or at least White. It is inhabited by people who are sane and care about life. The enemies are maniacal and careless with lives, including their own.

In a wonderful article entitled "Ambush at Kamikaze Pass," Tom Engelhardt notes the underlying common theme of the cowboy movie, the war movie, and the adventure film. They all portray the non-Caucasian world through the lens of the colonizer, offering us an archetypal scene: a circle of covered wagons or sometimes a fort or camp wherein humanity rests warm and secure. Suddenly, on the periphery emerge the screeching savages to kill the humans for no reason other than to quench their own bloodthirsty propensities. The White men, be they cowboys or cavalry, ready their rifles, knowing what to do: exterminate the attackers. This scenario "forces us to flip history on its head. It makes the intruder exchange places in our eyes with the intruded upon."[2] In real life, of course, the Indians faced ruthless invaders who were ready to exterminate them. But in these films, it is the Indians "who must invade, intrude, break in upon the circle—a circle which contains all those whom the film has already certified as 'human.' "[3]

For several decades this script, in different costume, was reenacted in movies dealing with Third World peoples. Whether in the Amazon jungle, the North African desert, the Sudan, the Transvaal, the South Pacific, or Indochina, the scene is the same: a group of Whites (usually Americans) fight off the swarthy hordes, killing enormous numbers of (Red, Brown, Yellow, Black) "devils," while, to the tune of plaintive music, losing but a few of their precious own. The swarthy hordes throw themselves against vastly superior firepower, not out of any desperate concern to defend their homelands and their people, but because they are propelled by a fanatical lust to kill and destroy. As Engelhardt notes: "It is not even 'bravery' as we in the West know it (though similar acts by Whites are portrayed heroically)."[4]

Lacking a normal range of human sensibilities, the enemy has no regard for its own lives. This is made clear to us in flicks like *The Halls of Montezuma* (1950): a captured Japanese officer is implored by U.S. Marine hero Richard Widmark: "You have a future—to rebuild Japan—to live for." But the smirky Nipponese, immune to the lures of tomorrow's Toyota market, replies: "Captain, you seem to have forgotten, my people for centuries have thought not of living well but dying well. Have you not studied our judo, our science . . . We always take the obvious and reverse it. Death is the basis of our strength." And to prove his point he commits hara-kiri first chance he gets.[5]

Meanwhile, Back at the Reality

. . . We came in sight of the camp of the friendly Indians afore-mentioned, and we were ordered by Colonel Chivington to attack the same, which was accordingly done. . . . The village of the Indians consisted of from one hundred to one hundred and thirty lodges, and, so far as I am able to judge, of from five hundred to six hundred souls, the majority of which were women and children; in going over the battleground the next day I did not see a body of man, woman, or child but was scalped, and in many instances their bodies were mutilated in the most horrible manner—men, women, and children's private parts cut out, etc. . . .

When it was day the soldiers returned to the fort—considering that they had done a deed of Roman valor, in murdering so many [Indians] in their sleep, where infants were torn from their mothers' breast and hacked to pieces in the presence of their parents and the pieces thrown into the fire . . . and other sucklings then cut, stuck, and pierced.

The memoirs of an American soldier quoted in Irving J. Sloan, *Our Violent Past* (New York: Random House, 1970), pp. 17, 20–21.

Imperialism has never recognized the humanity of its victims. By treating the colonized as subhuman, the colonizers can more easily justify exterminating them. John Wayne summed it up in one of his horse operas, *The Searchers* (1956): "There's humans and then there's Comanches." In World War II films, Japanese soldiers, played by Chinese-American actors, were portrayed as pitiless, sadistic demons. Hence, killing them posed no great moral problems. As the sergeant in *Guadalcanal Diary* (1943) explains: "Besides, they're not people." In that same film, one Marine asks about the enemy soldiers: "Where are the rest of the seven dwarfs?" Another answers: "They live in the trees like apes."[6]

In earlier times, imperialistic extermination could assume a more endearing form. In *Wee Willie Winkie* (1937), little Shirley Temple asks her grandfather, the British colonel, why he was mad at Khoda Khan, leader of the "warlike" tribes on India's border. "We're not mad at Khoda Khan. England wants to be friends with all her peoples. But if we don't shoot him, he'll shoot us," the colonel tenderly replies.[7]

In *The Real Glory* (1939) Gary Cooper plays an Army doctor who solves all the medical and military problems in the Philippine islands in the wake of the Spanish-American War. The movie offers not a hint of why the U.S. Army was in the Philippines, and nothing about how U.S. forces invaded the islands—crushing the Filipino liberation army that was fighting for independence, and killing hundreds of thousands of men, women, and children in the process—thereby paving the way for the takeover of the land, labor, and natural resources by U.S. firms. Instead, we get a benign image of U.S. imperialism in which the victimizer is transformed into the culturally superior benefactor. Perhaps only coincidentally, this film enjoyed a heavy television rerun in various cities in October 1990 at a time when President Bush was building up his interventionist forces in the Middle East, and again in January 1991 when the U.S. war against Iraq began.

The arrival of television by the early 1950s in almost every American home gave new life to old war films and even more so to the cowboy movies and matinee serials of the 1930s and 1940s. With their simple action plots and minimal picture frames, these relics were easily and inexpensively recycled for television. In short time, one of these heroes, Hopalong Cassidy, was featured in a new made-for-TV series that also generated a lucrative spin-off market for "Hoppy" toys, clothes, and other items. Hopalong's success cleared a trail to television for other movie and radio cowboy heroes, including Gene Autry, the Cisco Kid, and the Lone Ranger.[8] These juvenile westerns usually were free of the gore and savagery of the more adult cowboy-and-Indian slaughter flicks. But they were far from being merely entertainment. They supported such values as nationalism, conventional gender roles, and a particular view of law and order. Some of the commandments in Gene Autry's "Cowboy Code" (sent to little wranglers who watched him) were:

A cowboy is a good worker.

A cowboy respects womanhood, his parents, and the laws of his country.

A cowboy is a patriot.

The statement of standards put out by the production company that gave us "The Lone Ranger" said in part:

The Lone Ranger is motivated by love of country—a desire to help those who are building the West. . . . Patriotism means service to a community; voting; . . . the development of schools and churches. Patriotism includes also an obligation to maintain a home in which good citizens may be reared. Patriotism means respect for law and order, and the selection of officials who merit such respect. Patriotism consists of the preservation of the things for which our ancestors fought and died.[9]

George Trendle, creator of "The Lone Ranger" program, sees the masked rider as a patriotic, clean-living, God-fearing preserver of traditional values.[10]

Tonto, Gunga Din, and All That

In his struggle against evil and in his campaign to promote the work ethic and "build the West," the Lone Ranger was never without his trusty Indian sidekick, Tonto. Occasionally Tonto displayed a certain native resourcefulness, as when arriving in the nick of time to rescue his boss from a dangerous predicament. But Tonto (whose name means "stupid" in Spanish) rarely had an idea of his own that reached beyond the concerns of his White boss. His response usually consisted of a deep-voiced, monosyllabic concurring grunt: "Nnnnnnnh," not unlike the mooing of a steer. It would have been unimaginable for him to suggest that he and the Lone Ranger devote effort to righting the terrible wrongs committed against Tonto's people by those who were "building the West." When the dynamic duo took off across the wild brush with a hearty "Hi-Yo Silver," it was Tonto who swallowed dust, riding several paces behind his boss, on a horse that looked almost lackluster compared to the Lone Ranger's utterly magnificent steed.

In real life, the imperialists often manage to win the collaboration of some indigenous peoples. Because of the bleak options facing them, poverty, displacement, or tribal rivalries, the colonized can sometimes be coerced or bribed into joining the colonizer's ranks. In other words, instead of killing all the natives, the White conquerors use some in struggles against other segments of the native population.

The Lone Ranger and Tonto offer us a familiar media prototype of that kind of domesticated imperialist relationship. When Third-World people are not portrayed as heartless savages, they are cast as devoted subordinates, finding fulfillment in selfless service to or loving association with a White "superior," elevated to dependency upon that superior.[11]

Frequently the swarthy sidekick sacrifices his life for his White companion at the appropriate moment. The pathetic little hero of *Gunga Din* (1939) is shot to death while blowing his bugle to save the

The patriotic, clean-living Lone Ranger "builds the West" and vanquishes evil with the assistance of his faithful Indian companion, Tonto, who always rides several paces behind his White boss.

British imperialist troops from an ambush by his own compatriots. The Black trainer in *Body and Soul* (1947) gives his life to prevent his White boxing champion from throwing the big fight. The Mau Mau member falls on Punji sticks to save the child of his White friend in *Something of*

Value (1957). A Black officer in *Star Trek II: The Wrath of Khan* (1982) kills himself rather than harm his leader, Captain Kirk.

Usually, the darker peoples are used as little more than a background against which the White principals engage in their adventures. "The indigenous population served as nameless bearers to lug the imported paraphernalia of civilization along jungle trails," observes Robert Hart. "When the story needed to be invigorated by vignettes of incidental action, one or another of the expendable porters would topple off a cliff or be eaten by crocodiles, whereupon the foreign explorers would glance down and commiserate: 'Poor devil—what was he carrying?' "[12]

The numerous Tarzan movies of yore featured a Caucasian who lived like a native rather than a colonizer, albeit with a civilized White wife who had acquired a taste for roughing it. Yet Tarzan was unlike any native. He was a jungle superhero who outdid the savages single-handedly. And he did it all without a dark-skinned sidekick to assist him, at least without a human one. For Tarzan did have Cheeta, the chimpanzee who was allowed to display a bit more independence and pizzazz than Tonto. On occasion, Cheeta and a whole phalanx of other wild animals, including elephants, would respond to Tarzan's call and join him in a frontal assault upon his adversaries. Why these animals felt so partial toward Tarzan as opposed to other Homo sapiens was never made clear. Perhaps one is to understand that creatures of whatever species are happy to serve White superheroes.

In response to the protests of minority and progressive groups and the changing climate of opinion that came with the Vietnam era, the media began to offer a few improved scripts about Third World peoples. Films like *Little Big Man* (1970) and *Soldier Blue* (1970) and an occasional television drama actually showed sympathy for the Native American Indian and stood history back on its feet—for a few wobbly moments—by portraying the U.S. Army as the exterminating aggressors and the Indians as the victims. In *Soldier Blue*, the main protagonists are still White. In *Little Big Man*, a film about the plight of the Cheyenne, the hero is still a White man (Dustin Hoffman). In any case, Native Americans are portrayed as intelligent, human, and humane.

"Indian films" disappeared for the next twenty years, Hollywood having decided that the subject had no further commercial viability. In defiance of that market wisdom, Jim Wilson and Kevin Costner produced the three-hour epic *Dances with Wolves* (1990) about a Union Army cavalry lieutenant who finds himself drawn into a Lakota Sioux tribe and is condemned as a renegade by his army superiors. The script was written by Costner, who plays the White lead character. He is seldom off the screen and becomes tiresome in his omnipresence. Yet the film has some unusual and redeeming features: all the Sioux and Pawnee roles are played by Native American actors; the teepees and clothing are of authentic design; about one-fourth of the dialogue is in Lakota, with English subtitles; and the Sioux are portrayed as sympathetic human beings rather than screeching savages. (The Pawnee are the wicked ones in this film.)

Present-day struggles of Indians to retain control of their tribal life, reservation lands, and fishing rights have been accorded little attention by the make-believe media. The few exceptions would include *Loyalties* (1987), a Canadian film, which showed contemporary Native Americans to be imperfect but recognizable humans rather than either bloodthirsty or noble savages. It played well in Canada but could not get distribution in the United States. Similarly, *Powwow Highway* (1989) won a standing ovation at the New York Film Festival but no real distribution in the country.

More of the Same— With Some Exceptions

Whatever new developments in history, there is no shortage of the old colonial stuff in the make-believe media. Witness the way the motion-picture industry continues to treat Africa. There are a thousand fascinating stories that could be told about Africa. There are African mythologies and legends; Africans who built cities and empires long before the Europeans ever set foot upon their continent; Africans who suffered the loss of loved ones to slavers, experienced the destruction of their tribes and loss of tribal lands, and today face the famine and misery that is part of colonialism's legacy; Africans who have struggled with great courage for independence and revolution; Africans who try to hold their families and cultures together, confront generational and gender conflicts arising from changing social conditions, live in modern African cities and deal with the problems of urbanization, and fall in love and have dreams for themselves and their children; Africans who are underpaid laborers yet organize labor unions, churches, communities, and businesses, fight to get an education, and build mass political organizations under oppressive conditions.

A thousand powerful stories could come out of Africa, but when Hollywood finally did turn its attention to that land in recent years, all it could produce was *Out of Africa* (1985), a film that says nothing about Africans. *Out of Africa* is a major production about a minor literary figure, Isak Dinesen, an upper-crust Dane (Meryl Streep). It focuses on

Dinesen's tribulations as owner of a plantation in Africa. She is surrounded by natives who—like so many Gunga Dins—seem only concerned with serving her, addressing her reverently as "Sahib." The heroine's lover, played by Robert Redford, shows her the "real Africa," the Africa he loves, by taking her up in his airplane. What we see is the same old safari-flick footage of herds of zebras and giraffes running across the plains. His real Africa has no Africans in it.

Several years later came *White Mischief* (1988), another film with an African setting, which concentrates on a decadent colony of rich English. This movie offers adultery, murder, and a courtroom trial. What it doesn't have is any Africans—except servants and other such human background fixtures. To judge from such media productions, Africans lead lives of little interest to anyone.

As with Africa, so with India: in the early 1980s a spate of dramas about colonial India were released, including the British-made motion picture *Passage to India* (1984) and the television series "The Jewel in the Crown," both of which also focus almost exclusively on colonial Whites as the principals. The Indians we see are usually members of unthinking crowds or, again, are mute servants and lackeys who compose the social scenery of imperialism. *Passage to India* does recognize that colonizers might treat indigenous peoples unjustly. But the injustice is confined to an atypical incident: an emotionally unstable English woman falsely accuses an Indian man of having raped her, a charge that is exposed as bogus in court. Given the history of British imperialism, with its forced destruction of India's textile and manufacturing industries and forced impoverishment of India's population; its expropriation of India's lands, labor, markets, and capital; and its executions and massacres of India's resistance fighters, one easily could have found a more substantial example of colonial injustice than the old sexist standby of a woman falsely accusing a man of rape.

In *Gandhi* (1982), directed by Richard Attenborough and distributed by Columbia Pictures, we have a film about India that actually focuses on Indians—in particular, a great Indian leader, the struggle he waged against British rule, and his attempts to maintain peace between Muslims and Hindus. Here is a motion picture of quality that is absorbing and at times even inspiring. It does not flinch from showing the brutality of British colonialism, including the unprovoked massacre of hundreds of peaceful demonstrators and, in another sequence, the bloody beatings of scores of nonviolent protestors.

But *Gandhi* fails to explain what the British are doing in India. The film never mentions that the imperialists are pillaging the country for the enrichment of western investors. It never suggests that the awful poverty of India is linked to the immense wealth being extracted from that country. One is left with the impression that (1) the British occupy far-off countries just so they might strut about with swagger sticks and lord it over other folks, and (2) they simply lack the decency to go home when asked to.

The film emphasizes Gandhi's nonviolence without mentioning that his movement failed to bring about the social revolution needed to wipe out the poverty that today is still the lot of multitudes in India. *Gandhi* gives little attention to the organized popular struggle that won India's independence. Instead, a single individual is made to be the architect of India's freedom. Gandhi is presented as something of a saint. Little is said about the curious forms of his asceticism and the problems created within the movement by his religious obscurantism and his oddly preindustrial vision of India's future.[13]

Another rare anticolonialist motion picture, also directed by Richard Attenborough, is *Cry Freedom* (1987), the story of a White South African journalist who sides with the antiapartheid leader Steven Biko. The oppressions and terrors suffered by Black protagonists, including Biko, are treated seriously in the film, though given far less attention than the lesser travails of the journalist and his family. Perhaps the best way to reach White audiences is by showing how apartheid oppresses White people of conscience as well as others. However, since Black South Africans have faced far greater risks with fewer material resources at their command, one might expect a well-intentioned film to make their struggle the dramatic focal point.

Another anticolonial motion picture, a British production, *The Mission* (1986), exposes the way European powers stole lands and destroyed indigenous people in South America during the late eighteenth century. The missionaries join ranks with the tribes (something missionaries rarely have done in imperialism's history) against the higher clergy, crown officials, and big landowners in an unsuccessful attempt to save the Indian communities from displacement and extermination. Again, the principal protagonists are Whites. The Indians are never more than a supporting cast. Perhaps the film makes its most pertinent thrust in the printed crawl that appears at the end, announcing that the forcible extermination of indigenous peoples in the South American rain forests is still going on today.

A truly uncompromising anti-imperialist motion picture was the Italian-French production of over twenty years ago, *Burn!* (1969), starring Marlon Brando. From a political standpoint, it left little unsaid, noting the economic interests that were behind Caribbean colonialism, the comparative gains to be made from exploiting slave and free labor, and the problems of insurgency and counterinsurgency—all set in a late eighteenth-century West Indies setting. The film's only defect was its portrayal of the Black revolutionary leaders as too inexperienced to rule once they seized state power. In real life, the difficulties of revolutionary rule are caused mostly by the economic legacy of underdevelopment and the drain imposed by counterrevolutionary destruction and encirclement. This aside, *Burn!* stands almost alone in its willingness to deal so explicitly and intelligently with imperialism's *economic* interests. It is difficult to believe that such a motion picture could play in commercial movie houses in America. In fact, *Burn!* did not reach many theaters, nor stay very long in those it did reach. Produced during the height of the Vietnam war, it was yanked out of circulation by distributors after an unusually brief run.

Hardliners and "Antiterrorists"

The post-Vietnam era saw a resurgence of racist and anticommunist stereotypes in the media. In Francis Ford Coppola's *Apocalypse Now* (1979), montagnard tribespeople gather worshipfully around a great White god in the form of a renegade U.S. Army officer, Colonel Kurtz (Marlon Brando). The colonel, a borderline psychotic, believes wars should be fought the old-fashioned way, without pity or limitation. The United States, it seems, failed to match the enemy's ruthlessness and terror. Such an opinion misrepresents the facts in what was the most murderous war ever waged by a large industrial nation against a small underdeveloped country. At one point Kurtz observes that the Vietnamese liberation fighters, the Vietcong, chopped off the arms of hundreds of children as punishment for receiving vaccinations from U.S. health officers. This atrocity never happened in real life but was accepted as true by some viewers in the theater I attended, judging from their audibly outraged reactions.

Apocalypse Now also introduces us to a degenerated John Wayne prototype—assuming that's not a redundancy—Lieutenant Colonel Kilgore (Robert Duvall), who wears a cavalry hat and uses helicopters instead of horses to ride into a Vietnamese village, shooting it to pieces. Like the hunters who kill animals from trains and planes, the helicopter gunners run down their prey. Targeting one victim who is racing away, a gunner exclaims that he got her "right up the ass." When one of his choppers lands and is blown away by the liberation fighters, Kilgore angrily remarks that the enemy are a bunch of "savages." In a more relaxed moment, he notes: "I love the smell of napalm in the morning."

A standard image of Third World people—primitive montagnards guarding the stronghold of their great White leader, a renegade U.S. Army officer in *Apocalypse Now.*

The character of Kilgore is played satirically and the slaughter is shown with a less sympathetic camera than might be found in a John Wayne flick, yet it is ambiguous enough for us to wonder whether the war is being condemned or celebrated. Without a clear critique woven into the subtext, "all film tends to argue *in favor* of the behavior shown."[14]

In Michael Cimino's *The Deer Hunter* (1978), Vietnamese liberation fighters gleefully force American prisoners to play Russian roulette with a loaded revolver. Cimino admitted that the episode was a purely imagi-

Just Like in the Movies

War dramas in film and television may not create violence, but they seem to help define reality for the violent imagination. Hence, U.S. Marine Lance Corporal Eric Huffman enthuses:

"You know how in *Apocalypse Now* they go around putting aces of spades on the dead VC—well, that's where our squadron emblem comes from, from killing all those Vietcong. See, I double as door gunner when we rig for combat. I fire this .60 caliber gatling gun with six rotating barrels that can shoot off 4,000 rounds per minute. It's just like in the movie. I didn't like the last part of that film too much, but when they're flying into that village blowing all that shit away, I thought that was fantastic. I must have seen that movie about five times now."

When Huffman was asked about the possibility of war, he said, "Everyone's looking forward to it. I'd like to kick ass in Iran." What if we end up fighting elsewhere? "Any place is fine. I just want some action," he smiles with a sweet adolescent enthusiasm. "You see, they try and keep us motivated that way. It's all part of the plan."

Quoted in David Helvarg, "War Games," *In These Times*, June 4–17, 1980.

nary one, but he saw nothing wrong with this since he was striving for narrative effect rather than historical literalness. One wonders what the response would have been if a movie depicting French resistance fighters happily torturing German prisoners during the Nazi occupation of France were defended on the grounds of artistic license. The portrayal of the Vietnamese in *The Deer Hunter* might best be described as racist.

Neither *The Deer Hunter* nor *Apocalypse Now* nor the more antiwar films like *Platoon* (1986) or the underrated *Full Metal Jacket* (1987) take much time to depict the awful impact of the war on the Vietnamese. *Platoon* successfully captures some of the terror of jungle fighting—from the GI's perspective. It also portrays the torching of a village by U.S. forces, an operation that appears relatively benign compared to the widespread village massacres conducted by U.S. forces during the war. In the film, the Vietnamese children are protectively carried away from the burning huts by U.S. troops rather than being shot dead as they were at My Lai and other places. *Platoon* has the virtue of making no attempt to glorify the war. It points out that poor boys are the ones who have to do the fighting, and it admits the reality, albeit not the magnitude, of U.S. atrocities. At the same time, it offers unnecessary heroics and a final battle scene in which American soldiers wipe out a whole horde of attacking Vietcong, as they might Indians in a cowboy movie.

Casualties of War (1989) is unusual in that its central theme is built around a war crime. Some American soldiers abduct and rape a young Vietnamese woman. One of them is as willing and able a killer as the others but he is not a rapist. Bothered by the act, he informs his superiors who tell him to forget about it. To silence him, his comrades try to kill him at one point. Eventually a chaplain lends a sympathetic ear to the troubled GI, and the rapists are brought to justice. By focusing on this isolated crime and treating it as a deviant and aberrant act, the film implicitly invites us to overlook the fact that the entire war was a rape, involving indiscriminate mass killings and the systematic destruction of the Vietnamese countryside. If anything, the rape depicted in the film was unusual only in that it was prosecuted.

The 1970s and 1980s brought us movie director and writer John Milius, who dubbed himself a "zen fascist" and who wrote a number of war-and-gore scripts, including scenes for *Apocalypse Now* and *Jeremiah Johnson*, a 1972 release about a White hero who kills Indian after Indian. Milius's scenes had to be cut because they were too violent even for those films. Milius fit in well with the Reaganite cinema, declaring that, for the media, "I'm the Hermann Goering of my generation," and "There's something unspeakably attractive about war." To prove his point, he directed and cowrote *Conan the Barbarian* (1982), a movie that must have set a record for combat deaths by beheading, slashing, and bashing—delivered upon lesser mortals by the indestructible Aryan titan, Arnold Schwarzenegger.[15]

The military has always found a home in the entertainment media. In a more innocent day, we had the jingoism of John Wayne, who single-handedly won World War II—taking time off from killing Indians to kill "lotsa Japs" in *Back to Bataan* (1945), *The Fighting Seabees* (1944), *Sands of Iwo Jima* (1949), *Flying Leathernecks* (1951), and a dozen other flicks.

To say that Wayne won the celluloid war single-handedly is not quite true; he had the active support of the Pentagon itself. War films depend heavily on the military for expensive props, such as planes, ships, and tanks. Support is forthcoming only for scripts that fit the military's view of things. The films that fail to satisfy the Department of Defense's Motion Picture Production Board are denied equipment and banned from U.S. bases around the world, as happened to *Attack* (1956), *On the Beach* (1959), and *Steel Helmet* (1951). The latter's script called for the killing of an unarmed North Korean prisoner-of-war by a

GI. The army refused to go along with such a portrayal. It would have us believe that American soldiers have never done such things. Several scenes in other films, including *From Here to Eternity* (1953), had to be rewritten before the Pentagon would cooperate.[16]

As with movies, so with television. The Pentagon has spent millions of dollars on TV recruitment commercials and has allowed Bob Hope to telecast highlights of his overseas military base tours. The military has provided bases, materiel, and personnel for entire television series. In 1958, the army lent soldiers to be used as extras in "The Big Attack," thereby incurring the ire of the Screen Actors Guild. The military cooperated in the production of "Men in Space" (1959–60), a CBS science-fiction series—for whose scripts the Pentagon had approval rights. Other series such as "The Blue Angels," "The Silent Service," "Flight," and "Steve Canyon" received military equipment and file footage—in exchange for a positive image of the armed forces.[17]

This cooperation between the make-believe media and what some called "Pentagon Productions" continued through the Vietnam war. The military assisted in every conceivable way in filming *The Green Berets* (1968), a story of how Special Forces killer John Wayne guns down hordes of Vietnamese just as he did Indians and Japanese in earlier flicks, thereby seeming to win the Vietnam war. The military's cooperation continued throughout the 1980s with cold-war propaganda movies like *Rambo III, Red Dawn,* and *Invasion USA,* discussed in the next chapter. In both *Top Gun* (1986), a film about young bucks at an elite naval aviation training school who vie for macho glory, and *The Hunt for Red October* (1990), about a diabolic Soviet submarine commander, the U.S. Navy cooperated fully, providing the jet-fighter planes, nuclear submarines, and technical advisors. Naval crews were used as extras. Navy officials inspected and approved both films and were pleased with what they saw: a glorification of militarism and high-tech weaponry.

There have been good antiwar films, but they have been few and far between. Dalton Trumbo's *Johnny Got His Gun* (1971) is a powerful, wrenching story about one of war's victims. *Coming Home* (1978) less directly and less painfully deals with the victimization endured by war veterans. *Paths of Glory* (1957), starring Kirk Douglas, is often cited as an antiwar film and concerns trench combat in World War I and the unjust execution of several soldiers for cowardice. This film is really against *inefficient* war, a critique directed at the stupidity of field commanders who allow their troops to be slaughtered in a hopeless battle and then try to cover up their mistakes. The film does not question war itself; it just argues for better generalship and fewer unnecessary casualties.

The Military-Media Complex

In addition to providing its own productions and file footage to private companies, the Pentagon lent military bases . . . for on-location filming. It also provided experts to check on the accuracy of everything from proper military formations to Phil Silvers' [comic] references on "The Phil Silvers Show." The Defense Department even offered its academic campuses. The U.S. Military Academy at West Point was used in producing the Ziv series "The West Point Story." The U.S. Naval Academy at Annapolis was the site of many scenes in another Ziv product, "Men of Annapolis." In both cases, applications for admission to the academies rose as a result of these series.

J. Fred MacDonald, *Television and the Red Menace* (New York: Praeger, 1985), p. 119.

Standing almost alone as an antiwar film is *All Quiet on the Western Front* (1930), which offers a shattering, uncompromising depiction of the savagery of trench warfare. The effect on audiences is unambiguous. We have waited over sixty years for something that might come close to this classic. A fairly good remake of *All Quiet on the Western Front* did appear in 1979. In 1989 came Oliver Stone's *Born on the Fourth of July,* the true and moving story of Ron Kovic, a flag-waving, middle-American youth who joined the Marines and suffered a wound in Vietnam that left him paralyzed from mid-chest down. The film depicts the horrors of the VA hospital, Kovic's torturous struggle to convalesce and adapt to his paraplegic condition, and his transformation from militaristic superpatriot to peace activist. *Born on the Fourth of July* says little about the political issues behind the Vietnam war, but it strongly denounces the way war uses patriotism to victimize people, including the patriots themselves.

In the 1980s, the Reagan administration's "antiterrorism" hype helped the make-believe media in its endless search for villains. In 1984, while 17,000 Americans were murdered by their own compatriots (not counting the many other thousands wiped out by vehicular manslaughter), only sixteen U.S. citizens died in terrorist attacks abroad. In subsequent years, there were even fewer U.S. terrorist victims. Nevertheless, in 1986, many Americans canceled their plans for travel in Europe out of fear of terrorism.[18] During these years, hostage-taking and terrorism became a boom industry for Hollywood and television. Just a few examples should suffice.

In *Iron Eagle* (1986), a teenager purloins a U.S. Air Force F-16 and flies it from Arizona to the Middle East—nonstop—to kill an entire army of fanatical Arabs who are holding his dad as a hostage. In the course of this mission, the fearless lad takes full advantage of all the latest computer death technology, which makes the killing loads of fun. He also enlists the efforts of a retired colonel and Vietnam veteran, Louis Gossett, Jr., who is disgruntled about that no-win war but finds the promise of future victories in the killer instincts of a new generation. *Iron Eagle* makes explicit references to Reaganism. Thus, after his father is taken hostage, the young hero and his friends expect the government to do something. When one of them skeptically notes what happened to the hostages in Iran, another says: "That was different. Mr. Peanut [Jimmy Carter] was in charge. Now we got a different guy. Why do you suppose they call him Ronnie Ray-Gun?" As it turns out, even Ronnie Ray-Gun's government does not act, so the kid takes things into his own hands.

Delta Force (1986) shows us how really to deal with terrorists. Forget the tense, patient negotiations that freed the passengers of a number of hijacked airliners without loss of life. Send Chuck Norris, Lee Marvin, and other members of a U.S. commando team into Beirut where they can murder hundreds of Arabs and rescue all the hostages, losing only one member of their own team.

In *Death before Dishonor* (1987), the Marines are sent in to ease American frustrations about Qaddafi, Arab terrorists, and swarthy hordes in general. In this film, "the bad guys wear Vietcong-like black pajamas and the red-checkered *kaffiyeh* headdress usually associated with Palestinian nationalism. The good guys wear the camouflage jungle fatigues of the U.S. Marine Corps. It doesn't take long to figure out which side is going to win the shootout."[19] A Marine colonel is taken hostage by Arab terrorists. For sport, they disfigure him with a high-speed drill before he manages to plunge the whirring bit into the heart of his torturer. A beautiful woman, who ostensibly sympathizes with the Arab cutthroats, turns out to be an agent of the Mossad, the Israeli spy organization. She coordinates her efforts with the U.S. Marine Corps rescue force led by former Los Angeles Rams player cum actor Fred Dryer, who wastes dozens of villains with his automatic rifle. Indeed, just about every Arab in sight is killed before the last reel.

In an interview, Dryer noted that *Death before Dishonor* "is sticking to the American theme, which is the Marine Corps." His director, Terry Leonard, added: "I think a lot of America's frustrations will come out in this film. Americans are really fed up with this terrorism business. The hostages in Lebanon drive me nuts." To find relief, Leonard directed a

Israeli and Arab
Featured as Cowboy and Indian

Beginning in the 1950s, a popular new cinema genre developed around the Arab-Israeli conflict. At least ten films were made on this theme in the 1960s alone. . . . In these war movies, Israelis and their American friends are played by popular actors such as Kirk Douglas, Yul Brynner, John Wayne, Frank Sinatra, Paul Newman, and Sal Mineo. The Arabs, on the other hand, are cruel soldiers, unseen or seen only from a distance. In *Exodus* [1960], for example, they brutally kill a fifteen-year-old refugee girl, played by Jill Hayworth, and in *Cast a Giant Shadow* [1966] . . . the Arabs leer and laugh as they shoot at an Israeli woman trapped in a truck. . . .

These movies present the Israeli-Arab conflict in much the same way as cowboys and Indians: the Arabs are always the bad guys, the Israelis, the good guys . . . Cinema should refrain from gross oversimplifications which distort history and interfere with understanding the Middle East. . . .

The stereotyping of Arabs in American cinema has continued into the 1970s and 1980s. Some examples:

Network (1977) has a bitter anti-Arab scene in which a crusading television news commentator . . . warns that the Arabs are taking control of America. He calls the Arabs "medieval fanatics" (mistakenly referring to the Shah of Iran as an Arab). The film won four Academy Awards.

Black Sunday (1977) . . . concerns an Arab terrorist plot to kill the spectators at the Superbowl—including the President of the United States—with a horrible device to be detonated in a television blimp over the stadium. An Israeli major is the hero and the Arabs are the villains. . . .

In *Rollover* (1981) "the Arabs" destroy the world financial system. In publicity interviews, Jane Fonda has made her movie's message explicit: "If we aren't afraid of Arabs, we'd better examine our heads. They have strategic power over us. They are unstable, they are fundamentalists, tyrants, anti-woman, anti-free press."

Laurence Michalak, "Cruel and Unusual: Negative Images of Arabs in American Popular Culture," *ADC Issues*, January 1984, pp. 14–16.

film that drives *us* nuts. Yet, in the next breath he professed no intention of conveying a political message, insisting that "this is entertainment, just cowboys and Indians in the Middle East."[20] A revealing comparison.

New York Times film critic Vincent Canby passes judgment on antiterrorist action films:

The subversive thing about . . . films that exalt blunderbuss chauvinism is that, because they are action movies, they're very easy to sit through no matter what you believe in. Even as you're laughing at their absurdities and responding with acute dismay to their political subtexts, you stay in your seat to find out what's going to happen next.

America, the humiliated giant whose patience is exhausted, is the true subject of [these movies. They go] . . . well beyond what might be called international justice to glorify a kind of violence that is as mindless and wasteful as it is fanciful. . . . such movies aren't intended to be reasonable. Rather, they mean to give the mind a rest by playing on one's prejudices and on one's gut reactions to scenes of sadism, heroism and spectacular special effects.[21]

With the advent of the 1990s, the Bush administration gave us more U.S. military interventions around the world, and Hollywood obligingly provided more films about them. For instance, *Firebird* (1990) offers an explicit blend of entertainment and political propaganda, with an opening screen quotation from President Bush announcing his dedication to the war on narcotics. In this movie, a South American drug cartel, abetted by Cuban arms and helicopter teams, faces off against the U.S. military with its new Apache attack helicopters. Much of the movie seems to be a promotional for the new chopper (which was used to kill people, including civilians, in Panama when the United States invaded that country). One officer says, "We'll confront the forces of evil and kill them deader than hell," and "Your job is to come out of nowhere and blow your enemy to pieces." There is a female helicopter scout pilot who has forsaken a personal relationship with the lead male character. He wanted her to stay home and have babies but she finds more fulfillment killing Cuban Communists in air-to-air combat. In reality, Cuban helicopter teams have not been involved in the narcotics trade, and the United States has not done much against the drug cartels. Most of the American-sponsored "war on drugs" in Peru and Colombia really has been a counterinsurgency against political dissenters and national liberation forces. Like others of its kind, *Firebird* is an unrelenting glorification of high-tech military violence and a gross distortion of political reality.

The antiterrorist films, if that's what they really are, have all the ingredients of the swarthy hordes flicks: (1) White humanity is threatened by barbaric forces; (2) the White heroes use superior intelligence, technology, and limitless bravery to rescue their own from alien clutches; and (3) in doing so, they kill large numbers of Third World savages, thus demonstrating that force and violence are the necessary solution. Violence serves as the main vehicle for plot development (such as it is) and plot resolution. Far from being "antiterrorist," these productions are celebrations of state-sponsored terrorism, helping to set the stage for such events as the real-life, high-tech military destruction of Iraq in 1991.

Monsters and Galactic Aliens

Another variation of the swarthy hordes scenario can be found in science-fiction movies and television series. The basic formula is the same: a peaceable community is besieged by a wicked alien force. The cold-war era of the 1950s, preoccupied with a fear of "alien Communist" threats to the American way of life, offered a veritable plague of "big bug" alien invaders: *The Deadly Mantis* (1957), *Tarantula* (1955), *The Creature from the Black Lagoon* (1954), and *The Beginning of the End* (1957), the latter about some very unsporting oversized grasshoppers. In *Them!* (1954) gargantuan ants crawl all over Los Angeles and gorge themselves on its inhabitants. *The Monster That Challenged the World* (1957) features an elephantine marauding snail, slow but deadly. In *From Hell It Came* (1957) the devouring menace is none other than a deranged and remarkably mobile tree stump. And in *The Thing* (1951), a homicidal giant carrot with a vampiric appetite feasts on human blood and threatens to overrun the entire arctic region.[22] Other genetic mutations included jumbo roaches, wasps, squids, scorpions, reptiles, and serpents.

By the 1970s and 1980s, monsters were in less plentiful supply but still extant. *Island Claw* (1980) featured a colossal crab that preyed on the inhabitants of an otherwise idyllic island. Perhaps the ultimate creature was the one without any identifiable form: *The Blob* (1958). This huge mud-like ooze sneaked up on people through the plumbing and doorsills of their homes, increasing its mass and power with the number of victims it ingested. In 1972 came *Son of Blob* (also known as *Beware! The Blob*). And for those who think Hollywood is incapable of improvement, Blob Sr. was remade thirty years after the original—*The Blob* (1988)—with updated special effects that made the amorphous menace meaner, faster, and bigger.

One could go on. Huge dinosaurs and octopuses emerge intact from the murky depths after centuries of hibernation to consume hapless pedestrians, as in *It Came from beneath the Sea* (1955). The scrofulous *Godzilla, King of the Monsters* (1956) reappears in sequels every few

Along with periodically imposing his urban renewal program on downtown Tokyo, Godzilla occasionally takes on a competitor in a turf fight.

years (1969, 1972, 1976, 1985) to impose his urban renewal program
on downtown Tokyo. The loveable *King Kong* (1933, 1976) loses his
head over a pretty woman and begins to destroy the inhabitants of his
native island. Dragooned by his captors into residing within the unset-
tling confines of New York City, Kong understandably goes on another
rampage, finally climbing the highest towers in order to be alone with
his true love, only to be done in by the U.S. Air Force.

Armed with paralyzing stings or strangulating tentacles or crushing
pincers, the monsters smash through urban defenses and pulverize police and military. They are driven by an urge to destroy. Unlike the beasts
of the jungle, they are not sated after a kill; each new victim only further
stimulates their homicidal binges.

Just when all seems lost, the evil thing is stopped by the right
application of technological, chemical, or military counterforce or by
some clever antidote devised by the young hero, who is desperate to
rescue his girlfriend from the giant genius mutant ants or the regiments
of galactic humanoids.

In these films, as in almost all the other dramas produced by Hollywood and television, the mass of the people make no history. They can

only look forward to being either victimized by the menace or rescued from it. They are incapable of acting in concert against it. They spend most of their time screaming and fleeing for their lives, especially the women. Driven by panic, they sometimes get in the way of rescue efforts and are as much a problem as the invading creatures. The authorities themselves—police, military, scientists, and other community guardians—can also be part of the problem, as when they display an impenetrable skepticism that anything out of the ordinary is happening. Then it's up to the lone hero to vanquish the menace and show officials that he is not crazy.[23]

More sinister than the monster marauders with their easily identifiable antisocial behavior is the alien menace whose goal is to *take us over from within*. The big bug and lizard monsters want to lunch on us, but these diabolic infiltrators are aiming for totalitarian world domination. Not surprisingly, the witch-hunting, cold-war era of the 1950s provides us with some choice examples of this genre. In *Invaders from Mars* (1953), Martians lurk amidst us, taking control of distinguished citizens, parents, and even police by planting crystals in their brains and enslaving their wills. In *Invasion of the Body Snatchers* (1956, 1978), plant pods from another world take possession of our bodies and convert us into obedient automatons. When the heroes try to sound the alarm, they discover that the authorities themselves have been invaded by the pods. The subversion is everywhere. No one is to be trusted. The survivors exclaim: "They're taking us over, cell by cell," and "It's a malignant disease spreading through the whole country."[24] Similarly, in *The Aliens Are Coming* (1980), extraterrestrial beings from a dying planet possess the bodies of earthlings.

It is not too difficult to see that the ideological underpinnings for these kinds of productions are drawn straight from the long-standing right-wing fear of how Communism will spread among us like a "disease," infiltrating our lives, subverting our nation, and turning us into obedient robots, dominating us for the sheer sake of domination.

The 1989–90 television season saw improvement in the extraterrestrial department. A new kind of alien made an appearance in the Fox network series "Alien Nation." Despite the show's title, these aliens are anything but a nation. Instead of being conquering monsters, they are integrated into earthbound community life, holding jobs, owning homes, attending school, and the like. They speak perfect American English and are quite human in appearance, except for some notable differences like large bald heads, no eyebrows, two hearts, and unusual markings on their heads and backs. These features cause them to be the objects of defamatory slurs and ill-treatment of a kind that is pointedly reminiscent of ethnic intolerance. "Alien Nation" might be better titled "Alien Minority." In any case, it represents an improvement over the dreary aliens-enslave-earthlings fare we are usually fed.

If evil extraterrestrial hordes threaten our world, then it is only natural for hero earthlings (Americans) to venture into outer space in order to rectify matters. The two earliest cowboy heroes in futuristic dress who rode spaceships instead of horses were Flash Gordon and Buck Rogers. Both appeared in movies during the 1930s and early 1940s and in television series in the 1950s. Buck Rogers protected Earth in the twenty-fifth century from such threats as the "Slaves of the Master Mind."[25]

During the 1950s, television gave us Captain Video, the intergalactic do-gooder who saved people and planets from evil characters with un-American names like Vazarion, Marcus Gayo, Mook the Moon Man, Heng Goo Seng, and Kul of Eos. Captain Video was introduced at the beginning of each episode as the "champion of Justice, Truth, and Freedom throughout the universe!"[26] As MacDonald points out:

> Such clashes between hero and tyrant were not meaningless excursions in entertainment. They were value-laden fairy tales delivered with impact. . . . They were stylized Cold War fantasies in which the champions of democracy triumphed over totalitarianism. Certainly not every show in the series treated dictatorial plots, but the theme of victory over despotism permeated the programs.[27]

The 1960s gave us the "Star Trek" television series, featuring a team of crusaders from Earth who trundle about the universe, fighting galactic bad guys. The heroes' spaceship, significantly dubbed the *Enterprise* is piloted by the all-American Captain Kirk, "the ultimate cosmic policeman/meddler," who, along with his crew, "spread truth, justice, and the American way of life, including a life of high technology and eternal progress."[28]

Many movies end up as reruns on television or are made available for home viewing on videocassettes. Some even become the inspiration for TV series. The usual flow is from movies to television; less frequently does it go the other way. Such was the case with the "Star Trek" TV series which served as the basis for a movie in 1979, *Star Trek: The Motion Picture* (with film sequels in 1982, 1984, 1986, and 1989).

In another series of motion pictures, *Star Wars* (1977), *The Empire Strikes Back* (1980), and *Return of the Jedi* (1983), the subject is an evil cosmic power that is challenged by individualistic heroes. The heroes are obediently assisted by robots and "lower" nonhuman creatures

The NBC-TV sci-fi series "Star Trek" features intergalactic crusaders who explore the far reaches of the universe on their spaceship *Enterprise*, doing battle against creatures from other planets.

from other planets, high-tech versions of Tonto, Gunga Din, and Cheeta. As usual, right wins through might, with an assist from guile and technology. The evil military officers in *The Empire Strikes Back* have odd accents and wear Soviet-style uniforms; these touches earned the praise of right-wing commentators, who were pleased to point out the resemblances between the futuristic evil empire in the film and the 1980s evil empire in Moscow. A progressive media critic, Elayne Rapping, has this to say about the high-tech adventure genre:

> So much for political activity and democratic institutions. All is physical strength and technical trickery. . . . The films are anti-intellectual in their simplistic, often contradictory and loose-ended plots. They are antihuman in their total disdain for emotional sub tlety and personal relationships and problems, as well as their fasci-

nation with supernatural, magical, and spiritual explanations for their technically produced "effects." And they are . . . anti-democratic, specifically in their fascination with power, warfare, superior beings, and hierarchical class, sex, and race relations.[29]

In the White House, the State Department, and the Pentagon, on the big screen and the small screen, in real life and make-believe, the cowboy-explorer-soldier-space heroes guard us against alien threats.

3

The Media Fight the Red Menace

In the make-believe world of the media, swarthy hordes are dangerous, but Red hordes have been even worse. For decades, Communists were the diabolic enemies made for Hollywood and television. In fact, in all their various embellishments, the Communist demon was made largely *by* Hollywood and television.

Witch-Hunts and Stereotypes

From its earliest days, the motion-picture industry, like every other corporate enterprise, was hostile toward the Russian Revolution, domestic Communism, and labor unions. Putting these together, we get Bolshevik labor organizers in America who commit villainous acts—as seen in about a dozen silent films during the 1920s. They plant bombs, disrupt workplaces, and foment strikes. Luckily, they are always foiled by the authorities or by the film's hero.[1]

The advent of talkies provided additional opportunity to propagate negative stereotypes about Russian Communists and the Soviet Union. Two examples, *Ninotchka* (1939) and *Comrade X* (1940), offer almost identical plots: a debonair "Free World" male pursues an icy Russian female. In *Ninotchka,* Greta Garbo plays the humorless, puritanical, slogan-spouting Communist, a stock character to be seen in many subsequent film and television productions. Unlike most celluloid Reds, however, Garbo is eventually softened and humanized by the blandishments of bourgeois love and luxury.

During the World War II alliance between the United States and the Soviet Union, Hollywood turned out several openly pro-Soviet films, produced at the encouragement of President Roosevelt, who was report-

In *Ninotchka*, Greta Garbo plays a humorless, puritanical Communist who sensibly warms to the blandishments of bourgeois love and luxury.

edly interested in "flattering" Joe Stalin in order to keep him fighting.[2] Among these, *The North Star* (1943) gave rare recognition to the courage displayed and sacrifices made by the Soviet people against the Nazi invasion. Another film, *Mission to Moscow* (1943), was based on the experiences of Joseph Davies, the U.S. ambassador to the Soviet Union from 1936 to 1941. This picture presented the Soviet side of the story regarding the prewar years, including the Russo-Finnish war and the Hitler-Stalin treaty.

After the war in 1947 and again in 1951, the House Un-American Activities Committee (HUAC) launched a full-blown investigative campaign against "Communist influence" in Hollywood. HUAC had a number of goals:

First: expose movies that were "Communistic" or "sympathetic to the Communist point of view." Aside from the few openly pro-Soviet World War II pictures, none was actually found, unless one counts the various liberalistic pro-New Deal motion pictures that some committee members denounced.

Second: prevent any further production of films that harbored "un-American" views and dealt with social issues in a manner that might be detrimental to free-enterprise ideology. Even though HUAC found little to justify its anticommunist inquisition, it did succeed in imposing a chill on Hollywood's already lukewarm desire to make movies that explored iconoclastic political themes.

Third: purge leftist screenwriters, directors, and actors from the industry. Here the congressional inquisitors succeeded quite well. "Many progressive film-workers were driven out of the industry. . . . A few committed suicide, some were imprisoned, others went into exile, and many merely went underground. Those who continued working avoided political subjects or social issues."[3]

Fourth: curb labor militancy in Hollywood. Along with exercising

The Political Purge of Hollywood

During [the House Un-American Activities Committee] hearings, thirty members of the Hollywood community—in desperate and often unsuccessful attempts to save their jobs—named nearly three hundred of their colleagues as members or former members of the Communist Party. With communism appearing to be rampant in the film industry, the studios panicked and began cranking out anti-communist movies—which mostly contained old gangster movie plots, except that the gangsters were now replaced by communists who machine-gunned patriotic Americans and then sped off in fast cars. Two movies, Richard Widmark's *Pickup on South Street* and George Raft's *A Bullet for Joey*, actually portrayed the Mafia teaming up with the police to fight zombie-like communists. . . .

In the end, HUAC blacklisted or "graylisted" nearly two thousand artists in the motion picture, radio, and television industries. . . .

Meantime, [led by its president Ronald Reagan] the Screen Actors Guild [SAG] joined the "Crusade for Freedom," a counterattack against "communist lies and treachery." Reagan, saying that SAG would not defend those actors who defied HUAC, told his SAG colleagues, "It is every member's duty to cooperate fully." . . . Two years later, SAG would force its membership—and those applying for membership—to sign loyalty oaths, saying, "I am not now and will not become a member of the Communist Party nor of any other organization that seeks to overthrow the government of the United States by force and violence."

Dan Moldea, *Dark Victory: Ronald Reagan, MCA, and the Mob* (New York: Viking-Penguin, 1986), pp. 74–75.

an ideological control, the corporate-loving members of HUAC were interested in smothering the bitter labor agitation that the motion-picture industry was experiencing. Of course, the studio bosses cooperated fully with the committee's red-baiting of the Screen Writers Guild.

Fifth: make more anticommunist films. In 1947, HUAC members J. Parnell Thomas and Richard Nixon prodded the movie moguls to enter the fray against the Red Menace. Louis B. Mayer hastily rereleased *Ninotchka*, one month after the HUAC hearings. In short time, Hollywood joined the cold-war crusade with a score of Grade B, second-feature, anticommunist flicks that were usually financial disasters.[4] In this instance, ideology took precedence over box-office considerations. As Nora Sayre notes:

> For certain film makers, being asked to work on an anti-Communist picture was like a loyalty test: if someone who was thought to be a Communist refused to participate in the project, it was assumed that he must be a Party member. So, for some writers, directors, and actors, taking part in a film such as *I Married a Communist* was rather like receiving clearance—it meant they were politically clean. . . .
> The number of movies concerning other social issues decreased drastically between 1947 and 1954, although more than fifty anti-Communist films were produced.[5]

The efforts of the House Un-American Activities Committee should remind us that something more than entertainment was at stake. The committee correctly understood that the entertainment media was an important part of popular culture, and popular culture was a real factor in shaping popular consciousness, including political consciousness.

The image of the Communist as represented in these films and in the television dramas of the 1950s bore little relation to reality but fit well into the ideological stereotype. In movies such as *The Red Menace* (1949), *I Married a Communist* (1950), *I Was a Communist for the FBI* (1951), and *My Son John* (1952) and in the television series "I Led Three Lives" (1953–56) and numerous other TV spy and adventure stories, American Communists were portrayed as murderers, political assassins, terrorists, saboteurs, bank robbers, arsonists, blackmailers, racists, and—perhaps worst of all in the eyes of some witch-hunters—intellectuals.

In reality, there have been no documented instances of members of the Communist Party, USA, engaging in the kind of violent crimes portrayed in the media, although some members certainly have been guilty of being intellectuals. In real life, the party has a proud record of struggle for peace, East-West disarmament, industrial unionism, racial justice, and civil liberties. Party members were at the forefront of the CIO organizing drives of the 1930s, in the fight for civil rights and desegregation, and in the fight against the Ku Klux Klan and lynch-mob terrorism. Convicted under the Smith Act for "conspiring to teach and advocate the violent and forceful overthrow of the government," a number of Communist party leaders went to jail. Some, such as National Chairman Gus Hall, served upwards of nine years, not for acts of murder or sabotage, but for their political beliefs.

The media-made Communists of the 1950s are grim, unsmiling martinets who bark commands at lesser comrades and need to have jokes explained to them. They are cruel to animals and to each other. They prey upon impressionable and idealistic youth. They use sex to entice sweet young things (male and female) into the party—but they apparently never use sex for procreation, for they always seem to be childless. They rant and spout ideological slogans and talk (or, rather, snarl) about "bringing America to its knees" and "taking over this country." Their goal, according to Herbert Philbrick in "I Led Three Lives," is to "control everything and everybody by any means." These Reds are behind just about every labor-management conflict in America, instigating the otherwise contented but easily misled workers into such apparently un-American activities as strikes. Often Communists can be detected by their manner of cigarette exhalation: "they expel smoke very slowly from their nostrils before threatening someone's life, or suggesting that 'harm' will come to his family."[6]

Of course, these media-made American Communists are not really American. Their loyalty is to Moscow and their work dovetails with the foreign spies and saboteurs who seem to be everywhere. In the 1950s the Soviet Union was depicted in both the news and entertainment media as plotting to conquer the United States, either by subverting it from within or by obliterating it with a nuclear attack. In 1956, CBS went so far as to televise a pseudo-documentary, "The Day North America Is Attacked." Using newscaster Walter Cronkite as the announcer and numerous real-life military officers who played themselves, the network and the Pentagon depicted the U.S. military response to a Soviet nuclear bomber attack.[7]

As in news reports, so in the entertainment media—U.S. espionage is portrayed as a patriotic defense, while Soviet espionage is treated as proof of the Kremlin's aggressive intent. *Our* spies do heroic things to thwart the enemy. *Their* spies commit odious acts to undermine and conquer us. Week after week during the fifties, in television series such as "Passport to Danger," "David Harding, Counterspy," "I Spy," and "The Man Called X," the Free World's undercover heroes penetrated the Iron Curtain to rescue freedom-loving people, demolish Communist secret bases, and vanquish the Soviet agents. The efforts of the CIA, the military, and other government agents were supplemented by patriotic private citizens like the corporate executive in the television series "Biff Baker, U.S.A." His business affairs took him all over the world, enabling him to close deals for his company while doing a little espionage and sabotage for his government, thereby serving global capitalism in more ways than one.[8]

When it came to anathematizing Communism, the media has enlisted God, as well as the government and the military. Hollywood producer Cecil B. deMille wove anticommunist messages into his own films, drawing upon a celluloid religiosity to do so. In his remake of *The Ten Commandments* (1956), he appears in the prologue before a golden curtain to deliver a little lecture to the audience about "the theme of this movie." The question is, he says, "Are men the property of the state? Or are they free souls under God? This same battle continues throughout the world today."[9]

Television did its share in blending religiosity and anticommunism, offering an array of religious inspirational shows. Thus, we had "Zero-1960," produced by a fervent anticommunist organization called the Blue Army of Our Lady of Fatima. Nationally syndicated from 1957 to 1960, the show was more concerned with the horrors of atheistic Communism than with the joys of religion.[10]

From the mid-sixties to about the mid-seventies, a period of détente in U.S.–Soviet relations, the Soviets were less likely to be portrayed as the arch-villains in the news and entertainment sectors of the media. Indeed, they were sometimes made into not-such-bad-guys. Thus, in the television series "The Man from U.N.C.L.E." (1964–68), the American and Soviet agents actually team up under the aegis of an international law enforcement agency to fight a sinister crime organization plotting to control the world.

Rambo and the Reaganite Cinema

Not until the 1980s did the media war against the Red Menace again reach full force in both the news and entertainment sectors, faithfully following in the wake of the anti-Soviet propaganda campaign that was being conducted by the White House. The far right was back in the saddle, declaring the end of the noninterventionist "Vietnam syndrome" and the return of a mortal cold-war struggle with the Soviets.

President Reagan and his associates denounced Moscow as the "evil empire," the center of "international terrorism," and the source of "all the unrest" in the world.[11] On cue, Hollywood and the networks went into action. Here is a light sample from the "Reaganite cinema" produced in that era:

The Soldier (1982). The Soviet KGB threatens to blow up half the western world's petroleum supply with a nuclear device it planted in Saudi Arabia—unless the Israelis evacuate the West Bank in forty-eight hours. The Israelis refuse to budge. This upsets the U.S. president, who then decides to nuke the West Bank in order to vacate it and thereby save Western oil. The KGB are everywhere, having penetrated the highest reaches of the CIA itself. Luckily, a CIA counterterrorist team, who look like Young Republicans, side with the Israelis and refuse to knuckle under. They go in and kick Russkie ass. Moral of the story: Don't be led around by the spineless politicians in Washington. (Better to be led around by the tough ones in Jerusalem and Langley, Virginia.) Give the Soviet aggressors the only thing they understand: a bullet in the belly and a gun butt in the face.

Missing in Action (1984). Chuck Norris escapes from a Vietnamese prisoner-of-war camp years after the war. He then returns to Vietnam with a sidekick to liberate the other MIA-POWs from the clutches of the sadistic Vietnamese, who cackle a lot and simply cannot shoot straight. One wonders how they ever won the war. Norris shows how to fight the Vietnam war and win it this time—with individualistic heroics. Then came *Missing in Action II: The Beginning* (1985), literally the same stuff: Norris again escapes from a POW camp. He has trouble staying out of them. He rescues others, kills commies, refights the war, wins it yet again. Then in *Braddock: Missing in Action III* (1988), Norris returns to Vietnam to rescue his wife, kill commies, refight the war, etc.

There are over 78,000 missing-in-action servicemen from World War II. Nobody believes they are being held captive in beer cellars in Germany or Toyota factories in Japan. They are dead. So are the more than 2,000 MIAs from the Vietnam war. Hollywood reached a low point when it joined the Reagan administration's campaign to play upon the unrealistic hopes of bereaved families in order to fuel yet another anticommunist theme.

These films not only refight the Vietnam war, they rewrite it. Once more history is stood on its head, as the roles of aggressor and defender are reversed. Never a word is said about the colossal destruction and suffering wreaked upon the Vietnamese civilian population in a war of attrition by U.S. firepower many times greater and even more indiscriminate than that utilized in World War II.

The Public Believes Hollywood

Back in 1977, the House Select Committee on Missing Persons in Southeast Asia, chaired by Republican Representative Sonny Montgomery, concluded that "no Americans are still being held alive as prisoners of war in Indochina" and that "a total accounting by the Indochinese governments is not possible and should not be expected."

[Conservative activists], aided by a stream of Sylvester Stallone and Chuck Norris movies, have come to believe otherwise, and 82 percent of respondents, according to a recent Wirthlin poll, think American prisoners are still being held in Southeast Asia.

The Nation, June 4, 1988, p. 791.

An accounting of the Reaganite cinema should also include *Firefox* (1982), *Dangerous Moves* (1985), *White Nights* (1985), *Born American* (1986), and *Bulletproof* (1988), movies populated by ruthless KGB agents and brutish Soviet military who are bested by the individualistic heroics of two-fisted Americans or, as in *White Nights*, a heroic anticommunist Russian emigré.

The most notable representations of this genre are the Sylvester Stallone productions, beginning with *Rocky IV* (1985). The comedian Jay Leno once said that performers like Arnold Schwarzenegger and Sylvester Stallone deserve a lot of credit for having "opened up the acting profession to people who couldn't get into it when speech was a major requirement." Certainly this is true of Stallone's *Rocky IV,* the story of a highly inarticulate boxing champ, Rocky Balboa, who goes international to take on the Soviets. The Soviet boxer is a Nazi-style killing machine, created by high-tech training methods that include steroids and blood-doping. He kills Rocky's friend, African-American boxer Apollo Creed, in the ring to the delight of bloodthirsty Soviet spectators. Naturally, Rocky vows vengeance. Wearing American-flag trunks and facing a snarling Soviet crowd, Rocky demolishes the subhuman, superhuman Soviet boxer. The crowd, including the Politburo members and Soviet leader Gorbachev, do an ideological flip, rising as one to applaud their new hero, Rocky, who stands in the ring and instructs them on the meaning of world peace with such elegantly enlightening lines as: "It's how youse feel about me and I feel about you! Dat's wha' counts!" One critic observes:

As the fine line between Hollywood and the U.S. government grows even fainter, the actions of political leaders take on more of the character of wild fantasy and Hollywood films become more absurdly "political"—there is hardly a difference between a Reagan speech and a Rocky monologue.[12]

Stallone's celebration of a Reaganite cinema achieves its apotheosis in the Rambo series. *First Blood* (1982) introduces us to John Rambo (Stallone), another strung-out Vietnam veteran, an ex-Green Beret. Rambo gets into a scrape with a small-town sheriff who treats him brutally. This triggers bad memories of Vietnam, causing Rambo to go wacko. Things escalate into a one-man war against the police and the National Guard. In the last scene just before he surrenders, Rambo finally explains himself to his old Green Beret commander.

It wasn't my war. You asked me, I didn't ask you. I did what I had to do to win, but somebody wouldn't let us win. And I come back to the world, and I see all those maggots at the airport protesting me, calling me a baby-killer and all kinds of vile crap. Who're they to protest me? Back there I could fly a gunship, I could drive a tank. I was in charge of million dollar equipment. Back here I can't even hold a job.

Rambo, First Blood II (1985) finds our hero in the slammer because of the things he did in the previous movie. But he's given a deal: a presidential pardon if he goes to Vietnam, photographs his old POW camp, and shows that there are no more MIAs. He goes and finds Americans still being held prisoner. (Oddly enough, he does not run into Chuck Norris.) The officials back in Washington are embarrassed. They wanted him not to find any Americans missing-in-action so the issue could be put to rest. They order that Rambo be left to his fate in the jungle. (In real life, if Reaganite officials could have come up with a real, live MIA still being held in Vietnam, they would have joyfully squeezed every bit of propaganda advantage out of it.) Betrayed by the Washington bureaucrats and abandoned in this hostile environment, Rambo is captured and tortured by the Soviets. He escapes, liberates all the POWs, and then kicks, punches, and shoots his way to freedom, all the while being pursued by napalm-tossing Soviet helicopters. Armed with a bow (and arrows that explode), a serrated knife as big as a machete, and an occasional machine gun, Rambo kills the entire Vietnamese army and a battalion of Russians. He is assisted in this extraordinary feat by the fact that his adversaries all seem to be legally blind. They fire thousands of rounds at him and never so much as fluff his hair.

This Rambo rampage has enough distortions to keep any honest critic busy for a week. In reality: (1) The Vietnamese exchanged POWs with the United States after signing the Paris Peace Agreement, which ended the war. Since then, they have cooperated in trying to find the remains of MIAs. (2) U.S. prisoners-of-war were not tortured by the Soviets as depicted in the film. Torture was a regular practice of the South Vietnamese and U.S. Special Forces in Vietnam. (3) The Soviets did not drop napalm on anyone in Vietnam—it was the U.S. military that dropped large amounts of napalm and Agent Orange, mostly on the civilian population.

Rambo III (1988), opening in a record 2074 theaters throughout America, finds our hero in Afghanistan, where he singlehandedly kills scores of Russians. The film appeared just at the time the Soviets were withdrawing from Afghanistan. Rambo invades a Soviet fortress deep in

In *Rambo III*, our hero rescues a friend and fights his way out of a fortress inhabited by sadistic Russians who like to torture people and murder little children. Luckily, Rambo kills them all.

that country to rescue a friend, pausing only to squeeze an arrow out of his gut and cauterize the wound on an open flame. The Soviets are portrayed as sadists, rapists, and torturers who murder little children with explosive toys (a horror story originally propagated by the CIA). For fun, Rambo sends a Soviet captive plummeting with a noose around his neck to his death in a cave shaft, then for still more fun, Rambo dynamites him. Rambo gets along swell with the *mujahedeen* killers, feudal landowners, fundamentalist Islamic fanatics, and opium growers (all known in the United States as the "Afghan freedom fighters").

By the end of this third and worst of the Rambo films, our hero seems to have mellowed out. He gives his good-luck charm to an adoring twelve-year-old Afghan boy soldier, who himself is shown killing Russians on several occasions. War has been a healing, nurturing experience for Rambo, a rehabilitation through violence. He's found himself. As the movie ends, you feel he's going to move on, maybe head back to the States, buy a trailer, hunt bear, settle down and get married, join the National Rifle Association, and open up the nicest little gun shop in Texas.

Rambo's *Mujahedeen* Buddies in Real Life

Soon after the offensive at Jalalabad began March 7, there were reports of government troops being slaughtered after they surrendered or were captured. In one case, as Western journalists watched, a truckload of prisoners being escorted by relatively moderate rebels was stopped by extremists who casually shot the captives to death.

[Another report:] A motor column was supposed to bring dozens of women, children and old people from Jalalabad to Kabul. The buses and trucks were stopped by "a band of Afghan extremists" led by Saudi Arabian advisers. The drivers were lined up on the shoulder of the highway and shot. Small children were held up by their hair, shot in the face and their corpses thrown into Kabul River. Pretty women from the convoy were dragged off into the mountains by the rebels. The rest of the refugees were shot on the spot.

[The so-called free tribesmen, who go back and forth across the Afghan-Pakistan border on camels, have told stories of being kidnapped, separated from their wives and children and forced to fight for the *mujahedeen*.]

Dispatches from Afghanistan in the *Los Angeles Times* and other sources, as reported in Alexander Cockburn's column in the *Nation*, June 12, 1989, p. 803.

On second thought, it is not likely that Rambo would marry. Women do not figure big in his life. He channels his testosterone into more gratifying things like homicidal violence. Why fuss with females when you can get a bigger rush from killing Russians? Happiness is a warm gun.

When a woman does appear in movies about swarthy hordes or spies or vicious Reds, she is usually a seductive sexpot who turns out to be an undercover agent for one side or the other. Or she is merely an accessory, attached to the hero—quite literally, being yanked along by him a pace behind in heels and skirt, as they flee danger. Sometimes she is the U.S. ambassador's beautiful daughter or a reporter or just the hero's most recent sexual acquisition. In any case, she has a genius for getting herself into perilous predicaments from which she must be extricated by the hero. While occasionally allowed to hold or even shoot a gun in self-defense, she does it gingerly, as befitting her gender-typed deportment. More often she just stands uselessly aside, anxiously watching her hero fight off a platoon of attackers.

In *Rambo III*, women are so superfluous as to be altogether absent. In real life, many of the Afghan *mujahedeen* took up arms alongside their feudal landowners and opium growers because they bitterly opposed the laws favoring female education and emancipation promulgated by the Soviet-supported Kabul government. The Afghan "freedom fighters" believe a woman's place is in the tent. Rambo has no problem with that.

Images of Soviet aggression found sensationalist expression in movies like *Red Dawn* (1984) and *Invasion USA* (1985) and in television mini-series like ABC's "Amerika" (1987), all of which portray imaginary Soviet invasions of the United States. Coauthored by the self-described "Zen fascist" and war lover John Milius, *Red Dawn* tells how the Soviet Union, plagued by crop failures and food riots, launches a nuclear attack against Washington, D.C., and then occupies America's agriculturally rich heartland. The Soviets are assisted by domestic collaborators and by Cuba and Nicaragua, who have emerged as major military powers in the Western hemisphere. Luckily, in a small town in Colorado where most of the citizens have been murdered or sent to indoctrination camps, a group of youngsters escape to the hills, from which they launch armed attacks that make mincemeat out of the enemy. In the end, the "Wolverines," as they call themselves, carry out a suicidal raid to free other American youths, who then flee across the Rockies to unoccupied "Free America."

Invasion USA offers a variation on the same theme. Uniformed troops from the USSR, Cuba, and an unidentified Arab country disembark undetected on a Miami beach on a bright moonlit night. With the unimpeded ease of international drug smugglers, they pile into waiting trucks and fan out across the country. During this escapade, one of the Communist invaders sneeringly describes the Americans as "soft, spineless, decadent. They don't even understand the nature of their own freedom or how we will use it against them." The infiltrators commit terrorist acts that turn neighbors against each other and against the police. Nobody in America seems to grasp what is behind these strange doings. Nobody seems to know really what the danger is. Nobody, that is, except Chuck Norris, who eventually manages singlehandedly to rally outnumbered U.S. troops for a showdown fight that wipes out the invaders. Once again, we owe our salvation to individualistic heroics and abundant applications of violence.

In ABC's fourteen-hour television mini-series, "Amerika," a United-Nations army, led by the Soviets who dominate that organization, takes over the United States. The occupying army massacres large numbers of innocent people and puts even larger numbers into internment camps. America is turned into a Soviet satellite. Actually, after ten years of occupation (it is 1997), Soviet "Amerika" bears an ironic resemblance to Reagan's America. Sports and other propaganda are used as tools to distract the masses. Homeless people forage for food. Farmers complain of losing everything after years of hard work. Unemployment, alcoholism, and drug addiction are serious problems. Supposedly none of this existed until the Russians started messing up the American way of life.

Such films turn history on its head. The Soviet Union has never invaded the USA, nor has Cuba or Nicaragua. Rather, it is the other way around. The United States has invaded Cuba and Nicaragua and also Soviet Russia. In 1919–1921, the United States joined a fourteen-nation expeditionary force in an attempt to overthrow the revolutionary government in Russia. The invaders failed in their goal, but not until they had taken a terrible toll in lives and property. Most Americans are astonished to hear of it. This invasion of Soviet Russia remains something of a blank page in our school texts. Nor, to my knowledge, has there ever been so much as a movie or television story based on these events.

In order to justify one's own hostility toward others, one portrays "them" in the most negative way. "We want peace but they are aggressors; they want to bury us," goes the old refrain. It is always an embarrassment when the "enemy" acts like a friend, calling for talks, trade, arms limitations, cultural exchanges, and peaceful relations—as the Soviets kept doing through the decades after World War II and most effectively in the 1980s. To maintain public support for U.S. global interventionism and a huge military arsenal, our leaders often dismissed such overtures as just so many subterfuges designed to throw us off our guard.[13] Certainly the make-believe media have done their share in the campaign to nourish anticommunism, militarism, and nation-state chauvinism. In a promotional video for one of his Rambo movies, Sylvester Stallone, unlike most filmmakers who pretend they are not involved in ideological matters, openly described his movie as political: "I hope to establish a character that can represent a certain section of the American consciousness."[14] He succeeded all too well.

Red-Bashing on Madison Avenue

TV advertisers, keeping their eyes firmly on the evil empire, [have been] introducing a new technique: Red-bashing. Miller Lite beer was first. . . . They're showing an émigré Soviet comedian, surrounded by new capitalist pals at a bar, telling us he loves America and the wonderful things he's found here, including unopened mail. "Also," he says, "in America you can always find a party. In Russia, Party always finds you."

Then came MCI, the long-distance telephone service. . . . Its ads are set in a fish market somewhere in frozen Siberia. Its hero (or antihero) is a solitary consumer battling an implacable bureaucratic machine. The theme is anything but elusive: These poor folks have no choice in the goods and services they buy, much as Americans presumably had no choice in the bad old days when there was just A. T. & T. . . . "Fish no good," our beleaguered hero complains. "No refunds," comes the stern reply. . . .

The latest entry is Wendy's, the hamburger chain. Wendy's scenario is a fashion show behind the Iron Curtain in which an enormously fat model parades the same plain cloth dress. . . . The outfit's the same every time Olga comes down the runway. Only the accessories vary: In the beachwear version, she carries a beach ball. For evening-wear, she totes a flashlight. Hovering over the scene is a dim portrait of Lenin. Wendy's point is much the same: There's no choice over there. But there is here. . . .

A little levity in the East-West dialogue might not be a bad thing. It's nice, too, to be reminded that there's more choice here than in say, Irkutsk. But are these the products to demonstrate that wonderful truth? Sure, you can have Miller Lite. You can also have several other virtually identical lights. MCI vs. A.T.&T.? Well, it seems [A.T.&T.'s] prices are coming down while its competitors' prices are going up. And one fast-food burger is much like another.

Michael Olmert, *New York Times*, December 22, 1985.

As Communism disappeared from much of Eastern Europe, re-placed by right-wing anticommunist regimes, and as it receded in the USSR itself, the Red-Menace, Soviet-bashing films began to seem out-dated. When *The Hunt for Red October* (1990) appeared, it was prefaced with a disclaimer, reminding the audience that the film referred to events that (supposedly) occurred in pre-perestroika cold-war days. When Communists invite western capital into their countries and con-vert their socialist economies into "free-market" capitalism, they are no longer considered evil because they are no longer anticapitalist. But the end of the cold war and the decline of Eastern European state socialism does not mean the end of rabid anticommunism as far as the leaders of our national security are concerned. There are still popular revolution-ary forces in Central America and elsewhere that threaten overseas corporate investments, thereby inviting U.S. interventionism and counterinsurgency. And as long as such conflicts continue, they are likely to invite media productions about the dangers of leftist revolution-aries, narco-terrorists, and the like.

The Wide Weird World of Sports

Even the media's coverage of sporting events can provide occasions for anticommunism, militarism, and jingoism. In professional wrestling—or what passes for wrestling on television—we are treated to Hulk Hogan, whose promotional video couples military might with national chauvinism—specifically, a missile flying out of an American flag. Other "Wrestlemania" characters like "Iron Sheik," "Abdullah the Butcher," and "Haiti Kid" manage to debase Third World peoples, as does "Harpoon," a dark African-looking man who is not a crowd favor-ite. Perhaps worst of all are "Junk Yard Dog," an African-American dressed in a dog collar and chains, and "Rowdy Roddy Piper," who describes himself as the "last great White hope." Then there is "Nikolai Volkov," who would enter the ring and sing the Soviet anthem, which he could scarcely finish for all the boos and profanities the fans hurled at him. By 1990, as the international scene changed, so did Nikolai's act. He now wore a red jacket that had not only a hammer and sickle but a U.S. flag on it. Before one match, he was presented with a huge American flag. He waves it proudly and shouts, "God Bless America." How did he feel holding the flag, an announcer asks. "I never feel better in my life," he answers. The crowd cheers its approval.

Team sport contests between the United States and the USSR have provided ample opportunity for televised flag waving and Red bashing.

When the U.S. Olympic hockey team defeated a second-string Soviet team at Lake Placid, New York, on December 9, 1983, the ABC Nightline announcer crowed: "The Americans withstood an all-out Soviet assault." In an aftergame interview, U.S. coach Lou Vairo said he had told his players they "have something the Russians don't have . . . the American belief we can succeed at anything we do." Had the Soviets claimed such a faith in their own invincibility, it would have been taken as evidence of their implacably aggrandizing intentions.

When the Soviet Union beat the USA in basketball in the 1988 Summer Olympics, NBC treated it as the end of civilization as we know it. In post-game commentaries, NBC announcers described an American team seriously handicapped by insufficient practice time and the loss of a key player and thus unable to withstand "the Soviet onslaught." The Soviets, it seems, "never let up their attack," and were a "relentless juggernaut." The impression left was that the American players were facing the Red Army rather than another basketball team.

Reporting on the Washington Redskins' Superbowl victory in 1983, a *Washington Post* sportswriter rejoiced that "the capital of the Free World" now had a "world champion team." The writer suggested that the Redskin offensive line should be sent to President Reagan because they were "of such size, strength and irresistibility that they could carry the MX missiles around the desert" and "run the you-know-whos out of Afghanistan."[15]

Presidents of the United States make a regular practice of injecting their presence into sporting events. Ronald Reagan relied on a rehearsed script filled with painful quips when doing his public relations stint before fifty million TV sports viewers. In a split-screen telephone call to Los Angeles Raiders' coach Tom Flores immediately following the Raiders' 1984 Superbowl victory, Reagan said that "Moscow just called about Marcus Allen [the Raiders' running back]. They think he is some new secret weapon and they demand he be dismantled." And as if that weren't hilarious enough, Reagan added: "We could put your Raiders into silos—then we wouldn't need MX missiles." Thus the president associated a Raiders victory with White House militarism. He never thought to suggest that Allen and the Raiders be used as goodwill emissaries between the two superpowers.

The conclusion of the 1985 World Series found President Reagan once more milking a warmed-up audience of fifty million by calling the winning team for an after-game chat. Picking up on the ideological subtext, Kansas City manager Dick Howser told the president, "We think we did it the American way, with good hard work."

The media's telecasting of the Olympic games has been marked by blatant chauvinism. It is one thing for American viewers to favor their own country in international athletic contests, but quite another to be urged to do so by the media. The networks project an image of U.S. athletic superiority, focusing preeminently on American Olympic contestants to the neglect of those from other countries, including many who might give decidedly superior performances. There is also usually lack of coverage of events in which Americans are not favored or not engaged.

The Olympics are supposed to promote international good will and an enjoyment of the capabilities of athletes from all nations, not a shrill nationalism. ABC's coverage of the 1984 Summer Olympics was so shamelessly lopsided as to evoke an official reprimand from the normally placid International Olympic Committee. Similar complaints were registered by South Korean officials regarding NBC's coverage of the 1988 Summer Olympics in Seoul.

In a word, even a sector of the entertainment media such as sports reportage, which has no narrative line, can be permeated with anticommunist, militaristic, and chauvinistic imagery.

It should be evident by now that the political distortions of the entertainment media can be measured not only by what is said but by what is left unsaid. Aside from a few exceptional productions, the motion-picture and television industries have eschewed any treatment of the exploitations, atrocities, and other injustices perpetrated by the defenders of the "Free World" against peoples of the Third World. As in school textbooks, mainstream academic research, political life, and news media, so in the entertainment media: the United States global military and economic empire is nowhere to be seen; instead we have America the innocent, the just, an America threatened and even invaded by vicious adversaries. But also an America—as embodied by individual macho heroes—that gets tough against aggressors when the chips are down, kicks ass, wins the Vietnam war, and stops being soft on Communism and terrorism, an America that knows how to defend its way of life with fascistic violence. Thus, are the crimes and oppressions of the empire hidden from the empire's own people, who are themselves among its victims and among the consumers of its mythology.[16]

4

Make-Believe History

Americans are among the most ignorant people in the world when it comes to history. Opinion surveys have shown that large percentages of them do not know the difference between World War I and World War II. Many believe that Germany and the Soviet Union were allies in the latter conflict. As already noted, relatively few ever heard of the multinational invasion of Soviet Russia in which the United States was a participant. Many never heard of Hiroshima and have no idea that the United States dropped an atomic bomb on that city.[1] Many could not tell you what issues were involved in the Vietnam war or other armed conflicts in which the United States has participated. Nor could they say much about the history of aggression perpetrated against Native Americans and the slavery inflicted upon Africans in America. The centuries of imperialism imposed on Asia, Africa, and Latin America by the European and North American powers are, for the most part, nonevents in the collective American psyche. Not many Americans could put together two intelligent sentences about the histories of Mexico, Canada, Puerto Rico, or Cuba—to name the United States closest neighbors. Most would not have the foggiest idea about what was at stake in the French Revolution, the Russian Revolution, the Spanish Civil War, or the Chinese Revolution.

Americans themselves are not totally to blame for this. They are taught almost nothing of these things in primary and secondary school nor even at the university level. And what they are taught is usually devoid of the urgent political economic realities that allow both past and present to inform each other, making history meaningful to us. Nor do U.S. political leaders, news pundits, and other opinion makers find much reason to place current developments in an historical context, especially one that might raise troublesome questions about the existing social order. Popular ignorance is not without its functions. Those at the top prefer that people know little about history's potentially troublesome lessons (except those parts of history that have been specially packaged with superpatriotic, system-supporting messages).

As noted earlier, when portrayed in movies and television dramas, history is usually stood on its head or reduced to personal heroics. In this regard, the make-believe media reinforce the kind of history taught in the schools, mouthed by political leaders, and recorded by the news media. One can present almost any subject in the U.S. news and entertainment media: sex and scandal, deviancy and depravity, and sometimes even racial oppression and gender discrimination. What cannot be touched is the taboo subject of *class,* specifically the importance of class power and class struggle.

Nice Tyrants and Bad Revolutions

Even the class realities of earlier precapitalist eras are not considered a fit entertainment subject. The ancient world, for instance, as represented in the costume epics produced in such abundance by television and Hollywood, is viewed almost exclusively from its upper reaches, a perspective so rarified as to be devoid of class conflict, in fact, devoid of main characters from any class but the aristocracy and military. Such is the case with the television mini-series "I Claudius" and other less well-done productions. In movies like *Quo Vadis?* (1951, 1985) and *Caligula* (1980), the decadence of the imperial court and the violence of the Roman arena are presented in a sensationalistic manner but not the cruel class realities of Roman society, not the exploitation and impoverishment of the Roman people, and not the pillage and bloodletting perpetrated across the Mediterranean by Roman imperialism, all of which greatly advantaged the landed aristocracy.

Except for the occasional appearance of slaves who wait upon the lead characters, make-believe media offer hardly a hint that Rome was a place of terrible class injustices, heroic rebellions, and horrific repressions. An exception here is *Spartacus* (1960), produced by Edward Lewis, which tells of a famous uprising and puts Hollywood on record as being against slavery—at least of the ancient Roman variety.

When the common victims of Rome's rule do appear in the make-believe media, they usually turn out to be pagans or Jews who convert to Christianity after a stressful bout in a Roman dungeon or arena. During the anticommunist heyday of the 1950s, as already noted, producers like Cecil B. deMille consciously played up the allegorical link between Roman and Egyptian tyrants and the Kremlin—in movies like *Quo Vadis?*, *Ben Hur* (1959), *The Robe* (1953), and *The Silver Chalice* (1954). The early Christians in these biblical epics are like freedom fighters against a premature Red despotism. The most attractive actors are the ones who become Christians, a conversion that invariably makes their faces glow with joy as the entire screen is enveloped in rhapsodic music and radiant light. Often, God's presence makes itself known in a most direct way, by interjecting a command in an echoed baritone voice, as if God lived and spoke at the bottom of a well. In *Ben Hur*, the hero's mother and sister are saved from death and miraculously healed of all their wounds. Needless to say, they become faithful fans of the new messiah. Jesus power is able to transform gladiators into Christians and fierce lions into pussycats. Religion, specifically Christianity, emerges triumphant and affirmed.

The costume epics of later historical periods likewise evade social realities. Again, our attention is directed to the intrigues and ambitions of royalty. There is Queen Elizabeth I of the film *The Virgin Queen* (1955) and the British television series "Elizabeth R." and numerous other teleplays and movies. She stomps about her court, taking firm measures against those who would have the temerity to challenge the powers of her throne or the reaches of her empire, exclaiming "I *am* the *queen*!" She preserves her virginity so that no husband might infringe upon her royal powers. At the same time she repeatedly proclaims herself to be "loved by the people," though we never actually hear from the people themselves on this or any other question. Nor are we ever told which of her plundering aristocratic policies have won their love. Presumably "the people" did not include the Irish, whom "Good Queen Bess" killed in abundant numbers.

There is the hapless but benign King Louis of France in finery and poodle wig (*The Three Musketeers*, 1935, 1948, 1974), and the lovely, besieged Queen of Spain (*The Adventures of Don Juan*, 1948), calling upon their loyal swashbucklers to defend the crown's prerogatives against usurpers. There is Peter the Great, as depicted in the 1986 NBC mini-series by that name, whose ambitions and struggles are reduced to a family feud, devoid of class issues and considerations of social inequality.[2] From productions of this sort, one would never surmise that the British, French, Spanish, and czarist kingdoms were inhabited largely by impoverished peasants, tradespeople, and artisans, on whose backs lived so splendidly the very monarchs and aristocrats glorified in the narratives.

The make-believe media do not question the morality of absolute monarchy. In these epics, the throne is to be protected from predators or won back from usurpers. Loyalty to the crown is the highest virtue, although we are never really told why the incumbent is to be so revered. It is assumed that the country is a better place when ruled by the "legitimate" monarch. Hierarchy and aristocracy are the ordained order. An occasional passing reference to "the people" is supposedly enough to establish that the ruler is loved by his or her subjects. However, a wicked monarch will be hated by them, in which case some sword-wielding hero—never the people themselves—overturns the despot and props a nicer-looking, more clean-cut, and therefore more deserving pretender upon the throne.

The Adventures of Robin Hood (1938), an Errol Flynn swashbuckling flick, offers this simplistic scenario of good king vs. bad king. Bad King John is the usurper of the English throne, from whose rule good King Richard the Lion-Hearted must rescue the people. For reasons never explained, the common people are said to love Richard. Upon returning from the crusades, Richard regains his crown—thanks in part to the efforts of Robin Hood and his men. In reality, Richard the Lion-Hearted gave his people little cause to love him. His greatest contribution to history was to grab the lands of other nobles and plunder the hard-earned wealth of commoners. He also devoted much effort to pillaging villages and slaughtering people in the western provinces of France and other parts of Europe.

When the people do make an appearance as active agents of their own fate, seizing state power in a revolution, it is usually portrayed as a wicked thing. In *Orphans of the Storm* (1921), D. W. Griffith depicts the French Revolution as nothing more than rule by demagogues and mobs, who impose a despotism far worse than what any monarch might inflict. In *A Tale of Two Cities* (1917, 1935, 1958, 1980), the revolution is reduced to little more than guillotine terror, an irrational bloodletting by the mob that claims mostly innocents as its victims. Various versions of this film were rerun widely in 1989 across the United States in antirevolutionary commemoration of the French Revolution's bicentennial.

Another persistently marketed antirevolutionary treatment of the French Revolution is *The Scarlet Pimpernel* (1934), followed by *The Return of the Scarlet Pimpernel* (1938), *The Elusive Pimpernel* (1950), and the 1982 made-for-television version of the original. In these films, an underground hero disguised as a gentleman of the English court rescues French noblemen from the Terror. The common people are portrayed as vulgar bullies who take special delight in beheading finer folk. The film leaves little doubt that the world would be a better place if left in the hands of aristocrats and kept from the crude temper of the mindless mob.

As far as I know, there has never been a positive cinematic or television portrayal of the French Revolution. This great event, a turning point in the history of Europe and in the struggle for democracy in which the people overthrew an age-old class tyranny, has been accorded only unforgiving treatment. The closest we come to something different is the Polish-French production of *Danton* (1982) which provides a sympathetic treatment of the revolutionary leader Danton. It was Danton who once said that the rewards of revolution should go to the revolutionaries—that is, to the revolution's bourgeois leaders. No mention of this or of his own self-enrichening efforts are made in the film. The film's demon is Robespierre, who is allowed only one passing comment about the class realities behind the revolution, specifically a reference to the bankers and aristocrats who prey upon the people. Other than that, Robespierre comes across as little more than a tight-faced fanatic armed with a guillotine and the revolution itself as but a struggle among power-hungry personalities.

The Mexican Revolution is the subject of *Viva Zapata!* (1952). The revolutionary leader Emiliano Zapata is sympathetically portrayed as a peasant leader fighting to win back land for his people. But the film has little to say about the rich *latafundio* owners and cash-crop exporters who profited so handsomely by displacing the peasantry. The state, as personified by corrupt generals and politicians, is presented as the villain, not the privileged economic class that is so faithfully served by the state. The revolution succeeds, but state power corrupts the revolutionary leader himself. When Zapata realizes he is beginning to resemble the people he supplanted, he leaves office and resumes leadership of a peasant insurgency. The class conflict which was the heart of the Mexican Revolution is obscured by the film's more politically antiseptic message: power corrupts, so don't expect to achieve any kind of social betterment by seizing control of the state.

No Better Than the Textbooks

In the world of make-believe, American history is treated as badly as the history of other nations. On the relatively infrequent occasions the American Revolution has been the subject of movies and teleplays, it has been reduced to a contentless contest between patriots and redcoats. In this respect, our movies are no better than our history textbooks. An example is *Revolution* (1985), a motion picture burdened by a tedious and improbable script, which teaches us that the rebellion arose because the mean-spirited, sadistic British made a great sport of treating Americans poorly. In the closing scene, the Continental soldiers are cheated out of their severance pay by their own officers, thus leaving us—as in *Viva Zapata!*—with the oddly counterrevolutionary message: *plus ça change, plus c'est la même chose*. You just fought a revolution but don't expect to be treated any better than before; there's just too much corruption and injustice around.

Of the eighty years or so between the American Revolution and the Civil War, one hears little from the make-believe media—or certainly little that pertains to reality. One would never know that a working class was emerging during that period, consisting of horridly overworked and underpaid women, children, and men.

The Civil War era itself has been the subject of numerous films and television dramas, almost all shallow and sentimentalized, some downright pro-slavery. Still described by some critics as "the greatest movie ever made," *Gone with the Wind* (1939) looms as the prime example of an unabashed celebration of slavocracy. Life was sweet on the li'l ole plantation before the no-good Yankees came and ruined it all. The slaveholders are warm, lovable people. The slaves are devotedly childlike and simpleminded. Slave women fan the young white ladies as they take their naps in preparation for evening festivities. Mammies fuss and fret over the same young belles with loving admonitions. Field slaves work contentedly until "quittin' time," to a majestic offscreen musical score that makes their toil seem like an uplifting outdoor recreation. The bad times come with the war, when the Yankees burn Atlanta and plunder the plantations. Worse still is the postwar Reconstruction era, when people—especially Blacks—no longer know their place. Society is

Television's Little Pseudo-history Morons

Historical illiteracy starts early in life. Even the mythical stories that are passed off as American history suffer terribly at the hands of preschoolers and other youngsters who are raised primarily on television. Playskool, a toymaker, asked 151 children, all four-to-six-year-olds, who sewed the first American flag. Most frequently named was Barbara Bush, followed by actress Joanna Kerns (Kirk Cameron's mother on the television sitcom "Growing Pains"). Betsy Ross placed a poor third and Debbie Gibson was fourth.

USA Today, April 10, 1990.

thrown into the squalor and disorder that comes when slavery is abolished. The Southern gentlemen of the former slavocracy are obligated to use vigilante violence to deal with ruffian ex-slaves and low-life Whites.

In the absence of anything better, *Gone with the Wind* has been, for several generations of Americans (thanks to movie and television reruns and videos), the most vivid and reliable image of what the antebellum South must have been like, an image only partly blurred by the more recent television series "Roots," which did portray some of the brutality of slavery.

Even more notorious is D. W. Griffith's silent era *Birth of a Nation* (1915), which paints a frightening picture of the Reconstruction period, complete with corrupt and villainous Black legislators, arrogant mulat-

Treated as a film classic, *Birth of a Nation* offers a glorified version of the rise of the Ku Klux Klan during Reconstruction. The film helped promote a revival of the racist Klan outside the South.

toes who treat old Confederates with bruising insolence, and leering Black soldiers who lust after White women. Only the night-riding Ku Klux Klan is able to rectify matters. *Birth of a Nation* helped promote the revival of the Klan outside the South. The movie's message was received so seriously that schoolchildren throughout the country were taken to see it in order to learn "history."[3] It was rereleased in 1921, 1922, and 1930 and continues to be featured in film series as a "classic" and in university film courses as a "landmark production" of early cinematography.

The more recent six-part television series "North and South" (ABC, 1985), adapted from a pulp novel by that title, also parades a conservative view of the Civil War—though sanitized for modern audiences to avoid some of the more egregious racial stereotypes common to earlier Hollywood productions. The principal characters are two West Point cadets. One is from a rich Southern slave-owning family, the other is the son of a rich Philadelphia industrialist. Wicked Southern politicians plot secession in order to increase their power. Likewise, fanatical Northern abolitionists do their frothy best to drive the country into a divisive war. "North and South" tells us that the Civil War was an unnecessary conflict between brothers, instigated by pro- and antislavery extremists. Both the slaveholders who uncompromisingly defend their interests with violence and the people who uncompromisingly oppose slavery are treated as moral equivalents. The show's negative image of abolitionists is in keeping with many school texts. The true history of the multiracial and democratic abolitionist movement is a far more compelling story than the blather offered in "North and South," yet it is rarely touched by the entertainment media.[4]

To prove that "North and South" was not make-believe history at its worst, ABC gave us the even more insufferable "North and South, Book 2" in 1988, which carries the narrative through the Civil War itself—with scenes that might have come out of *Gone with the Wind*. There is the Confederate officer who, as he leaves for the war, tells his belle of his dedication to their slavocracy: "We would be without pride and honor if we let the North tell us how to live. There are some things worth fighting for, this land, this home, a way of life." He is helped onto his horse by his faithful slave, a young Black man who hands him his sword and reassures him about the White women he is leaving behind: "Don't worry 'bout nothin, master. I'll look after them." A Virginia belle who brings medical supplies to the Confederate troops at the lines has a smiling slave at home named "Washington," who, along with his son, faithfully serves her. One would never know that in real life almost all slaves sympathized with the Northern cause. Some killed their overseers and openly rebelled. Many fled to Northern lines, and 180,000 Blacks fought in the Union Army.

The women in "North and South," as in so many costume dramas, have little to do except look pretty and act appreciative in the presence of their men. Both the Confederate and Yankee lead characters are told in separate scenes by their women that they look handsome in their uniforms. The women are there to admire and adore the men as they go off to slaughter each other, voicing their regrets with lines like: "Oh, Ah jest don't want to see you go."

Glory (1989) provides a refreshing exception to the way the Civil War is usually presented. Based on a true account of a Black regiment led by White officers, it effectively tells us about a part of the war that is unknown to most Americans. To be sure, the film has its drawbacks: it is told mostly from the White officer's perspective; it takes liberties with actual events; and it implicitly supports the view that Blacks must "earn" their equality and win the approval of Whites by performing in heroic ways. Yet *Glory* also takes time to give us the Black soldiers' struggles and thoughts. It is a powerful, moving, and tragic drama of African-American people fighting for their freedom in a war they helped to win, a representation of real history rather than Hollywood's usual pseudo-history.

Skipping the better part of a century to World War II, we find that media presentations of that conflict are almost too numerous to count. As mentioned in an earlier chapter, the films that came out during or soon after the war itself were mostly of the Grade-B John Wayne shoot-'em-up variety. Postwar productions like *The Longest Day* (1962) and *A Bridge Too Far* (1977) offer a more realistic, less propagandistically heroic impression of combat. Occasionally an exceptional film like the British-made *The Bridge on the River Kwai* (1957) attempts a statement about the dehumanizing aspects of war and militarism. Then there is the glorified blood-and-guts warrior of *Patton* (1970) and the supposedly basically good Nazis of movies like *The Young Lions* (1958). There are films that present the war from a German, but not pro-Nazi, point of view such as *The Last Blitzkrieg* (1958) and *Das Boot* (1981)—or *The Boat* in the dubbed American version. *The Hindenburg* (1975) goes a step further and features a Nazi officer as the hero who tries to prevent sabotage of the 1937 airship. None of these films ever get around to saying much about the political issues underlying the war.

The most notable attempt to dramatize some of the politics of World War II was the ABC-TV eighteen-hour series "The Winds of War" (1983). Based on a novel of that title by Herman Wouk, this historical romance offers a surface treatment of the rise of Nazism and the origins of the war. The hero, Pug Henry, or other members of his family manage to be present at just about every crucial event of the period, meetings with Hitler, Churchill, and Mussolini, dinner with Roosevelt and later with Stalin, Pearl Harbor, the Blitzkrieg over London, and the bombing of Berlin. Pseudo-history is spread all over the script in a meaningless hodgepodge that violates real history. The series has nothing to say about the way western leaders tolerated and even collaborated with the fascist takeovers in Spain, Austria, and Czechoslovakia, nor the way they and the western press looked favorably upon Hitler as a bulwark against Communism in Germany and upon Nazi Germany as a bulwark against Communism throughout Europe.

In one scene President Roosevelt extolls Pug Henry for being one of the few people to have foreseen the German-Soviet Non-Aggression Pact, thus playing on the old fiction that Stalin betrayed the West and sided with Hitler, a view that ignores the USSR's strenuous opposition to Munich, its willingness to stand by Czechoslovakia, and the way Moscow was repeatedly rebuffed by Great Britain and France when it tried to form an anti-Nazi alliance with them. Much of the dialogue of Wouk's book is used verbatim in the teleplay, but there are a number of revealing omissions. As Anne Rizzo notes, in Wouk's novel a member of the U.S. Foreign Service remarks after the signing of the German-Soviet pact:

> Lord, how the British have been asking for this! An alliance with Russia was their one chance to stop Germany. They had years in which to do it. All of Stalin's fear of Germany and the Nazis was on their side. And what did they do? Dawdle, fuss, flirt with Hitler, and give away Czechoslovakia.
>
> Finally, finally, they sent some minor politicians on a slow boat to see Stalin. When Hitler decided to gamble on this alliance, he shot his foreign minister to Moscow on a special plane with powers to sign a deal. And that's why we're within inches of a world war.[5]

This passage never made it into the teleplay. It says too much. Actually, it doesn't say quite enough. The British did more than dawdle and flirt with Hitler. They actively allied themselves with him in the dismantling of Czechoslovakia. They ignored Stalin and strung him along, hoping ultimately to isolate the Soviet Union and set it up for an invasion by Nazi Germany—which indeed happened. Having witnessed how Nazism wiped out the socialist left within Germany, Chamberlain and the other western collaborators hoped that Hitler might do the same to Russia. Indeed, the plan almost worked. At least 85 percent of the fighting in the European war took place on the Eastern front. The Soviets emerged victorious only after suffering horrendous losses.

In "The Winds of War," there inevitably appear the good Nazis who complain about Hitler's mismanagement of the war but not about his actual war policies and his Nazism. We are supposed to look favorably upon these characters because of the limited criticisms they utter about the Fuehrer. There are Americans, including officials, who wine and dine with Nazis right up to Pearl Harbor—with no questions raised in the script about the acceptability of such associations. There is a kinder, gentler Hitler playing sweetly with a little girl. There is the shallow, hare-brained female character, Pug's wife, whose only concern is to wear the right clothes and hobnob with the rich and famous. She dashes about Berlin, searching for the perfect outfit for a Nazi reception, squealing: "Hitler likes pink."[6]

Television mini-series like "The Winds of War," "War and Remembrance," and "Holocaust" all touch upon the crimes of Nazism, sometimes quite effectively. But they do not venture a mention of how German industrialists supported and financed Hitler at home and abroad benefiting from fascism once it seized state power—and profiting from the forced labor of concentration camps.[7] In both the make-believe media world and in the mainstream scholarly literature of the last several decades, Nazism is treated simply as a kind of mass insanity most commonly afflicting the baser elements of society. One would never know from these sources that the core of Hitler's support actually came from the more affluent classes and that the majority of the German working class opposed Hitler's accession to power, as did a majority of the Italian proletariat oppose Mussolini.

Speaking of whom, an NBC three-part series, "Mussolini: The Untold Story" (1985), displays open admiration for the fascist dictator. Mussolini is presented to us not as the tyrant who overthrew Italian parliamentary democracy, destroyed labor unions, reintroduced child labor, drastically reduced or in some instances totally eliminated taxes for the rich, sold off public holdings to private interests at bargain prices, subsidized corporations with state funds, slashed wages and human services for the working poor, greatly increased military spending, jailed, tortured, and assassinated political opponents, and waged wars of aggression in Africa and the Balkans. What we get instead is "Springtime for Benito," Mussolini the loving father, the sexually energetic fellow who has numerous affairs until he falls for his favorite mistress and settles down with her. We are invited to sympathize with Il Duce as he mourns the loss of his son while killing thousands of people in Ethiopia. As Norman Markowitz notes: "The concluding segment portrays Mussolini as a tragic figure, undone by his alliance with the Nazis, not as the Fascist war criminal who blazed the trail that Hitler would follow. Mussolini himself would have had no quarrel with much of this presentation."[8]

A spate of television docudramas in the 1970s and 1980s offered more of the same. There was the Cuban Missile Crisis—as the story might have been told by the White House. There was Harry Truman firing Douglas MacArthur in a teleplay that divided its sympathies equally between the president who exercised constitutional authority and the general who violated it. There were the travails of Eleanor and Franklin Roosevelt and the repeated dramatizations and documentaries about Edward VIII and Wallis Simpson. Again, the subject matter was either faithfully mainstream in its safely limited political perspective or so trivial in its content as to be not very political at all.

One exception is the surprisingly honest 1989 CBS docudrama "Day One," which tells the story of the decision to drop the atom bomb on Hiroshima and Nagasaki. The teleplay actually gets into the underlying cold-war politics, revealing that the White House's major concern was not defeating Japan but intimidating the Soviet Union and impressing Congress. The film maintains that Japan was ready to surrender before the bombs were dropped and that many of the scientists originally involved in production of the bomb opposed its use. "Day One" is a rare example of revealingly accurate history, a media dramatization of major historical events that departs from the usual mainstream apologetics.

In the minds of many Americans, movie and television dramas are the final chapter of history, the most lasting impression they have of what the past was like, what little of it they may have been exposed to. For the most part, make-believe history is an insipid costume epic, a personalized affair, the plotting, strutting, and yearnings of court figures and state leaders. Tyrants become humanly likeable as the social realities of their tyranny are ignored. The revolutionary populace is represented as tyrannical and irrational, while the sources of their anger and misery remain unexplained. Conflicts and wars just seem to happen, arising out of personal motives and ambitions. In these ways make-believe history reinforces the historical illiteracy fostered in the schools and in political life in general.

5

Blue-Collar Blues

As we have seen in the last chapter, Hollywood and television either ignore or misrepresent the history of great events. In a similar fashion, they mistreat the history of working-class struggle in the United States and throughout the world. In general, the entertainment world indulges in a class bigotry that remains unchallenged by the media's producers and critics.

Workers from Nowhere

In the war between labor and capital, there are thousands of untold stories and unsung heroes: men, women, and children; Anglo, African-American, Latino, European, and Asian; immigrant and native-born. Workers have struggled against poverty, recession, low wages, unemployment, lockouts, blacklists, takebacks, wage reductions, contract violations, plant closings, union busting, and court injunctions. They have endured the violence of gun thugs, Pinkerton detectives, Klansmen, state militia, police, racketeers, company goons and spies, and the U.S. Army. In defense of their rights, working people have used strikes, boycotts, industrial sabotage, picket lines, slowdowns, sit-ins, and retaliatory violence.

In the late nineteenth and early twentieth centuries, a distinct working class culture existed with its own songs, poetry, and sagas, celebrating the struggles of working people. Much of this culture has been pushed out of existence by the motion picture and television industries. Just as labor history and labor's present-day struggles are seldom taught in the schools (except for a passing reference to strikes and the industrial violence of earlier times), so are they rarely given fair treatment—

or much treatment of any kind—in the make-believe media. Not surprisingly, working people have no sense of their own history, no idea of the origins of the minimum wage or the eight-hour day.[1]

By what process of struggle did workers greatly reduce the use of child labor in the United States? How did they abolish property restrictions on voting? How did they win the right to assemble and exercise free speech in labor-organizing campaigns, the right to collective bargaining, and the right to pensions, paid vacations, and retirement and disability benefits? Hollywood and television do not begin to tell us. Nor do the people who produce the make-believe world have a very firm idea about these events. Were they to think about it, they probably would not even consider such subjects to be marketable for teleplays and films.[2]

History aside, the upper-middle-class producers and writers and the upper-class media owners show little interest in the present-day struggles of working people: the loss of pensions and seniority, the struggle for occupational safety and unionization, the suffering from work-connected injuries and diseases, the scourge of unemployment, the constant worries about money, the regressive and unfair tax burdens, the extreme exploitation of labor in Third World countries—including hundreds of millions of children, and the homicidal violence perpetrated in many U.S.-supported Third World states against labor organizers.

A study of prime-time television dramas by the International Association of Machinists and Aerospace Workers (IAM) found that working people are consistently underrepresented and portrayed in negative, marginal, and patronizing ways. There are many times more prostitutes, pimps, government officials, secret agents, doctors, butlers, police, military personnel, and private detectives than there are production-line workers.[3] Other studies find that blue collar and service workers compose sixty-seven percent of the U.S. work force but only ten percent of television characters, usually waiters, bartenders, and store clerks. Even then their presence is rarely central to the plot. The most common prime-time shows in recent years have been about law enforcement, national security, and private investigation of crime, in that order.[4]

Serious work-related difficulties do not seem to exist or are perceived mostly from a management perspective. Economic hardship is rarely part of the script, except when a person needs money because of an unexpected adversity. In such instances, money problems are usually resolved by individual ingenuity within the show's time frame. Nearly everyone in the make-believe media appears to be managing well, free of financial worries and living in circumstances that only the affluent can afford.[5]

Buffoons, Bigots, and Loveable Boys

Generally, workers are portrayed as good-natured, simple sorts, more funny and friendly than middle-class professionals, but also more foolish, less competent, less educated, less attractive, and less able to act as leaders.[6] The 1950s NBC television series "The Life of Riley" (adapted from radio) offered one of the first TV stereotypes of the blue-collar worker as a good-natured, laughable buffoon. In every show, the dim-witted Chester Riley, without ever straying far from his living room, manages to get himself into a muddle, only to comment: "Whadda revoltin' development dis is!" a running gag evoking much canned laughter. Riley's wife, an intelligent, practical-minded housewife with middle-class diction, patiently tries to set him straight now and then.

Another notable working-class buffoon spewed up on the small screen was Ralph Kramden (Jackie Gleason) of "The Honeymooners," a sitcom that ran in the mid-fifties and was inflicted upon us repeatedly as reruns right into the eighties. Kramden is a bus driver and a loud-mouthed, potbellied nincompoop. When bested in argument by his more articulate and intelligent wife, he holds his fist up to her and bellows: "One of these days, Alice, POW! right in the kisser!"—a threat of male spousal violence that is accorded roars of canned laughter. Kramden's neighbor and buddy, Norton, who speaks in a moronic, adenoidal voice, is a maintenance worker "in the sewers." Any reference he makes to his line of work is sure to be accompanied by offscreen laughter, as if an occupation of that sort is so undeserving of respect as to be inherently amusing.

In 1971, the new situation comedy series "All in the Family" (a Norman Lear creation, running later as "Archie Bunker's Place") touched upon the controversial social and political issues that entertainment television had ignored throughout the 1960s.[7] In this respect, the series represented a breakthrough in "socially conscious" entertainment. The main character is a blue-collar bigot, Archie Bunker, who fulminates about ethnic minorities, welfare "chiselers," liberals, intellectual "wimps," feminists, hippies, peaceniks, gays, and the like. Although he is usually bested in argument by his relatively enlightened son-in-law or some other character, studies show that "viewers took away whatever attitudes they brought to the show; racists felt confirmed in their racism, liberals in their broad-mindedness and sense of superiority."[8]

Under the guise of presenting a sophisticated "camp" humor, the show has Archie using ethnically defamatory terms like "coon,"

While "All in the Family" pokes fun at Archie Bunker, a loudmouthed ignorant bigot, the program practices a bigotry of its own in its portrayal of working-class stereotypes.

"polack," "mick," and "sheeny." While such utterances are supposed to reflect poorly upon him, they actually seem to gain respectability, given the playful context in which they are expressed. The violence, fear, and suffering that bigotry has spawned throughout history is hard to imagine when viewing "All in the Family." As incarnated in Archie, bigotry becomes nothing more than the expressions of a foolish, almost loveable lout.

While "All in the Family" ostensibly pokes fun at the bigoted Archie Bunker and thereby at bigotry in general, it practices a *class* prejudice of its own. It repeatedly pokes fun at Archie because he is a potbellied, beer-guzzling, *working-class* ignoramus. Thus, when he mispronounces or misuses a word, this is accompanied by generous offerings of audience laughter, the implication being that a malapropism—uttered by a working person who has been deprived of a decent education—is cause for great merriment.

Like the Riley and Kramden spouses, Archie's wife is a devoted housewife, though seemingly not as intelligent as the aggressively articulate Archie. She speaks in a mincing, almost imbecilic high-pitched voice, while remaining the properly domesticated female, supportive of her spouse, even as she occasionally urges him not to be so combative with others.

Some months before "All in the Family" premiered, the film *Joe* (1970) featured a working-class, antihero bigot as the central character, a hard hat hippie-hater who is both repelled and fascinated by the counterculture. Like Archie Bunker, he is a visceral, flag-waving superpatriot, lacking in sensibility, schooling, tolerance, and information. Films like *Joe* and television shows like "All in the Family" tell us that even if all workers are not bigots, certainly all bigots are workers. In fact, one way to telegraph the bigots' undesirable nature is through their stereotyped "lower class" traits: slovenly speech and appearance, crude personal deportment, simplemindedness, and the like. In real life, we can observe plenty of affluent persons who are as bigoted as any worker might be, even if their prejudices are cloaked in the more circumspect terminology and educated accents of Bronxville, Grosse Pointe, and Shaker Heights. Yet, such persons do not fit the media's own class-related stereotype of a bigot—as embodied in the blue-collar worker.

A Teamsters Union publication, *Focus*, complained that Archie Bunker and other characters like him present a distorted image of working people. "For some reason, the writers of those shows decided the average worker is a dingbat—fat, more than a little dumb, a committed racist and most of all, very comical." No wonder that "most of the folks who design the policies . . . in high government circles, no matter what party is in power, have no idea of what a working person is like and what he needs."[9] Likewise for most of the folks who produce entertainment shows.

Nor do media people seem to have any interest in the workplace travails that people must confront. Chester Riley is never shown sweating away on the production line. Ralph Kramden is never seen putting in a long day on the bus route. Archie Bunker is not to be found in his cab or on the loading dock (when he worked as a foreman). The two Milwaukee brewery workers of the "Laverne and Shirley" show are rarely at work, and when they are, production work seems more like "simple-minded fun," for they spend more time in "slapstick sexual antics" than in actual toil.[10]

Even if, as some might argue, workplace struggle is not an apt subject for situation comedies, the workplace certainly is a suitable mise-en-scène for more serious treatment. Yet, even in dramas about working people, the action rarely involves actual work problems (with the few notable exceptions to be discussed later in this chapter). One of the better television series situated in the workplace was "Taxi," which ran for five years. But most of this show's interaction occurred while drivers were waiting to go out on their shifts and usually involved personal problems rather than work-related ones. In the made-for-television movie *Hard Hat and Legs* (1980), a construction worker is the central character, but he is never seen actually working nor even reflecting upon the problems and dangers of his work.

Hard Hat and Legs does offer the familiar theme of the rough-hewn worker who courts a well-educated middle-class woman (Sharon Gless), a beauty who in this instance happens to teach, yes, sex education. Being a blue-collar macho-man, he has a lot to teach *her* about that subject beyond the book-learning stuff. First, however, he must overcome her defenses, created in part by his own stampeding approach and, more importantly, by the class differences that exist between them. This latter point is never explicitly made; after all, this is an American film, not a British one. The script just assumes that a college-educated, cultivated lady in her right mind would not have any reason to seriously entertain the overtures of a lovesick, unschooled construction worker—at least not at first. In other words, rather than *examining* class prejudice, the movie implicitly *practices* an unacknowledged class prejudice of its own, as is so commonly done in the make-believe media. We are never invited to question why there is so much social distance between these two people in a society like ours where such barriers supposedly do not exist.

The whole plot in *Hard Hat and Legs* centers on whether our blue-collar hero is enough of an adorable diamond in the rough to compensate for the deficiencies of his class background. Will he display sufficient pizzazz, brash charm, and savvy (he's wonderful with her children) to bridge the gap between beauty and the boor? She, in turn, contributes to bridging gaps when he takes her home to dine with his working-class, Italian-American family. Like any band of primitive villagers, they eat with gluttonous intensity, pausing only to scowl suspiciously at her civilized presence. But when she demonstrates a fluency in Italian, these simple creatures are suddenly overcome with joy; they rush to embrace her, squealing: "Ooouuuh, she speaks Italian! Ooouuuh, she speaks Italian!"

The blue-collar worker as the untrammeled, unschooled boy pursuing a higher-status woman appears also in *Jackknife* (1989), a film vaguely reminiscent of *Marty* (1955), though without any of the latter's quality and charm. The lead character, a somewhat emotionally damaged Vietnam veteran (Robert De Niro), is keen about a lonely, plain-faced schoolteacher, the sister of an even more damaged war buddy of his. Our hero is predictably enthusiastic: "Wowie, I got a date with a lady, a real laaaady." He is really good at working with cars: "If it's got an engine, I can fix it." In this respect, he's not unlike Marty, who was "just a butcher" but a good butcher. It seems that if occupants of the lower rungs are especially good at what they do, they might be deserving of something better than what their station in life normally allows—for instance, "a real laaaady."

At one point, the two find themselves in a fancy yuppie restaurant. The waitress asks if they wish to order cocktails. This causes De Niro's face to go blank. Duh, cocktails? What's that? Instead he orders two beers, and we are supposed to be amused by his untutored ways. It's a variation of Archie's malapropisms. Like any good blue-collar bozo, he is a brew addict. He even talks about "breakfast beer," which "really wakes you up and gets you going." He introduces his lady friend to the lusty joys of beer guzzling, and—after storming her uptight defenses—he introduces her to the lusty joys of bedding down. He compliments her on her figure by noting: "Hey, I think you're built like a brick shithouse." Another adorable working-class diamond in the rough.

She asks him to accompany her to the school prom, which she has to chaperone. He rents a white-jacket tuxedo with a chintzy gold cummerbund and tie, while the other males are in black tie and jacket. Thus, even when dressing formal, he displays his tacky working-class taste. But he wows them all at the prom by cutting fancy steps on the dance floor, again overcoming his presumed class deficiencies by being superproficient at what he's doing.

Class and Virtue

The entertainment media present working people not only as unlettered and uncouth but also as less desirable and less moral than other people. Conversely, virtue is more likely to be ascribed to those characters whose speech and appearance are soundly middle- or upper-middle class.

Even a simple adventure story like *Treasure Island* (1934, 1950, 1972) manifests this implicit class perspective. There are two groups of acquisitive persons searching for a lost treasure. One, headed by a squire, has money enough to hire a ship and crew. The other, led by the rascal Long John Silver, has no money—so they sign up as part of the crew. The narrative implicitly assumes from the beginning that the squire has a moral claim to the treasure, while Long John's gang does not. After all, it is the squire who puts up the venture capital for the ship. Having no investment in the undertaking other than their labor, Long John and his men, by definition, will be "stealing" the treasure, while the squire will be "discovering" it.

To be sure, there are other differences. Long John's men are cut-throats. The squire is not. Yet, one wonders if the difference between a bad pirate and a good squire is itself not preeminently a matter of having the right amount of disposable income. The squire is no less acquisitive than the conspirators. He just does with money what they must achieve with cutlasses. The squire and his associates dress in fine clothes, speak an educated diction, and drink brandy. Long John and his men dress slovenly, speak in guttural tones, and drink rum. From these indications alone, the viewer knows who are the good guys and who are the bad. Virtue is visually measured by one's approximation to proper class appearances.

Sometimes class contrasts are juxtaposed within one person, as in *The Three Faces of Eve* (1957), a movie about a woman who suffers from multiple personalities. When we first meet Eve (Joanne Woodward), she is a disturbed, strongly repressed, puritanically religious person, who speaks with a rural, poor-Southern accent. Her second personality is that of a wild, flirtatious woman who also speaks with a rural, poor-Southern accent. After much treatment by her psychiatrist, she is cured of these schizoid personalities and emerges with a healthy third one, the real Eve, a poised, self-possessed, pleasant woman. What is intriguing is that she now speaks with a cultivated, affluent, Smith College accent, free of any low-income regionalism or ruralism, much like Joanne Woodward herself. This transformation in class style and speech is used to indicate mental health without any awareness of the class bias thusly expressed.

Mental health is also the question in *A Woman under the Influence* (1974), the story of a disturbed woman who is married to a hard-hat husband. He cannot handle—and inadvertently contributes to—her emotional deterioration. She is victimized by a spouse who is nothing more than an insensitive, working-class bull in a china shop. One comes away convinced that every unstable woman needs a kinder, gentler, and above all, more *middle-class* hubby if she wishes to avoid a mental crack-up.

Class prototypes abound in the 1980s television series "The A-

The "Better" Class Knows Best

A television public-service advertisement on behalf of the news industry was run on ABC in June 1989. It showed an overweight, casually dressed man sitting at a restaurant table, holding forth in a boorish voice: "If you ask me, I think the media distorts everything. So I don't watch the news. Like, take that guy Noriega in Paraguay. So who cares about him anyway?"

While saying this, he reaches over and grabs fried potatoes from his companion's plate and slurps them into his mouth. The camera moves to his female companion, who turns out to be an extremely well-dressed, upper-crust, blond beauty. How often in real life do we see this combination eating french fries together?

"Panama," she says.

"Huh? What about Panama?" he says.

"Noriega is from Panama, not Paraguay," she says in a velvety, polished tone that contrasts significantly with his Archie Bunker delivery.

The scene fades and is replaced by a printed announcement telling viewers that the news helps them understand what is going on.

What is interesting about this ad is the contrast between the two characters. The unfavorable individual who does not trust the news media is represented as a loud-mouthed working-class ignoramus. The one who corrects him and with whom we are invited to side is a "quality," "better-class" kind of person.

Team." In each episode, a Vietnam-era commando unit helps an underdog, be it a Latino immigrant or a disabled veteran, by vanquishing some menacing force such as organized crime, a business competitor, or corrupt government officials. As always with the make-believe media, the A-Team does good work on an individualized rather than collectively organized basis, helping particular victims by thwarting particular villains. The A-Team's leaders are two White males of privileged background. The lowest ranking members of the team, who do none of the thinking nor the leading, are working-class palookas. They show they are good with their hands, both by punching out the bad guys and by doing the maintenance work on the team's flying vehicles and cars. One of them, "B.A." (bad ass), played by the African-American Mr. T., is visceral, tough, and purposely bad-mannered toward those he doesn't like. He projects an image of crudeness and ignorance and is associated with the physical side of things. In sum, the team has a brain (the intelligent White leaders) and a body with its simpler physical functions (the working-class characters), a hierarchy that corresponds to the social structure itself.[11]

Sometimes class bigotry is interwoven with gender bigotry, as in *Pretty Woman* (1990). A dreamboat multimillionaire corporate raider finds himself all alone for an extended stay in Hollywood (his girlfriend is unwilling to join him), so he quickly recruits a beautiful prostitute as his playmate of the month. She is paid $3,000 a week to wait around his superposh hotel penthouse ready to perform the usual services and accompany him to business dinners at top restaurants. As prostitution goes, it is a dream gig. But there is one cloud on the horizon. She is low-class. She doesn't know which fork to use at those CEO power feasts, and she's bothersomely fidgety, wears tacky clothes, chews gum, and, y'know, doesn't talk so good. But with some tips from the hotel manager, she proves to be a veritable Eliza Doolittle in her class metamorphosis. She dresses in proper attire, sticks the gum away forever, and starts picking the right utensils at dinner. She also figures out how to speak a little more like Joanne Woodward without the benefit of a multiple personality syndrome, and she develops the capacity to sit in a poised, wordless, empty-headed fashion, every inch the expensive female ornament.

She is still a prostitute but a classy one. It is enough of a distinction for the handsome young corporate raider. Having liked her because she was charmingly cheap, he now loves her all the more because she has real polish and is a more suitable companion. So suitable that he decides to do the right thing by her: set her up in an apartment so he can make regular visits at regular prices. But now she wants the better things in life, like marriage, a nice house, and, above all, a different occupation, one that would allow her to use less of herself. She is furious at him for treating her like, well, a prostitute. She decides to give up her profession and get a high-school diploma so that she might make a better life for herself—perhaps as a filing clerk or receptionist or some other of the entry-level jobs awaiting young women with high-school diplomas.[12]

After the usual girl-breaks-off-with-boy scenes, the millionaire prince returns. It seems he can't concentrate on making money without her. He even abandons his cutthroat schemes and enters into a less lucrative but supposedly more productive, caring business venture with a struggling old-time entrepreneur. The bad capitalist is transformed into a good capitalist. He then carries off his ex-prostitute for a lifetime of bliss. The moral is a familiar one, updated for post-Reagan yuppiedom: A woman can escape from economic and gender exploitation by winning the love and career advantages offered by a rich male. Sexual allure goes only so far unless it develops a material base and becomes a class act.[13]

No-Good Unions

Like workers themselves, labor organizations are either ignored or poorly represented in the media. Unions have won victories on behalf of working people and have supported many worthy causes beyond the workplace, including consumer safety, human services, progressive income taxes, and environmental protections. But the make-believe media seem not to have noticed.

Hollywood and television moguls have regularly waged war against the labor unions in their own industries. Not surprisingly, they have shown little inclination to treat unions sympathetically in films and teleplays. When labor difficulties *are* portrayed, as in *They Drive by Night* (1940), a film about the trucking industry, it is the individual, in this case a wildcat trucker, who resolves the situation by acting on his own. Commenting on this movie, Eric Smoodin notes: "Frontier individualism, which the film makes appear so attractive, works as the alternative to collective action by the truckers—that is, unionism—a potentially radical solution to labor unrest, and therefore a solution which Hollywood cannot support."[14]

The Oscar-winning film *On the Waterfront* (1954) was originally turned down by a number of studios because, as Hollywood mogul Darryl Zanuck commented at the time: "Who gives a shit about labor unions?"[15] In that movie, the villains are the corrupt union leaders. Not a critical word is uttered against the owners, even though they had a real-life history of collaborating with union racketeers. Victory comes when Terry, the hero, turns against the hoods and testifies before a federal investigative agency. In retaliation, the labor racketeers beat him mercilessly in front of an entire workforce of longshoremen who stand by meekly. But when Terry staggers to his feet and leads them back into the workplace, they cheer their battered hero and follow him like happy sheep. The corrupt union boss, who has been trying to get them back to work all along, is now furious that they are returning in tow with Terry; this supposedly represents a real defeat for the bad guys.

Terry never considers the possibility of collective action with his fellow workers to reform the union. Instead, he goes to the feds to get revenge against the labor crooks who killed his brother. As usual, we are given individual motives rather than collective goals, individual heroics rather than organized mass action.

In *Sometimes a Great Notion* (1971), family owners of a logging company overcome the violence and harassment of their striking workforce. The strikers sabotage the equipment, an act of destruction not designed to win audience sympathy. But the plucky family devises a way to deliver a large order on schedule. There are those who don't want to see the work done, such as the strikers, and those who get it done no matter what, such as the dedicated owners. The workers come across as a mean-spirited bunch, less concerned with providing for society than with destroying productive things in order to extract more gain for themselves.

In *F.I.S.T.* (1978), the union is again the villain. An honest worker eventually becomes a labor boss linked to the mob, more interested in power than in improving the conditions of workers. Once more, we have a favorite Hollywood theme: power corrupts. Likewise, in *Blue Collar* (1978), the union is an undemocratic instrument of corruption, coercion, and terror within the Detroit automotive industry, murdering one of its own rank-and-file members and buying off another, pitting older workers against young, Black against White. In contrast, the company representative and the FBI man appear downright benign. The film suggests that the FBI is committed to freeing workers from the bondage of union corruption. In real life, the FBI participated in the McCarthyite purges of progressive leaders from unions, thus leaving them open to infiltration by mobsters.[16]

There is nothing inherently wrong with portraying union corruption, for there are corrupt unions. But corruption is concentrated in less than one percent of all locals.[17] (In comparison, 11 percent of the biggest corporations have been caught in unlawful acts, many of them repeat offenders.) It is wrong, however, to concentrate on union corruption to the exclusion of other realities regarding labor organizations. In this respect, the entertainment media are very much like the news media.[18] In the case of *Blue Collar*, the misrepresentation is particularly egregious since the United Auto Workers is one of the most honest and democratic unions, with a record of fighting racism within its own ranks and with hundreds of rank-and-file organizations and caucuses that elect delegates to union conventions.[19] Detroit autoworkers have a long and remarkable history of insurgency and struggle against the exploitation of corporate bosses, but the make-believe media seem not to know it. Instead, in movies like *Blue Collar*, reality is again stood on its head. The unions are portrayed as enemies of workers, with nothing said about who the workers' real enemies might be.

Even when unions are not the main villains, they still usually do not come off well. In *Silkwood* (1983), the local union is of no help to the courageous Karen Silkwood, who discovers that the company she

Upper-Middle-Class Fantasies

Studies have concluded . . . that behavior modeled on television does invade the fantasy life of the viewer. While the relationship between fantasy life and real life is unclear and varies from viewer to viewer, there may be some cause for alarm if upper-middle-class characters can transmit their morality, their picture of the "good life," and their beliefs and attitudes to the fantasies of 200 million American viewers. If the dreams and inspirations of American workers are induced by television rather than from direct experience, the labor movement is likely to feel real effects in organizing drives, collective bargaining, solidarity, and collective political action. Upper-middle-class television certainly does not make every little boy or girl fantasize about belonging to a union when they grow up, nor does it induce men and women to fantasize about the positive changes and contributions that can be brought about through collective action.

Ralph Arthur Johnson, "World without Workers: Prime Time's Presentation of Labor," *Labor Studies Journal*, 5, winter 1981, pp. 205–206.

works for, Kerr-McGee, is guilty of serious radiation safety violations. The national union is staffed by officials who seem to have little time for her until they find they might be able to use her for purposes of their own. (In real life, union leaders did not exploit Silkwood and took some risks on behalf of her cause.[20]) The other workers seem ambivalent about supporting Silkwood's struggle. The film never makes clear how culpable Kerr-McGee is. It fails to note that in real life Silkwood's own mysterious contamination was traced to a batch of plutonium available only to Kerr-McGee management personnel. Still, this motion picture gives us some sense of workplace struggle and the venality of a corporate power that puts profits before people. It has the added virtue of portraying a real-life *female* protagonist, a woman who is not passively attached to some man but who actively struggles for causes of her own.

A worthwhile made-for-television film that has received relatively little attention is *The $5.20-an-Hour Dream* (1980). A divorced working mother gets a job on a traditionally all-male assembly line and has to deal with the sexism and resentment of her coworkers, along with mistreatment from management. The film shows people actually working under harsh factory conditions. Management's attempt to exploit

Silkwood gives us a somewhat watered-down version of Karen Silkwood's struggle against the unsafe and criminally deceptive practices of a Kerr-McGee plutonium fuel-rod plant.

both male and female employees causes some of the men to make
common cause with the female worker. But the union-shop steward is
portrayed as less interested in helping the workers than in collecting
their dues and cozying up to management.

Unions do not fare well on prime-time television. In "Trapper John,
M.D.," a nurses' strike is shown as obstructing the critical routine of
the hospital. The series "Skag" so distorted the image of steelworkers
and their union representatives—the latter portrayed as brutal bullies—
that the United Steel Workers union criticized the show for its lack of
authenticity.[21]

Even a series with a liberal orientation like "Murphy Brown" does
not treat unions seriously. In one 1990 episode when the television

Television's No-Good Unions

TV shows rarely present working people as central characters, let alone talking about their struggles as workers and unionists. But when the subject does occasionally come up, it is usually treated in an offensively distorted and self-serving manner by the big business-dominated media. . . .

Such was the case with the CBS crimefighter series "Wiseguy," a five-part story . . . which centered mainly on attempts by a clothing manufacturer to resist mob infiltration. [The story] digressed for a time to focus on a Chinatown sweatshop plagued by substandard and inhuman working conditions. . . A militant young woman, played by Joan Chen, leads the angry workers on a strike for a minimum wage and safe working conditions.

Chen fights eloquently and passionately for the strikers, denouncing manufacturers who "want to keep you oppressed and silent," and "enforce the system which dehumanizes labor for money" even

as "they build big houses and send their children to fancy colleges, while you live in squalor." . . .

The program, which starts out as seemingly one of the most daring and outspoken pro-worker TV dramas ever, takes a sharp right turn midway through. Chen turns out to be personally . . . inflexible, and "unreasonable" toward the manufacturer, who is willing to change and compromise. The union is revealed to be "in bed" with the mob, and none other than the notoriously union-busting FBI turns up as labor mediator, replacing the indifferent union and correcting the system on behalf of the strikers.

Shows like "Wiseguy" make a shameless, calculated, and dishonest display of sympathy for working people, redirecting worker anger away from big business and toward the mob, while defaming the union movement . . .

Prairie Miller, "Teleprobe," *People's Daily World*, January 26, 1989.

camera crew goes on strike, Murphy (Candice Bergen) decides to bring the boys to their senses by inviting union and management representatives to her home for refreshments. Her plan is just to get them to "sit down and start talking," then the strike would be settled. The adversaries scowl at each other in her living room, breaking the hostile silence only to hurl supposedly wild accusations. The management representative says the workers are lazy louts who need three people to do one person's work. The union representative more accurately says that management just tries to squeeze every ounce of sweat out of employees with no regard for them as human beings. The script implicitly supports

Murphy's assumption that the strike is just the outgrowth of ill-willed grumpiness and a lack of communication rather than a struggle over real material interests. If only both sides would take the chips off their shoulders and come to their senses, the silly old strike would be over, as indeed it is by the end of the half-hour episode, thanks to Murphy's cheerful efforts.

People, including workers themselves, supposedly want to escape rather than confront the realities of the workplace. In violation of that notion, I would argue that it is the *lack* of reality that makes the make-believe media unconvincing and boring. As Dan Cohen puts it:

> Some people suggest that the reason for the dearth of working-class shows on TV is that people who work all day don't want to come home and watch TV shows about work. That's probably true—given the kind of shows the networks produce. But imagine a show based in a factory or an office that was . . . well-written and political . . . Imagine a series that showed all the absurdity and meanness that workers have to deal with every day, imagine seeing them prevail, sometimes, by collective action. Imagine a show with consistent anticapitalist politics. Find me the worker who wouldn't stay home to watch that one.[22]

A television situation comedy beginning in the 1989–90 season, "Roseanne," featuring an obese, working-class woman as the lead, offers an occasional glimpse of how the make-believe media can be entertaining *because* it deals with class reality (though falling far short of what Dan Cohen asks for in the above quotation). In one episode, Roseanne protests her boss's order to speed up production on the assembly line. The employees are already overworked, she argues. The boss and she enter into a secret pact: he will retract the order if she will stop criticizing him at the plant. When he weasels out of the deal, she leads a wildcat strike. The situation remains unresolved by the end of the episode. Of course, this being a prime-time sitcom, we can expect just so much. Hence, no union is in sight. Whatever the show's limitations, there is no evidence that episodes like the one just mentioned cause the show's ratings to drop. People do not call in to complain that they are bored with a story about job-related realities. Work is still the experience that occupies the major portion of most people's waking hours. Sympathetic treatments of that experience would be watched with interest by large audiences that otherwise have been known occasionally to tire of the usual silly, shallow sitcom fare.

Doing It Better

Among the handful of films and teleplays that give labor organizations a fair shake is *Norma Rae* (1979), based on a true story about a young woman fighting to unionize a Southern textile mill. Rather than indulging in the usual individualized heroics, she rallies her fellow workers for collective action and coordinates her efforts with a union organizer from New York. The union is actually portrayed as committed to the workers' interests. (Even here, however, the union representative must stave off his superiors who urge abandonment of the organizing effort because results are slow in coming.) As with *Silkwood*, this film has the added virtue of presenting a woman as a rank-and-file leader. It also shows Black and White workers overcoming racial barriers and working together.

A made-for-television movie, *A Matter of Sex* (1984) even more explicitly combines the themes of workplace struggle and women's rights. It is based on a true story about eight female bank employees in a small town who walk a picket line for many months seeking equality in pay and promotion. The union plays a positive, if not very effective role, attempting to drum up support for the women strikers in a community that reacts unsympathetically through most of the struggle.

An excellent film about the West Virginia coal-mining wars of the 1920s is *Matewan* (1987), written and directed by John Sayles. Despite Sayles's past successes, his script was rejected by every major studio. He eventually produced the film independently, taking years to scrape together sufficient private funding. In *Matewan*, the coal miners organize against oppressive conditions and a heartless management. Joined together in the face of much hardship, they overcome the ethnic divisions between native Whites, African-Americans, and Italian immigrants (the latter two groups were originally recruited as scabs). The union organizer is actually depicted as courageously dedicated to the workers' cause. With equal accuracy, the coal company is portrayed as determined to starve the workers into submission and break the strike with scabs, company spies, gun thugs, and every other strong-arm method. Small wonder Hollywood would not touch this script. The film played in New York and other major urban locales, but in many sections of the country it failed to get distributed.

An above-average made-for-television movie, *Heart of Steel* (1983) portrays the sufferings of workers facing unemployment after the steel mill closes. In one scene, they accuse management of milking the plant for profits: "You've been stealing from us!" exclaims the lead character. The United Steel Workers representative in the movie is portrayed as quite comfortable with management, but even he is forced to note: "The American worker and his family are now taking a beating for mismanagement by this company and this government since World War II. No matter what happens, remember your union never quit on you. We're still here, still fighting." With time, however, the hero becomes disillusioned with the union. He says to his dad: "You always told me to work hard, stick with the union, love your country. I did all that. I got nothing. I ain't got a job. I lost my truck. I'll go on welfare and when that runs out, I'll feed my kids out of garbage cans." An otherwise devoted husband and father, he becomes increasingly abusive toward his family. Other families break up; one worker commits suicide.

Unfortunately, the movie ends on an ideologically predictable and almost silly note. The workers break into the abandoned mill and spend a day making a record amount of steel. No syndicalist worker takeover here; they just do it for one day as a gesture designed to bolster their "self-respect," the hero says. Everyone in town comes to cheer the workers as they depart from their symbolic day at the mill, including the hero's previously alienated family. In the end, the hero reverts to good old American individualism: "I can't count on the union or the government. We got to rely on ourselves." With much upbeat fanfare, he hits the road to find a job, leaving most of his coworkers and community behind him. He'll come back for his family when he finds work. Suddenly, unemployment is merely an individual problem in need of an individual solution.

John Sayles's excellent *Eight Men Out* (1988) deals with the notorious true story of how the Chicago White Sox baseball team agreed to take gambling bribes in return for throwing the 1919 World Series. Of special interest is the film's treatment of the exploitative and corrupting nature of management-player relations. The players' resentment at being cheated and underpaid by their boss drives them to accept bribes. If the team owner cannot be honest with them, they eventually see no reason to be honest about the game. Unable to get a decent wage from an owner who grows increasingly rich off their labor, they succumb to temptation when the opportunity presents itself. The players then discover that the same law that is too feeble to secure them collective bargaining rights is strong enough to come down hard on them when the gambling fix is exposed.

How corporate America has been taking over the land, water, and mineral resources of the country is a subject not given much close attention by Hollywood and television. One had to wait until 1940 for *The Grapes of Wrath* (directed by John Ford) to see a film that portrayed the victimization of small farmers by bankers and big growers—with much of the blame also put on such innocently impersonal forces as "hard times." Now considered a classic, this film suffers from a deficient political subtext. As Christensen notes: "Survival, not change, is the theme. Nowhere is the system as a whole challenged; never is faith in the American way shaken. . . . The film reassures."[23]

The Milagro Beanfield War (1988), produced by the Chicano activist

The Same Story in Great Britain

My second documentary . . . was "Conversations with a Working Man." This was the story of . . . a dyehouse worker [whose] job was monotonous, filthy and injurious to his health, yet he derived a pride from "doing it well". . . . [He is] a gentle man with tolerant, principled views, and a loyal member of his (now defunct) union, the Dyers and Bleachers. In other words, he is not unlike millions of Britons.

"Conversations with a Working Man" was to be a documentary given over to the views of an articulate trade unionist without intrusion by those who often claimed to speak for him. . . . One executive worried a great deal about "what the [International Broadcasting] Authority will think". . . . What was made very clear was that the commentary would have to undergo numerous changes to be "acceptable to the Authority." Two of the changes are unforgettable.

The Authority, I was told, would not tolerate the term "working class" because it had "political implications." It would have to be changed to "working heritage." Then there was the problem of the term "the people," which was a "Marxist expression" and therefore anathema to the Authority. I had not read much Marx, so I did not know. But surely "the people" had existed before Marx.

Behind this nonsense was, of course, serious purpose. Twelve years later the film director Ken Loach, whose films about trade unionists were to be the object of censorship, wrote:

Working people are allowed on television so long as they fit the stereotype that producers have of them. Workers can appear pathetic in their ignorance and poverty, apathetic to parliamentary politics, or aggressive on the picket line. But let them make a serious political analysis based on their own experiences and in their own language, then keep them off the air. That's the job of professional pundits, MPs [members of parliament] and General Secretaries. They understand the rules of the game.

John Pilger, *Heroes* (London: Pan Books, 1986), pp. 478–79.

filmmaker Moctesuma Esparza and directed by Robert Redford, tells of a resistance by small farmers against big-land developers and collusive government officials in New Mexico. Finding their water supplies cut off and facing ruinous taxes that are intended to subsidize these same developers, the Mexican-American farmers take united action against a common enemy.

Among the superior films that deal with the struggles of the working class, one should list foreign productions such as: *Gaijin* (1982), an excellent treatment of Japanese and Italian immigrant workers in Brazil confronting plantation bosses in an early part of this century; *The Organizer* (1964), which deals with industrial workers who struggle for better wages and reduction of the twelve-hour workday in Turin at the turn of the century; and *The Working Class Goes to Heaven* (1973), about present-day workers in Italy, trapped between a speed-up on the assembly line and a tinseled consumerism.

One of the most uncompromising and politically advanced films about class struggle ever made is an American one, *Salt of the Earth* (1954). It is based on a real-life 1951–52 strike led by Mexican-American workers against a zinc mine in New Mexico. The miners complain about poor safety conditions and discriminatory wages. They are paid less than Anglo workers as a way of holding down the wages of both groups. One worker notes that the land on which the mine stood once belonged to his grandfather. The sheriff and his deputies are faithful servants of the bosses. The strikers get support from workers and union locals around the country, a kind of labor solidarity seldom recognized by either the news or entertainment media. The miners' union is portrayed as democratic, with the international section backing the local rather than dictating to it. The union representative, an Anglo, is dedicated, politically aware, and willing to learn from the Mexican rank and file. The film also shows how money problems, oppressive work conditions, and bigotry take their toll on family life.

An impressive feature of *Salt of the Earth* is that it is told preeminently from a feminist perspective. The women—all housewives—join the fray, as auxiliaries to the striking miners, then as active participants when the miners are barred from picketing by a Taft-Hartley court injunction. The women are shown as capable, courageous, well-organized, and disciplined in their struggle against the sheriff's thugs and against those of their own men who resist their newly claimed "unwomanly" roles. During the strike, their husbands learn firsthand about the difficulties of domestic toil. In response to her husband's complaint that her activism and her demand for equality are violating his manly "dignity," the female lead character says:

Have you learned nothing from this strike? Why are you afraid to
have me at your side? You still think you can have dignity only if I
have none. . . . The Anglo bosses look down upon you and you hate
them for it. "Stay in your place, you dirty Mexican." That's what
they tell you. But why must you say to me, "Stay in your place"?
Do you feel better having someone lower than you? Whose neck
shall I stand on to make me feel superior? And what will I get out
of it? I don't want anything lower than me. I'm low enough. I want
to rise up and push everything else up with me.

Salt of the Earth is one of those rare films that offers the solution of
collective action against the interrelated evils of class oppression, ethnic
prejudice, and male supremacism. Independently produced with a cast
of mostly nonprofessional actors, the movie was sponsored by the International Union of Mine, Mill and Smelter Workers, a union forced out
of the CIO during the postwar witch-hunt days because it had a Communist leadership. The film's producer, director, and writer had all been
blacklisted after appearing before the House Un-American Activities
Committee.

The movie took three years to complete in the face of violent vigilante attacks by armed townspeople on location. The Mexican actress
who played the lead, Rosoura Revueltas, was deported three times
during the shooting of the film. There were difficulties hiring a cast and
a crew because many professionals feared being blacklisted should they
work on what was said to be a Communist project. (*Salt of the Earth* is
both a fine film and indeed made by Communists or persons closely
associated with the Communist party's struggle against class oppression, racism, and sexism.) Hollywood's resistance to this movie was so
thorough that even laboratories, usually uncommitted to anything except cash, refused to handle the film's processing. Officials of the projec-
tionist union refused to allow its members to screen it. The movie was
attacked by members of Congress and by the American Legion for being
a "Moscow propaganda tool." Distributors boycotted *Salt of the Earth*. It
ended up playing in only eleven movie houses out of the nation's
13,000. Since then, it has been confined to an occasional union hall or
leftist conference and college campus.[24] To my knowledge, it has never
been shown on television, but it is available on videocassette.

Another excellent pro-union film unable to win much distribution
is *The Killing Floor* (1985), the powerful story of African-American and
White slaughterhouse workers in Chicago in 1919. Based on actual
events, the film dramatizes the struggles of workers who strive to overcome racial barriers and create the foundations for industrial unionism.

The Killing Floor was financed by some thirty unions, with additional funds from organizations like the National Endowment for the Humanities and American Playhouse. Made available on videocassette in 1989, it is still unknown to almost all viewers, having been accorded very limited distribution.

Better treated was *Roger and Me* (1989), a full-length documentary that gives an acerbic yet humorous account of the industrial demise of Flint, Michigan, and the role played by General Motors. Made on a shoestring budget by rookie filmmaker Michael Moore, the film briefly and hastily notes that GM makes bigger, quicker profits by closing plants, reneging on pension funds, and moving to cheaper labor markets abroad. *Roger and Me* spends most of its time on satire, poking fun at a variety of people, with its prime target being GM chief Roger Smith. Almost no footage is devoted to an analysis of the political economy that enables GM to do what it does to people and communities. Nevertheless, the film's pro-worker, anticorporate sympathies are clear. Surprisingly, it was picked up by Time Warner Inc. for mass distribution, probably the only documentary of its kind to enjoy that privilege. It soon proved to be a box-office success. Despite the movie's originality and popularity, the Motion Picture Academy failed even to mention it for an Oscar nomination in the documentary category.

The handful of worthwhile films that deal with the actual realities of working-class struggle have some things in common:

1. With few exceptions, they are either independently produced or foreign made; they do not come out of Hollywood or from the networks.

2. They usually are accorded a decidedly limited distribution, reaching much smaller audiences than the shopping-mall cinema productions that saturate America.

3. They rarely have money for the kind of pre-release publicity that might help create a broader market appeal.

4. They are far less likely to become reruns on prime-time television. If televised, they are apt to be shown at obscure hours.

Along with its mistreatment of working people and their unions, the entertainment industry propagates a more diffuse kind of class prejudice. This is evident in its treatment of the affluent strata, as will be seen in the next chapter.

6

Affluent Class and Corporate Brass

Despite the widely publicized notion that just about everyone in the United States (except for a few millionaires and beggars) is "middle class," there are marked differences among us in income, status, education, and life-style. But class is not just a matter of these demographic differences. More important is the way class acts as a force of power and wealth. Thus, there are the rich and powerful, those who own and exercise a preponderate control over the command positions within corporations, banks, industries, communications systems, and media. Class power permeates our economic, political, military, educational, and cultural institutions. The realities of class are omnipresent in our society, ingrained in our everyday experience, helping to shape the quality of our lives. Yet people are taught not to think in class terms. And references to class power are often dismissed as conspiracy theory or Marxist ideological mouthing.

Increasingly, attention is given in our media and public life to just about every subject one might imagine. Even racism and sexism, while insufficiently confronted, are at least recognized as bigotries, certainly more so today than in earlier generations. But, as noted in previous chapters, *class* bigotry continues to be an unchallenged and unperceived form of prejudice. The realities of class power and class oppression remain largely a forbidden topic. The expressions of class bigotry in our literature and textbooks, in our institutions and daily lives, and in our films and television shows go unexamined. Class is the colossal reality right before our eyes that we Americans are trained not to see.

Escaping Class

If the make-believe media are "escapist," it is in large part because they have long downplayed or avoided altogether the harsh realities of racial, gender, and class oppression. For many decades, through the magic of the entertainment industry, racial oppression was transmogrified into a happy-go-lucky tap dance routine. Women's oppression was reduced to love problems or the difficulties that arose when women strayed from traditional roles and ventured into a man's world. The economic injustices of capitalism were dismissed as just a matter of "hard times." Instead of dramatizing the class dimensions of political power, the media gave us morality plays about the personal venalities of individual politicians. To quote one critic:

> For the most part the movies continued to reiterate in the talkies of the 1930s the familiar, threadbare themes of the silent 1920s: that the rich, too, had their troubles, and were not to be envied; that a woman's life, however useful, acquired meaning only in romance; . . . that the ills of existence were mostly moral ills; that the cure for these ills lay in preserving an unquenchable optimism and a sense of good-neighborliness. The mores of Hollywood remained more or less the same in spite of the Depression.[1]

In the Frank Capra films of the thirties and forties, America is a nation of small towns and modest but comfortable homes, inhabited by ordinary but sometimes heroic folks who try to set aright any greedy or snobbish individual. Capra's *It's a Wonderful Life* (1946), frequently replayed on television at Christmastime, gives us the character of George Bailey, who spends most of his life lending a helping hand to folks in his town. George makes a populist speech before the financial tycoons of the town. Think about the little people, he says, who built this community with their hard work. They don't have big sums of dough to shell out. The building and loan institution gives them a chance to own a home. It's the only alternative to living in one of the slums that the evil banker, Mr. Potter, owns. Potter, the "cruelest, richest man in town," knows it all too well and he wants to close the building and loan. But the other moneybags on the board are touched by George's plea and they vote Potter down, if you can believe it. In violation of all market imperatives, they decide to float the building and loan even though it's in the red (for having been too soft with people who were down on their luck). They then appoint George as its executive officer.

But the building and loan falls on hard times. Potter tightens the screws and denies George financial aid, telling him to get help from "the riff-raff you love so much." George wishes he was dead and for a short while, with the aid of his guardian angel, he gets his wish and sees what the community he loves would have been like if he hadn't been there: a tacky, tawdry, heartless rundown town with honky-tonks and strip joints, dominated completely by Potter. George realizes that one person can make a big difference. In the final scene, the hometown folks come through for George. The same crowd that previously had been besieging the building and loan to get their money out now congregate spontaneously in George's living room to sing Christmas carols and empty their pockets of thousands of dollars (where did they get all that money?) in order to bail out George and save the building and loan, so grateful are they for all he has done.

It's a Wonderful Life tells us that there are bad greedy business people like Potter, the monopolist banker, who operate on the imperative of "accumulate, accumulate, accumulate," and good business people like George Bailey who are the purveyors of good works and faith and want what is best for ordinary folks. It is vintage Capra, a fairy tale.

In Capra's *Mr. Smith Goes to Washington* (1939), the decent, honest Senator refuses to play ball with cynical, corrupt malefactors. Good meets evil but evil is still personal and never systemic. "The evil of [Capra's] corrupt characters never rubbed off on the institutions they controlled or the social and economic system that shaped their behavior and allowed them to succeed."[2] Probably the most influential director of his time, Capra created the kind of mythical, celluloid America that Ronald Reagan was still selling us in the 1980s.

To gladden the troubled spirits of people gripped in the Great Depression, Hollywood in the thirties also created Shirley Temple, the adorable song-and-dance imp. In *Bright Eyes, Curly Top, Dimples,* and *Poor Little Rich Girl,* Shirley plays the loveable little child who heals other people's lives. She teaches us not to hate the rich; they are just grumpy old people whom nobody loves. She softens their hearts and transforms them into warm, caring folks. Shirley also helps friendless servants, Blacks, and hoboes. She dispenses love and affection to all who need her. Happiness is a matter of having the right attitude. The Depression is just a silly thing that should not be taken seriously. Anyone can be an old sourpuss about malnutrition and unemployment, but under Shirley's spell we learn to sing away our poverty and dance away our despair.[3]

The Academy-Award winning *The Best Years of Our Lives* (1946) tells us that small-town America is the best place to be. The affluent bank officer, a returning veteran, pals around with two other veterans, ordinary working guys, one of whom gets romantically involved with the banker's daughter. Early in the film, the three men drive past the fire station, the diner, and the ballpark, places which they supposedly share in common: one town, one class of people. The women are maternal and caring, except for one wife with loose morals, who refuses to be domesticated and is not worthy of audience sympathy, as the film makes clear.[4]

Films about small-town America depict a society taken straight from a Norman Rockwell painting. Class is not a factor of life because everyone is middle-class. Ethnicity is not a factor because everyone is White-Anglo-Saxon-Protestant, except perhaps for the Black maid and the Latino delivery boy. Sexism is not an issue because women know their place.

Forty years after *The Best Years of Our Lives* not all that much had changed. *Down and Out in Beverly Hills* (1986) gives us a class view that fits the Reaganite mythology. It tells us that the homeless "choose" street poverty as a preferred life-style. A street person works his way into a nouveau-riche household, manipulates all the family members, and steals the hearts of the rich man's wife, daughter, and maid. Needless to say, he prefers this rip-off life to honest hard work, even refusing a management job in the rich man's factory. In somewhat similar fashion, an African-American homeless friend of his refuses a sandwich offered in a restaurant, preferring to steal some food from the same

Down and Out in Beverly Hills reaffirms the Reaganite mythology that the homeless "choose" street poverty as a life-style.

restaurant. The film lets us know that you just can't be nice to these lowlifes. It also tells us that the rich are not to be envied for they are bored and unhappy. In search of diversion, the rich man goes slumming with the bum and has the time of his life, partying with the indigents, learning to beg and eat garbage. "It was great!" he says. *Down and Out in Beverly Hills* transforms the desperate plight of the homeless into a diverting escapade. It panders to class prejudices by portraying the poor as little more than lazy predators.

Make-believe Moneyed Media

The revolution in the standard of living on TV [during the Reagan years] has been the most extraordinary jump since man has been on the planet, far surpassing anything that real-life economists could even conceive. . . . There are no longer *any* Americans on TV who are not well-to-do, except for cops and servicemen, and they get to have nice clothes anyway. . . . Just about every other newcomer is out and out stinking rich or at least lives as if he were. You can grab the shows by the handful and hear the sound of money: "Glitter," about two well-to-do reporters for a *People* mag clone, surrounded by nothing but rich people; "Paper Dolls," in which fashion plates, teeny-bopper models, lecherous older men and aging vamps let their fingernails grow, but keep their coupons well-clipped; or "Hunter," in which a man and woman chase criminals from behind the raw silk curtain. . . .

In situation comedy land, the days when Harriet Nelson or Mrs. Cleaver slaved over an ironing board are even more obsolete. To-day's sitcom world has about 12 shows with middle-class, white, two-parent families with children. All but one of them has full-time domestic help . . . only "Family Ties" shows a family *without* a live-in servant. . . . (There are, relatively speaking, about 110 times as many servants on TV as in real life.) . . .

Why did it happen? As usual in Hollywood, the product is caused by a little input from the outside world and a lot of input from the Hollywood pros. To some extent, Hollywood's TV apparatus is reflecting an increased (and alarming) fixation on wealth in American life generally. . . . Today's heroes are the money makers, not the spearheads of the proletariat. . . . The message coming out of the TV screen is now exactly the same as the message coming out of all the means of mass communication in America: "Enrichissez-vous."

Benjamin J. Stein, "In Prime Time, Everybody's Rich," *Washington Post*, October 17, 1984.

Trauma in Soapville

Soon after conquering America, television gave us the soap opera, a dramatic form carried over from daytime radio. Relatively inexpensive to produce, yet commanding large audiences and high advertising revenues, the afternoon soaps provide the networks with more profits than does prime-time television. Here is a make-believe society devoid of politico-economic oppression, inhabited mostly by White, economically well-off, professionals (lawyers, doctors, architects, and business executives and their families) who spend their waking hours wrestling with a never-ending succession of personal crises. Relatively few Latinos, African-Americans, and Asians and even fewer blue-collar workers appear as principals.[5] Soap characters have little to say about the struggles of working people, the injustice of the tax system, the price-gouging of consumers, the destruction of neighborhoods, the impossible cost of housing and rents due to realty speculation and landlord greed, the undemocratic powers of corporations, and the fast-buck desecration of our environment—dramatic issues that affect us directly and personally.

In Soapville there are seldom any class differences and certainly no class conflict. All behavior is seen as morally motivated. The woman from the wrong side of town who schemes and lies to get a man and the man who schemes and lies to get a job are seen simply as evil people.

The afflictions of the elderly are another neglected theme. Emphasis is on relatively youthful persons, those considered to be at the top of the hill, not over it. Occasionally an attractively greying older individual or couple who are in perfect health and financially secure appears as part of the family montage. But the special travails of the aged rarely figure significantly.[6]

Motherhood is lauded, yet children are in scarce supply in Soapville. Pregnancies are numerous but so are miscarriages and stillbirths; however, abortions are unheard of. The little ones who survive childbirth often do so with their paternity in question. They are kidnapped and fought over in custody battles. But once the controversy is resolved, they usually are conveniently killed in accidents, die of rare diseases, or just drop out of sight. In this way, the adult characters are less limited in the number of times they might marry, divorce, switch partners, have mental breakdowns, disappear, engage in money schemes, and plot murder. The fortunate few kids who escape all dangers grow up at a supernatural rate, are shipped off to school, and are only occasionally referred to in adult conversation. In no time, they suddenly reappear almost full-grown to become a source of family conflict and to start romances of their own.[7]

The Good and the Bad
of Soap-Opera Sex

Promiscuous sex is . . . a vital ingredient. But while everyone does it, the good guys and the bad buys have different motivations.

Good guys have affairs when: (a) they are married to a very bad person who treats them terribly and they fall in love with someone else; (b) they are caught in a moment of weakness and despair; or (c) they are trapped in a cave in a snow storm and think they are going to die.

Of course, to keep the soaps interesting, these are fairly common occurrences. The other factor that separates the good from the bad is guilt. The good guys always feel guilty. The bad guys are not tethered by such feelings. They have affairs when: (a) they want a rich lover to marry; (b) they want to keep someone away from his or her true love; or (c) they are feeling lusty.

Rose Rubin Rivera. "The World of Afternoon Soap Operas." *World Magazine*, February 17, 1983. p. 13.

The few social problems that make their way into soap scripts, such as alcoholism, drug addiction, unemployment, and crime, are reduced to purely personal phenomena. People are victimized by aberrant mishaps or by other ill-willed people and never by socioeconomic and political injustices. In time, virtuous individuals rectify the situation and sometimes even reform evildoers.

Reality gives us millions of isolated, lonely people living in congested, automobile-dominated, crime-ridden urban sprawls. Soapville gives us a secure, comfortable, small-town community that resembles an extended family, filled with concerned people who drop by to chat and who give themselves totally to each other's troubled affairs, defending their friends from treacherous interlopers.

Reality gives us the overworked, sleep-starved, single mothers who spend long hours toiling at underpaid jobs, raising children, and doing household chores while worrying about how they are going to make ends meet. The soaps give us mostly well-heeled, childless women—wives and lovers—who sometimes have careers of their own but who, in any case, seldom worry about grocery bills, tuition costs, mortgage payments, and old-age retirement. Their waking hours, like those of their men, are consumed by endless rounds of romance, seduction, and interpersonal conspiracies. These experiences are acted out in comfort-able upper-middle-class living rooms, bedrooms, kitchens, or executive offices by beautifully groomed people, who, even if just lounging about the house, look as if they are prepared for a photo session with a fashion magazine.

But one should not think that life is easy in Soapville. It is a series of perpetual catastrophes. Characters are forever contracting fatal ill-nesses; dying in accidents; attempting and sometimes succeeding at suicides; being blackmailed, murdered, raped, or kidnapped; going in-sane; suffering amnesia; developing split personalities; falling victim to nefarious financial schemes; and—judging from the accidental preg-nancy rate—engaging in sexual encounters without the slightest knowl-edge of modern birth control techniques. Here are some examples cover-ing only one week (May 22–26, 1989):

> On "Another World," Cass accuses Nicole of killing Jason; Gwen
> constantly reminds Evan that Rachel killed his mother; Evan admits
> to Rachel that he wanted to get revenge against her, but has
> changed his mind; after walking out on Vicki, Jamie decides to have
> blood tests to see if he is Steven's father.
>
> On "Guiding Light," Sonni is arrested on kidnapping charges;
> Reva realizes that Sonni is innocent of the charge; Josh is devastated
> when the police fish Rose's body out of the lake; Roger and Alan
> fight over a gun in the church organ loft during Phillip's wedding
> ceremony; Alan gets the drop on Roger then threatens to blow up
> the church if Roger doesn't reveal his true identity to everyone; Alan
> shoots Roger when he tries to get rid of the bomb; just as Phillip is
> about to say "I do," he is shot by a stray bullet; and, of course,
> Meredith and Rick are still at odds because she is carrying Phillip's
> baby.
>
> On "Days of Our Lives," Tom urges Robin to tell Mike that Mike
> is the father of her infant son; Marcus is upset that he can find no
> record of his own birth; Roman regains consciousness and tells Abe
> that he is sure he was shot by Cal; Adam kisses Kimberly, who tells
> him she loves Shane; Alfred kidnaps Shane and admits sending
> threatening letters to Kimberly to get her and Shane to leave town.[8]

Just ordinary moments in the lives of ordinary people.

The soaps teach us that individuals cannot join together to work toward a harmonious, collective solution of difficulties. Indeed, the message is that interpersonal contact *causes* rather than solves difficul-ties. The picture is of a bourgeois society composed of clashing, throbbing egos, devoid of common social and political goals, caught up in an interminable succession of treacheries, seductions, crimes, and monumental mishaps.

On the rare occasions when explicitly political material is worked into the script, it is not likely to be very edifying. Thus in 1983 during the Reagan era, one story line on "General Hospital" involved a scientist, Dr. Putnam, whose education was financed by the "Party," a secret sinister political organization. He is under the dictatorial control of a "Party" agent who herself is under the command of "Comrade Grigory." This comrade, it turns out, is part of a mysterious international spy ring in the service of a foreign power. Facing repeated commands from Party agents such as: "The Party demands you do this!" Dr. Putnam has no choice but to obey. He engages in acts of espionage and murder on behalf of his superiors, in a script that is little more than an anticommunist caricature.[9]

While issues regarding class power remain untouched, the 1980s did see the incorporation of various contemporary cultural themes into soap scripts—in that superficial co-optive way designed to contain rather than activate an issue. Thus, without ever actually challenging existing social arrangements, the soaps can come away seeming very relevant by touching upon subjects such as gender roles, rape, incest, spouse abuse, homosexuality, and AIDS. But, again, these things are usually presented as personal problems to be tackled by personal means.

Sometimes these cultural issues are accorded broader treatment. In 1988, "All My Children" was the first soap opera to feature a lesbian as a major character and the first to have the show's characters grapple— as a community—with prejudice against homosexuals. This same soap also portrayed a community effort to educate people about AIDS and to protect an AIDS victim, in this case a working-class single mother, from vigilante harassment.[10]

These exceptions aside, the political text of the soaps has not changed much in forty years. "The nuclear family, motherhood, heterosexual monogamy and capitalism are permanent, unquestioned norms. Abortion is still forbidden. Characters are either 'good' or 'bad' from birth, and their moral condition has no relation to their class or work."[11]

The Rise of the "Oil Operas"

During the early 1980s, a novel variation of the soap opera emerged, geared to prime-time evening viewers instead of the afternoon audience, appearing weekly instead of daily. Shows like "Dallas," "Dynasty," "Falcon Crest," and "Flamingo Road" are set in the South or West and focus on the big business and domestic struggles of corporate patriarchal families. The leading characters are business moguls, usually oil barons, who manifest a single-minded dedication to lust, wealth, and power. Whether pursuing money or women, they are ruthlessly self-serving, betraying little need for companionship and affection. They plot and scheme in their palatial homes, private planes, executive suites, and swank resorts, tended to by small armies of disciplined and devoted servants.

There are few if any virtuous lead characters. One usually must choose between "bad guys" and "worse guys." Occasionally, a somewhat less venal character might agonize for a moment, as when Bobby Ewing of "Dallas" gets drunk and groans: "There must be a way to run Ewing Oil without lying and cheating." He is quickly proven wrong by his older brother, the notorious J.R.[12] The oil operas pretty much do away with questions of social conscience. There are no moral values as such, only instrumental values which either work or don't work in advancing one to still greater heights of wealth and corporate power. Bribery, blackmail, fraud, corruption—no tactic is too reprehensible if it works.

Occasionally, a female power monger like Alexis in "Dynasty" might fight her way into this man's world of high finance—thus, letting us know that, given the chance, a woman can be as determinedly rotten as any man. More often, however, women are just one of the properties that the moguls fight over and acquire. Although set in places like Dallas and Denver, the oil operas have few Latinos, Blacks, or working-class Whites. When such characters do appear, they have no interests apart from the rich employers to whom they are bound.

The oil operas are not intended to incite resentment against the rich. If anything, they invite the audience to enter vicariously into a lavish world. In the absence of any specific statements to the contrary, these soaps promote implicit acceptance and even enjoyment of the wild and wicked doings of the rich and powerful, those who reduce sex, family, land, career, and most other things to property acquisitions.

None of these tycoons do any productive work; they are too busy skimming the cream. "This is a world where the tables and floors are always cleaned, the food is always cooked, the mansions are always built and maintained in just the right way—and the oil is pumped out of the ground at a steady rate. All taken completely for granted."[13] Missing from the picture are the working people who do the work that enables the oil barons to live the way they do.

As the ruthless Alexis, Joan Collins does her bit in the ABC-TV series "Dynasty" to promote acceptance of the wild and wicked doings of the rich and powerful.

Benign Bosses and Bad Bosses

For decades, the make-believe media have represented the socioeconomic power of our society as being in good hands. With some exceptions, the Establishment figures who preside over the businesses and other institutions come across as dedicated, fair-minded, and deserving of our trust, rarely racist or sexist, and not apt to pursue policies that hurt the poor and the powerless while favoring the rich and powerful.

Of course, bad apples come along occasionally, those who play ruthlessly and violate the established rules. In the case of the oil operas, as just noted, such venal tycoons are elevated to a kind of amoral hero status. In most instances these undesirables are set straight by more scrupulous individuals or are likely to meet a deservedly unfortunate end. Whatever the outcome, their evil is seen as being personal to them rather than representative of the business system and other institutions from which they draw their power.

Then there are the *good* business people, who sometimes are indifferent to other people's troubles only because they are so preoccupied with their own business affairs. Once they are properly apprised of the problem, they are "capable of legendary generosity and humanity."[14] A rare species in real life, these selfless types have been around for quite a while in the make-believe media. In *The Devil and Miss Jones* (1941), for instance, a crusty mogul poses as a clerk in his own department store in order to ferret out union organizers. However, he is soon won over to his employees' cause and becomes a caring, sharing kind of boss.

Equally unlikely is Frank Capra's *Mr. Deeds Goes to Town* (1936). Longfellow Deeds inherits $20 million and decides to give it all away to needy people. He comes across as an admirable, humane person, one of the loveable, nurturing rich. In *Million Dollar Baby* (1941), a wealthy lady takes a fancy to a young working woman and gives her a million dollars. The sudden acquisition of so much money causes strains between the young heroine and her penniless but proud boyfriend (Ronald Reagan). In the final scene, she solves everything by dashing about town, tossing away her entire fortune to passersby, who happily grab at the fluttering dollars. The message: wealth is best left to the wealthy; not only does money fail to guarantee happiness, it seems to cause unhappiness when placed in the hands of ordinary folks; no use resenting the rich; the best things in life are free.

Money is given away more sedately and systematically in "The Millionaire," a television series that ran through much of the 1950s (updated and redone in 1978 as a made-for-TV movie). Through a trusted assistant, a never-seen millionaire hands out million-dollar cashier's checks to people of modest means. The acquisition of such funds changes the lives of the characters, sometimes in ironic ways, since they often don't know how to make the best of their bounty.

A wealthy elderly lady in *Christmas Eve* (1986) hands out money to the poor with the assistance of her chauffeur. As proof of her eccentricity she gives cash and does not even bother to get receipts for tax deductions. At one point she is arrested for interfering with a police round-up of street people. When her embarrassed son ("It's in all the newspapers") comes to bail her out, she won't go unless all her poor friends go, so he has to bail out all of them. She also refuses to go along with her high-powered son who wants to swing a lucrative business deal involving a new housing complex. No, she says, we won't build a new complex until we have a place for the poor people living there now. "That's the way your father did it"—which makes one wonder how father managed to get so rich investing in real estate. Stories about generous millionaires almost never focus on the less-than-generous ways they or their families accumulated and sustained their fortunes.

The best thing for workers is to cooperate fully with a benign management so that together they might ward off foreign competitors. Such is the message in *Gung Ho* (1986), an otherwise lightweight movie about a Japanese company that reopens a shuttered auto plant in the United States. The conflict between labor and management turns out to be only a *cultural* one. The workers don't take their morning exercises seriously the way Japanese workers do. Worse still, they goof around on the assembly line. Finally, when it becomes a matter of produce or perish, they learn to work hard as a compliant team under management's guidance, performing their tasks and even their exercises with a rigorous martial-arts dedication. The plant stays open; no unions are in sight; no mention is made of the profits that go to the owners; workers and bosses hug each other; everyone is happy.

The inventive, independent entrepreneur who tilts against corporate giants is the theme of *Tucker: The Man and His Dream* (1988), directed by Francis Ford Coppola. Far superior to the usual Hollywood fare, this film draws from the real-life story of the Michigan small businessman who dreamed of building the car of the future in the 1940s with safety and performance features that were reluctantly adopted decades later by the same giant automakers who originally resisted him. Seeing Tucker as a threat to their market, the automotive cartel and its political allies destroy him. His steel supplies are cut off; he is placed under surveillance by the FBI, attacked by a Michigan senator and by an unsympathetic business-owned press, and hit with trumped-up charges by the Securities and Exchange Commission. During the course of events, Tucker gets in a few telling lines, as when he notes that the big guys "don't give a damn about people; all they care about is profits. They're guilty of criminal negligence."

But like other promising films, *Tucker* goes only so far. Thus, Tucker's enemies—Ford, General Motors, and Chrysler—are never mentioned by name, being evasively referred to only as "the Big Three" or "Detroit."[15] (Presumably, the "Big Three" are identifiable to most people, though one young viewer with whom I attended this movie wondered if Toyota was included among them.) Nor do the corporate conspirators arrayed against Tucker ever appear on the screen to tell us exactly why their oligopolistic interests require that he be crushed.

In a final courtroom speech, Tucker irrelevantly blames his troubles on a red-tape society created by "bureaucrats." Today Benjamin Franklin would need a permit to fly his kite, he quips. In fact, the government bureaucrats who do appear in the film helpfully provide Tucker with a large surplus war plant for his auto-building—at no cost and with a minimum of red tape.

Tucker also irrelevantly blames his troubles on the fact that "we" have a self-inflated view of ourselves as a nation because "we" invented the atomic bomb and are now resting on our laurels. He says not a word about the business oligopoly that is actually destroying him. Instead, we get a preachment on the need to return to the purer private enterprise system of the small entrepreneur, free of irksome government regulations. No right-wing libertarian could ask for more.

Special attention should be given to Oliver Stone's *Wall Street* (1987). Though a good film, it illustrates better than most "anti-business" movies the limits of a liberal critique. The main character, inside trader and cutthroat corporate raider Gordon Gekko (Michael Douglas) represents *bad* Wall Street. In Gekko's world, no room exists for fair play or friendship; as he tells young Bud, a would-be protégé:

In *Wall Street*, corporate raider Gordon Gekko tells young Bud that greed is good and that the free market prevails over democracy. Luckily, the good capitalists eventually prevail over the bad ones like Gekko.

"If you want a friend, buy a dog." Leading a takeover fight at a stock-holders meeting, he declares: "Greed is good. Greed is right. Greed works." Turning to Bud, Gekko delivers one of the rarest commentaries one is likely to hear on the big screen:

> Capitalism at its finest. The richest one percent of this country owns half our country's wealth, five trillion dollars. One-third of that comes from hard work [?]; two-thirds from inheritance, interest on interest accumulating—and from what I do: stock and real-estate speculation. It's bullshit: You got 90 percent of the American public out there with little or no net worth. I create nothing. I *own*. We make the rules, pal. The news, war, peace, famine, upheaval, the price of a paper clip—we pick that rabbit out of the hat while every-body sits out there wondering how the hell we did it. You're not naive enough to think we're living in a democracy, are you, Buddy? It's the free market and you're part of it.

But closer scrutiny reveals that this is not a Marxist film. Coun-terposed to Gekko's *bad* Wall Street is *good* Wall Street, embodied in Lou, the crusty old broker, one of those who create the "one-third" of investor wealth that supposedly "comes from hard work." Lou puts a fatherly arm around Bud's shoulder and warns him against playing fast with illegal insider information:

> There are no shortcuts, son. Quick-buck artists come and go with every bull market. The steady players make it through the bear mar-kets. You're part of something here, Bud. The money you make for people creates science and research jobs. Don't sell that out.

The film accepts the capitalist mythology that Wall Street's money is "created" by the investors and speculators who gamble with it, rather than by those who actually work at the "science and research jobs" and other occupations. We are being asked to believe that *good* Wall Street serves the nation, not itself. Bad guys like Gekko are at fault, not the system that produced them.

In the end, the Securities and Exchange Commission steps in and arrests Bud for inside trading and nabs the evil Gekko. Crime does not pay, not even on Wall Street, at least not if it's a crime against other financial interests. This is Gekko's sin: he is bilking other investors. While the film leaves us with the impression that the SEC protects the public interest, it really protects the corporate speculators from each other—on occasion.

The wicked businessman is not an unfamiliar character in the make-believe media. George Gerbner, dean of the Annenberg School of Communications at the University of Pennsylvania, reports that "good" business characters in prime-time television outnumber the "bad" ones by two to one. In contrast, the ratio for doctors was sixteen to one and for police twelve to one.[16] So while the image of business people is more positive than negative, it is less positive than other establishment professions. Perhaps this is a concession to popular sentiment, specifically the resentment felt toward the tycoons who treat the productive forces of society as just so many gaming pieces in the contest for self-enrichment.

To the extent it exists, the media critique of the business world goes only so far. Consider the classic *Citizen Kane* (1941), which was based on the life of press mogul William Randolph Hearst. The film's twenty-six-year-old star, director, and coauthor Orson Welles produced a movie that was exceptional more for its dramatic composition, narrative structure, and camera techniques than for its politics. In fact, the film's political theme was the usual Hollywood fare: power corrupts and money does not bring happiness.[17]

At its best, the mainstream entertainment industry tiptoes up toward the truth but never quite embraces it. From *Citizen Kane* to *Wall Street,* the focus is on the ruthlessness of individual moneybags. Their wrongful ways are not born of the system in which they operate but are personal to them. "If television is unkind to businessmen," notes Gitlin, who could also be describing Hollywood, "it is scarcely unkind to the values of a business civilization. Capitalism and the consumer society come out largely uncontested."[18]

While the media teach us that money does not bring happiness and often makes us miserable, we should remind ourselves that in real life the rich live quite well. Very few of them voluntarily give up their fortunes so that they might pursue the deeper satisfactions of putting in a ten-hour day driving a taxi or plucking chickens in a poultry plant. One need only recall the candid remark made in 1984 by Barbara Bush, wife of then Vice President George Bush, that she and her husband were not ashamed of being rich; they enjoyed their wealth.

At the very least, even if money does not guarantee happiness, it certainly makes life much easier; it makes it easier to deal with adversities or to escape altogether the many kinds of unhappinesses caused by not having enough money for one's needs. Money creates the best possible life chances in a capitalist society, providing privileged opportunities for professional success and for comfortable living in spacious homes; the best schooling; diverse and advantageous social contacts;

superior access to political careers, power, and favored treatment by government and the law; greater opportunities for travel, leisure, and recreation; the finest health and therapeutic care; quality retirement conditions; and a host of other services that are not readily accessible to those of lesser means and not available at all to the poorest among us.

Money can raise persons of limited talent and inferior intelligence to remarkable heights. As the career of Vice President Dan Quayle demonstrates, money can magically transform the mediocre into the meteoric. When portraying the luxurious world of the rich, the make-believe media say little about all this. Instead, we are fed images of generous millionaires, amorous playboys, embattled tycoons, and bored heiresses.

7

Superdocs and Shoot-'em-ups

Of the professionals overrepresented in the make-believe media, police and doctors have been among the most prominent. Were we to believe the portrayals fed to us, law officers and physicians want nothing more for themselves than the satisfaction of a job well done in the service of others. As usual, the media ignore the social and economic realities in which these professionals operate.

The Magic Medicine Show

In movies of the 1940s and 1950s and television series of the 1960s and 1970s (but no longer around by the 1980s), doctors like Kildare and Welby displayed qualities of wisdom and devotion regularly found only among deity. They tirelessly went beyond their normal duties to save and redirect their patients' lives. They possessed almost preternatural powers of counseling and a never-faltering fair-mindedness and forbearance. "All Marcus Welby has to do is give his stop-feeling-sorry-for-yourself speech and the character undergoes a drastic personality change."[1] Their ability to diagnose the most exotic ailments bordered on the clairvoyant. They were always right and always rather modest about it. Such physicians were free of professional jealousies and rivalries, single-mindedly dedicated to service, and oddly indifferent to monetary rewards.[2] Some of them, like Marcus Welby, even made house calls.

These shows gave no hint that large numbers of people lacked the financial means to command the medical care their television sets seemed to promise. During its first five years, "Marcus Welby, M.D." received some 250,000 letters, mostly from individuals seeking medical advice.[3] This audience response was symptomatic of (1) many viewers' inability to separate fact from fiction and (2) the pathetic and unattended needs of many who could not afford doctors or who, no longer having any faith in real ones, sought the free and apparently omniscient care extended by television's superdocs.

No mention was ever made on these shows of how the costs of getting an M.D. degree closed that profession to many capable persons, leaving us to draw our medical personnel not necessarily from the most competent population but from the more affluent. Nor was there ever a hint that a good portion of medical-school costs in this country were federally subsidized, so that ironically many lower-income people could not afford the very services they helped support with their taxes.

The medical series "Ben Casey," running from 1961 to 1966, represented a partial departure from the perfectly idealized superdoc in the nice spotless hospital. Casey worked in an urban hospital which bore some resemblance to a real one. He also occasionally confronted a hidebound medical establishment that was not always considerate of patients' rights. In his spare time, the young handsome doctor pursued his amorous interests. As with the more standard superdocs, Casey's seemingly superhuman technical exploits always vindicated the moral and medical worth of his profession.[4]

The early 1980s saw a more sophisticated version of the superdoc with "Trapper John, M.D.," a Korean war veteran. (In fact, the show was a spin-off from "M*A*S*H" with fewer jokes.) As to be expected, Trapper John was wise, calm, and selfless, and like all his other television medical colleagues, he manifested no concern for higher fees, tax shelters, stock investments, realty speculations, summer houses, and yachts.

In contrast to the superdoc shows, the 1970s TV series "Medic" was willing to deal with the more realistic subjects hitherto avoided on television, such as childhood leukemia, mastectomy, postpartum psychosis, and medical malpractice. The hospital personnel in "Medic" served on what Hal Himmelstein calls the "urban frontier,"[5] a place where a few courageous Whites did battle amidst—if not necessarily against—the swarthy hordes, not as cowboys and soldiers but as doctors, police, lawyers, and social workers, administering to troubled and troublesome inner-city denizens.

Unlike the superdocs who did everything superbly, the urban-frontier doctors were portrayed as weary, imperfect humans, attempting with mixed success to carry on. Paddy Chayefsky's film *The Hospital* (1971) is a perfect example of this genre. White doctors try valiantly to hold together an urban hospital in a poor multiracial neighborhood.

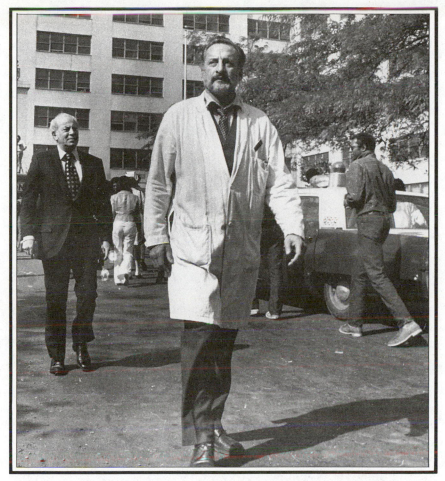

George C. Scott is the valiantly dedicated doctor in *The Hospital* who battles against the skullduggery, incompetence, and chaos caused by lesser people.

They treat patients in crowded messy wards, train younger personnel, and deal with mysterious fatal mishaps. Little is said in the film about the wider realities of political economy that leave municipal hospitals underfinanced and overburdened. The hospital itself is depicted as victimized not by the warped economics of the private medical industry but by some unfathomable human folly, perpetrated—we are invited to surmise—by the minorities who crowd into the wards and the senseless foul-ups committed by lower-level staff.

The White physicians in *The Hospital,* like the White missionaries of earlier films, try to preserve some semblance of civilization while surrounded by inept or hostile "natives." At one point in the film, two veteran doctors think of quitting the struggle, but they quickly discard that notion, magnanimously choosing to stay at their posts in what one of them calls "this cockamamy hospital" in "this cockamamy world." Such is the liberal's plight. Since there are no rational explanations for what is wrong, there are no rational solutions. Just hang in there. That is as far as Chayefsky's politics—and Hollywood's—will let us go.

By the 1980s, a television series, "St. Elsewhere," portrayed a whole hospital as the hero. The format, resembling that of the cop show "Hill Street Blues," was originally borrowed from the soap operas: several plot lines going simultaneously, interspersed with quick cuts and not all resolved by the end of a particular episode. The doctors in "St. Elsewhere" were almost all White males, but they were also imperfect and humanly motivated. Devoid of superheroes, the show had an intelligent and often amusing script and sometimes dealt with real hospital problems. It went off the air in 1988.

All these medical shows—both the idealized and the more realistic ones—have one thing in common: they leave unexamined the political economy of modern medicine. Media doctors never charge exorbitant fees, as do some of their real-life counterparts. In the make-believe medical world, physicians never cheat Medicaid and Medicare out of hundreds of millions of dollars by consistently overcharging for services, by fraudulently billing for nonexistent patients or for services not rendered, or by charging for unneeded tests and treatments, and making unnecessary hospital admissions. Media doctors seem to know nothing about the estimated two million unnecessary operations that are knowingly performed annually by real-life doctors, costing about $4 billion and leading to the death of some 10,000 patients and an undetermined number of disabilities each year.[6]

Media doctors are not likely to involve themselves with reaping enormous profits by running methadone clinics. Nor are they ever shown running hospitals that break strikes and underpay their service staff or deny treatment to people who cannot show proof of ability to pay or eject patients in the midst of an illness because their insurance coverage has run out. Unlike their real-life counterparts, media doctors never mobilize their political muscle to get state legislatures to impose monopolistic bans on alternative health treatments. Nor do they incorporate themselves to avoid taxes while doubling their fees and investing their money in the very pharmaceutical and medical supply industries whose prices have helped jack up hospital bills five times faster than the overall cost of living. Nor would media doctors be seen as self-enriching directors of private hospitals that are interested exclusively in the highly profitable market of insured paying customers, while remaining inaccessible to the poor and the uninsured. Private hospitals are rarely, if ever, depicted in the media for what many of them are: lucrative ventures for rich private investors.[7]

In a word, media doctors, even those stationed on the urban frontier—like just about everyone else in the make-believe media—are divorced from underlying material realities. They might conflict with privileged people but not with the privileged class system. They might deal with some of the effects of poverty but not with its causes. As with other media drama, medical shows are seldom able to recognize the existence of real social problems that require something more than individualized attention. When such problems *are* acknowledged, it is assumed they are beyond solution.

Bang! Bang! You're Dead

Media doctors, like media western gunfighters, were nearing extinction by the early 1990s. Not so with media law officers. The "cop-and-crime" shows remained the leading staple. While many specimens of this genre flop in less than a season, fresh replacements pour forth, along with various action-adventure and crime-and-violence shows in which the police do not figure as a significant factor. In these latter productions, a layperson, being either the would-be victim, a friend, or a vigilante, eventually dispatches the villain.

It is not enough to denounce media crime and violence; we also need to explain why it is so prevalent. Studies find that over 60 percent of prime-time shows portray at least one crime. Murder and assault rank respectively as the two top criminal acts on television (and probably in the public imagination). In real life, the two most frequent felonies are burglary and larceny.[8] It is no accident that the media would give more attention to more violent crimes. Burglary and larceny have less shock value, less visual impact, than do murder and assault. Therefore, by media standards, they have less dramatic content.

Actually like almost any other human activity, any crime can be endowed with dramatic content. Ordinary life situations—sometimes because of their very familiarity—can be most compelling, if handled convincingly. The make-believe media, however, are more interested in presenting contrived and sensationalist shortcuts than in developing stories of depth and subtlety. Violent crime offers just the kind of ready-made, jiffy-quick "action drama" that Hollywood and television feel they must produce in superabundance. The heinous crimes are more capable of fulfilling the dramatic void left by the absence of real-life content. To hold our attention, the terrorized woman careening about in a large, dark house had better be stalked by a determined killer rather than by some nervous burglar who is only after her silverware.

On one Sunday (January 20, 1985) in Washington, D.C., the following movie reruns were aired on television:

Airport (1970): Someone bombs a passenger jet, killing many passengers.

Raid on Entebbe (1978): Israeli commandos stage a daring airfield raid, killing lots of "terrorists."

The Sentinel (1977): A woman faces terror in a house whose only other tenant is a blind priest.

Women of San Quentin (1983): Female prison inmates have a violent confrontation with female guards.

Straw Dogs (1971): A couple is terrorized by local toughs, resulting in much savagery and multiple killings.

Open Season (1974): Three thrill killers kidnap and leisurely murder a young couple. They, in turn, are killed by a vengeful relative of one of their earlier victims.

Nightmare in Chicago (1964): A deranged killer terrorizes passengers on a Chicago turnpike for seventy-two hours before the police blow him away.

Family Plot (1976): A spiritualist searches for a missing heir who is a professional kidnapper.

The Catamount Killing (1976): A couple meet their violent downfall after going to criminal lengths to escape the emptiness of their lives.

That same Sunday also offered a few standard TV cop-and-crime reruns, along with a mystery show about a mutilated body found buried in a strange grave. After enough days, months, and years of consuming this kind of fare, we might well be ready to vote for authoritarian law-and-order candidates, support the death penalty, increase military spending, bomb Iraq, buy a gun, and shoot anyone who strolls across our lawn after dusk.

Media violence is not confined to criminals, of course. In "Kojak," "Baretta," "Starsky and Hutch," and other TV police series nefarious violence is met with righteous violence, although it is often difficult to distinguish the two. Whether perpetrated by good guys or bad guys, violence on crime shows and in action-adventure films and teleplays is nearly omnipresent, often linked to sex, money, dominance, self-aggrandizement, and thrill-seeking.

The cop shows, known in the trade as "tire-screechers," focus on action: high-speed car chases, helicopter pursuits, rooftop shoot-outs, back-alley slugfests, and police with guns ablaze. This emphasis on violence subverts the very concept of law and order that police are supposed to uphold. One study concludes that the police behavior portrayed on entertainment television habitually violates the constitutional rights of individuals. The message communicated is that crime can be best met by state-sponsored illegality and brutality. Due process is something that has to be brushed aside so police can successfully subdue evil. Law officers are shown carrying out illegal searches and break-ins, coercing suspects into confessing, and employing homicidal violence against suspected criminals in shoot-'em-up endings.[9] According to another study, only about 5 percent of the apprehended criminals are ever shown going to trial or have their trials mentioned. Justice, as represented in the judicial process, seldom makes an appearance on screen, except in explicit courtroom dramas.[10] On most television and Hollywood cop shows, justice seems to flow from the barrel of a gun.

> Scores of citizens uninvolved in the crime under investigation are roughed up, shaken down, or harassed—by police. Homes, offices and cars are broken into regularly—by police. With a sixth sense that only scriptwriters can generate, every such invasion of personal privacy turns up the real, and usually demented criminal, or is justified because the victim was probably guilty of some crime anyway. Honest, law-abiding citizens are miraculously never hurt by these methods. There are no trials, no plea bargains, no defense, no argument about illegal police conduct affecting the guilty, the innocent, or the society as a whole.[11]

Here is TV detective D'Angelo, from the series by that name, telling it like it is during one episode in 1978:

> *D'Angelo:* What do I know about the law? I'm not a lawyer. I'm a cop.
> *Inspector Keller:* It's your job to enforce it.
> *D'Angelo:* It's my job to protect people from the mugger, the rapist, the armed robber, and the killer. People like Joey, like my partner Mickey, did the law help them? Did the law stop that killer?

All the laws in the world won't stop one man with a gun. It's going to take me or somebody like me. And you know what? I'll do it anyway I can.

    Inspector Keller: You're a dangerous man, Bert.

    D'Angelo: That's right. You'd better be damn glad I'm on your side.

A number of movies appearing in the 1970s and 1980s featured rogue cops like Clint Eastwood's *Dirty Harry* (1971), and its sequels, *Magnum Force* (1973), *The Enforcer* (1976), *Sudden Impact* (1983), and *The Dead Pool* (1988). Like their television counterparts, such films reaffirm the views of right-wing police organizations and politicians, who see the law as "handcuffing" the police. *Dirty Harry* argues that the law is guilty of protecting the rights of a homicidal psychopath. In real life, however, "the majority of suspects are poor, inarticulate and ignorant petty criminals open to police bamboozlement."[12] Detective Harry's angry remarks to his superior sound like D'Angelo's: "[What about the rights] of that old lady who had a sawed-off shotgun in her ear. Or doesn't she count anymore? What the hell is going on around here? . . . We're more concerned with the rights of the criminals than of the people we're supposed to be protecting."[13] This charge was to be made relentlessly in real life and with great effect by conservative politicians for years on end.

    The authoritarian message comes through again and again: The law

TV Doesn't Help Real Cops

Captain Thomas Gallagher, commander of the 44th Precinct in the Bronx, N.Y., offered this observation about police work and television:

    Unlike TV policemen, we don't always come up with the bad guy. We have a lot of restrictions, many of them constitutional. Some TV viewers feel we're not as good as Kojak, that we're not doing the proper job because we don't get our man in an hour. So TV doesn't help us in that regard. Nor does it help us when so many illegal acts are performed by TV police. . . .

    I realize there's right-wing pressure on the Supreme Court to crack down on offenders. The public seems to feel there's too much crime and that we have to wipe the criminals off the street, regardless of their constitutional rights. Television picks up on this.

Interview in *Saturday Review*, March 19, 1977.

does not protect you; it hinders those who wish to protect you. Only severely repressive direct action by persons freed from the manacles of the law can prevent the social order from falling apart. It is a mistake to describe such offerings as "law-and-order" shows. If anything is being boosted, it is lawlessness perpetrated by self-appointed vigilante cops.

This vigilantism is not new. It is as old as the earliest cowboy flicks, in which angry members of the posse would exclaim: "A trial is too good for that coyote! Let's string him up now!" In the 1930s, vigilantism was enthusiastically endorsed in crime films involving the Federal Bureau of Investigation. The "G-Men," as FBI agents were then known, violated all due process when hunting their quarry. Their vigilantism was encapsulated in films with titles such as: *Let 'Em Have It*, *Muss 'Em Up*, *Don't Turn 'Em Loose*, *Show Them No Mercy*. This cinematic protofascist motif was commented on by Milton Meyer, one critic of that day:

> It is the spirit that seeks order at the expense of justice. It advocates "treating em rough," whether "em" are laborers on strike, Communists at talk, or criminals in flight. It embraces the creation of a police army to fight crime, with the general view that police armies may be put to a number of uses.[14]

Such films were not far removed from reality, in that the FBI's real-life campaigns against Communists, labor radicals, and other dissidents evidenced little regard for due process.

The FBI was further glorified in a movie, *The FBI Story* (1959), and in a subsequent ABC television series, "The FBI" (1965–74), creations that won the cooperation and approval of FBI director J. Edgar Hoover. Needless to say, no hint was given in any of these shows that the FBI had a generally dismal record against organized crime and an almost nonexistent record against racist violence. In the postwar era, the FBI became so preoccupied with the surveillance and repression of Communists, civil-rights advocates, Black militants, peace protestors, Third World solidarity supporters, and others deemed dangerous to the status quo, that the reputation G-men had as gangbusters was forgotten by many people.

The entertainment media served the FBI in other ways. In an episode of "Kojak" on CBS, the tough cop was pitted against a "terrorist" Puerto Rican organization whose members were characterized as violent fanatics and assassins. The organization's name was "El Comite," the same as a real-life group founded in 1970 and committed to Puerto Rican independence, a group without any history of violence. Shortly after the show was aired, the ever-alert FBI, not inclined to let a good opportunity pass, began a series of harassing raids on the homes of real-life members of El Comite.[15] This was more than just a matter of life imitating art. Such cop shows give vivid support to right-wing political propaganda and help create the very climate of opinion that allows for real-life repression.

When the conservative Republican candidate Barry Goldwater pledged during the presidential campaign of 1964 to fight crime in the streets, the proposal fell flat. Few people thought the federal government should involve itself in an area considered to be largely the preserve of state and local authorities. Some were amused by the image of Goldwater as a kind of presidential sheriff. By the 1980s, however, after many more intensive years of shoot-'em-ups on television and in movie houses, the crime issue had become a major campaign theme of every conservative Republican presidential candidate. The Republicans tirelessly accused the Democrats, especially liberal ones, of being "soft on crime," a charge that began to stick in the minds of some voters.

It would seem that, along with right-wing political propagandists, the make-believe media deserve blame for the fact that public apprehension about crime has accelerated more precipitously than the actual crime rate in recent decades. A study conducted by two social psychologists compared the responses of light television viewers with heavy viewers and found the latter to be significantly more fearful about crime and generally more convinced that additional police were needed to contain unlawful activities. The study concluded that television violence cultivates exaggerated notions about danger in the real world. "The exaggerated sense of risk and insecurity may lead to increasing demands for protection and to increasing pressure for the use of force by established authority."[16] Other studies show that adults became more belligerent after large doses of television crime shows and more fearful of racial minorities, cities, and criminal attack.[17]

Some crime shows have been little more than urban-frontier remakes of the swarthy hordes epics discussed in Chapter Two. Thus, in the film *Assault on Precinct 13* (1976), a police station in a rundown part of town is attacked by weirdly painted youth gangs, as might a fort be attacked by Indians. The last few survivors in the station are rescued when other police—like the cavalry of yore—arrive on the scene. *Fort Apache, The Bronx* (1981) is another example of the urban-frontier drama in which the White cops protect the besieged ramparts of civilization from vicious swarthy hordes. Not surprisingly, the film offended the feelings of the Latino and African-American communities.

As if to celebrate the advent of the Reagan era, the networks opened the 1981–82 season with eight new shoot-'em-ups, along with several law-and-order westerns. Included was "Today's FBI," a series designed to restore the bureau's image after the scandals of a few years before. FBI agents were assigned to the show—at taxpayers' expense— to okay scripts and offer suggestions about plot lines.[18] Though net- work bosses had concluded that the nation was in a strong law-and- order mood, almost all the new cop shows, including "Today's FBI," "Strike Force," and "McClain's Law," were dismal flops. Every cop show of that year slumped in the ratings. The public was showing signs of having overdosed on shoot-'em-ups.

Nevertheless, toward the end of the decade, macho media cops were still blasting away. On the big screen, Dirty Harry returned in *The Dead Pool* (1988)—a box-office flop—to target a new villain—the news media. In this film, attention-hungry criminals are driven to all sorts of deranged acts by the provocative news media. Dirty Harry's own police department seems to be staffed mostly by publicity hounds. The manipu- lative methods of the media are treated as something self-generated by reporters and editors. Harry moralizes about our sick culture and tries to set it all straight by shooting some people and punching out others.

Another Reagan-era Hollywood shoot-'em-up and another box- office flop was *Cobra* (1986), with the screenplay by Sylvester Stallone, who took a break from playing the homicidal Rambo in order to play a homicidal vigilante cop named Marion Cobretti, better known as "Co- bra." Like so many of its genre, this movie pretends to be opposed to violence while joyfully wallowing in it. Against the protests of the press and the hesitations of his own police department, Cobra becomes a one-man army and slaughters a gang of psychopathic killers. These psychos are trying to take over northern California or the nation or the world—it's not clear. In one scene, Cobra is in an abandoned steel mill which, for some odd reason, is fully operative. He impales a villain on a giant hook and watches him twist in agony as he is carried off into a flaming furnace. Cobra pours gasoline over another foe and sets him on fire, sneering: "You have the right to remain silent." As busy as he is killing punks, Cobra finds time to punch out the bookish liberal wimp who has been speaking out against excessive violence.

Cobra does not bother with sissy things like arrest, incarceration, and trial. "This is where the law stops and I begin," he announces as he annihilates another enemy. For those in the audience who might miss the political point of this movie, the office Cobra occupies at police headquarters sports a Big Brother–size portrait of President Reagan.

With cops like these, who needs criminals? Indeed, in the lawless urban jungle, who needs cops? Eventually private individuals take lawlessness into their own hands. In *Taxi Driver* (1976) and more pointedly in *Death Wish* (1974) and its numerous sequels (1982, 1985, 1987) and imitations, self-appointed citizen vigilantes set about to rid the streets of criminals the old-fashioned way—by direct annihilation. As the publicity poster for the spy movie *Lassiter* (1984), starring Tom Selleck, exclaimed: "When the law has a job they can't handle, they need a man outside the law."

Making It Look "Realistic"

Beginning in the late 1960s, a whole genre of "relevant" television dramas emerged such as "The Young Lawyers," "The Interns," "Storefront Lawyers," "East Side, West Side," and "Mod Squad," which supposedly dealt with every social problem from inner-city drug rings to political protests. While ostensibly fashioned from the raw side of life, these shows tended to caricature the reality they were supposed to faithfully portray. As Les Brown describes it:

> Ideological types, as they were depicted in TV shows, had little resemblance beyond the external trappings to their objective counterparts in the real world. The psychopath looked like a hippie but was not in any philosophical sense a hippie. Yet the message was: beware the hippie, within lives a psychopath. In other shows, [political] militants were not angry revolutionaries but paranoics or agents of hostile countries; draft evaders not really opponents of the war but neurotics rejecting their fathers in return for having been rejected by them; bigots not true haters but merely persons who lived too long in isolation from other races; drug users not the disenchanted but victims of ghoulish weirdos and organized crime. Television faced the gut issues with false characters, and instead of shedding light on the ailments of the social system and the divisions within it, the playlets distorted the questions and fudged the answers.[19]

In contrast to the supercop epics, "organizational cop" television shows emerged, such as "Police Story" and "Hill Street Blues" (premiering respectively in 1973 and 1980), which had a more realistic overlay. Shifting scenes, unresolved conflicts, interspersed plots, hand-held cinéma-vérité camera work and busy, cluttered backgrounds gave "Hill Street Blues" a messy slice-of-life flavor. The individual hero cop was replaced by the police organization caught up in its grubby everyday struggles. Police officers resembled real people. Here were cops who had drinking problems, marriage problems, or problems with coworkers, cops who fouled up their assignments and took out their frustrations by using brutality, cops who harbored racist and sexist attitudes, even a cop who took bribes and perjured himself. And on occasion, a glimmer of larger social problems peeked through, as when in one episode an inner-city man is driven to domestic violence by unemployment and economic desperation. "Hill Street Blues" was a critical success, receiving an amazing twenty-one Emmy nominations after its first year, more than those received by any other prime-time comedy or dramatic series. In time, its ratings also climbed and it became a favorite, even among real police officers.

These more realistic shows, however, went just so far. "Hill Street Blues" dared not say much about the problems created by class oppression and the role of police in keeping the lid on that oppression. The Black and Latino police "clientele" of such shows come through as being beyond redemption, although a few might achieve salvation thanks to the paternal efforts of individual cops. The fashionably jaded themes are palmed off as realism.[20]

Other cop shows like "Miami Vice" and "Private Eye" offered some technical innovations in the late 1980s, such as a visual texture, musical score, jagged plot line, and a kind of mise-en-scène realism that made them resemble films more than television programs. They also contained plenty of the old formula: car chases, gratuitous violence, tough talk, ethnic villains, and an absence of depth in plot or character. And, of course, facing the venality of vice kings and drug lords, they, too, let us know there were no solutions. In the absence of solutions, the only thing left to do is kill lots of bad guys. In eighteen episodes of "Miami Vice" during 1988, supercops Crockett and Tubbs killed forty-three people, five times as many as the entire Miami police force killed during that whole year. To get a further perspective on real-life police work: on average, a Chicago police officer fires his or her gun in the line of duty once every twenty-seven years.[21]

Like the medical shows, the cop shows can be faulted not only for what they offer but for what they leave untouched. It is no crime to be against crime. Even those of us who would not make common cause with right-wing crime-scare campaigns might wonder why the police don't do a better job of fighting crime. Is it really because their hands are tied by the law? I would suggest other reasons:

1. In regard to crimes caused by widespread poverty, racism, underemployment, wage exploitation, poor housing, and other forms of

In eighteen episodes of
the NBC-TV series "Miami
Vice," supercops Crockett
and Tubbs killed forty-
three people, five times as
many as the entire Miami
police force killed during
that whole year.

economic oppression, the police are not equipped to deal with
the immense realities they face. The best they can do is keep a
lid on things—which is their class function.

2. As for dealing with crimes caused by individual pathologies and
   personal venality, of which there are a good many in our society,
   the police can sometimes be grossly unresponsive or not very
   competent.

3. In the case of crimes perpetrated in high places by influential persons, the police are limited by the class biases of the law and the
   law enforcement system. As has been said, the poor have little
   reason to respect the law and the rich and influential have little
   reason to fear it.

4. When it comes to organized crime, the police are sometimes complicit with the criminals, as are some judges and officials.

These various realities are seldom, if ever, dealt with in cop shows. Just as the conservative politicians run on law-and-order platforms and accept campaign endorsements from police associations while saying nothing intelligent about the real crime problem, so, too, the make-believe media, for all their preoccupation with shoot-'em-ups, have little to say about the real causes of crime and the chronic failures of real-life police performance. They seldom, if ever, portray the outrageously sloppy, lazy, incompetent police work that allows thrill killers, serial rapists, and serial killers to get away with multiple victimization for years.[22] The media do not show the police as they really are: a patchwork quilt of poorly trained local organizations that regularly ignore missing-persons reports, that frequently botch forensic investigations, and that often fail to share information with each other and check reports on killers.

One would never guess from cop shows that a major function of the police is to serve as strikebreakers, protecting owners from workers and landlords from tenants. One would never imagine from the shoot-'em-ups that some police departments have devoted more time and energy to harassing low-income residents and intimidating political dissenters than to fighting organized crime. In fact, Illinois Police Superintendent James McGuire announced in 1971 that there were more police throughout the country "on political intelligence assignments than are engaged in fighting organized crime."[23]

One would never surmise that not only are there a few bad apples on the force who take bribes, but that entire police units have been on the take, systematically protecting organized rackets and drug cartels, railroading Black community leaders into jail when they attempt to resist the drug trade in their communities. Relying on the entertainment media, one gets hardly an inkling of the widespread collaboration between police and drug lords in this country. The Knapp Commission, for instance, found that the biggest drug pushers in New York City were the New York City police.[24]

Crime itself is defined in most shoot-'em-ups as something that happens in the streets and not in the suites. Relatively little attention is given to white-collar corporate criminals, the kind who in real life are seldom caught, or if caught, seldom punished, or if punished, seldom severely. By resorting to unfair and often illegal market practices and by violating occupational, environmental, and product safety standards, corporate crime causes more deaths and injuries and greater money losses to the American public than does street crime.[25] But you would never know it if you got most of your information about crime from the entertainment media, as, indeed, millions of Americans do.

On rare occasions, police corruption is portrayed as involving something more than a few bad cops. In *The Big Easy* (1987), for instance, just about the entire police force is on the take, pocketing small amounts from strip-club owners and the like. When challenged about this by the female assistant D.A., the hero cop brushes it off as just the way things are done in New Orleans. But when he discovers that some of his fellow cops are bringing in boatloads of heroin, *that* is just too evil for him, so he shoots it out with them and brings the whole thing to a halt.

There are two glowing exceptions to this otherwise dreary inventory: *Serpico* (1973) and *Prince of the City* (1981), both films by Sidney Lumet. What makes them superb is that they are free of the conventional cop-crime scenario. They are true stories that deal with real-life individual members of the New York City police who try to come to grips with the widespread corruption within the department and beyond. *Serpico,* the better of the two, gives a compelling account of how public investigations turn out to be cover-ups, much to the frustration of the honest officer who tries to cooperate with the investigators. The theme of this film is that the existing law enforcement system does not have much room for scrupulous people who cannot look the other way and who are inclined to point the finger at those in high places.

Also worthy of mention is the television detective series "Cagney and Lacey" (1982–88). The show had some exceptional features. First was its empowerment of women as effective and believable law enforcers—the two lead characters were female detectives—a refreshing contrast to the pandering presentation of sexpot "crime-fighters" in shows like "Charlie's Angels." Second, "Cagney and Lacey" dealt with political, social, and racial themes from a sometimes pronounced liberal perspective. One episode concerned a Chilean political emigré who heroically stops a criminal and is then threatened with deportation by the Immigration and Naturalization Service; he gets sanctuary in a church and wins the complicity of Cagney and Lacey. There is an episode about a woman who engages in civil disobedience against a business firm that is dumping toxic waste. Another episode casts an unfavorable light upon the advocates of compulsory pregnancy who are engaged in bombing abortion clinics. Lacey's husband is a working-class man with political opinions; he opposes aid to the Nicaraguan contras and he's grappling with unemployment. Cagney is a victim of date rape in one episode and she has a drinking problem—a recurring theme in other episodes—

which she refuses to recognize until she comes to terms with it by going to Alcoholics Anonymous.

These exceptions aside, most of the cop-and-crime shows, like so many other media offerings, are dehumanized superficial contrivances that are impossible to believe and hard to enjoy, unless the viewer has been sufficiently conditioned to find enjoyment in brainless, violent action.

8

Black Images in White Media

The make-believe media are predominantly White media. Of the sixty or seventy major performers in the new TV shows each season, relatively few are African-American. It took the television industry over four decades before it could get around to featuring African-American talk-show hosts such as Oprah Winfrey and Arsenio Hall. For other people of color, the situation has been at least as bad. As of the late 1970s, Asian-Americans, Native American Indians, and Latinos (that is, all persons of Spanish-speaking origin, including Chicanos and Puerto Ricans) together constituted less than 3 percent of the characters in teleplays and sitcoms.[1] Nor has the situation improved markedly since then.

In 1982, when it sought to give an award to an African-American for excellence in the cinema, the National Association for the Advancement of Colored People (NAACP) discovered that Cicely Tyson's performance in *Bustin' Loose* (1981), an artless, lightweight comedy, was the only lead role by a Black woman in more than two years.[2]

On the production side, not more than 3 percent of the people working behind the cameras are African-American. As of 1989, there were no major Black executives or agents in the movie and television industries. In 1988, Hollywood's two highest-ranking African-American executives lost their jobs. The same underrepresentation prevails in the news sector. A 1985 survey by the American Society of Newspaper Editors found that people of color composed less than 6 percent of the journalists employed (a good number of whom worked for Black publications).[3]

Smilin' 'n' Servin'

In the early years of the movie industry, the images of African-Americans were unrestrainedly racist—as reflected in such silent films as *The Wooing and Wedding of a Coon* (1904), *For Massa's Sake* (1911), *Coon Town Suffragettes* (1914), and *The Nigger* (1915). Whether he was called Sambo or Rastus, whether played by Blacks or black-faced Whites, the cinematic African-American male was usually a simple-minded buffoon, quick to laugh, irresponsible, lazy, fearful, and rhythmic. His female counterpart was good-natured, motherly yet sometimes sassy, able to work but complaining about it, and employed as a cook, seamstress, or servant.[4] One Black actor, Lincoln Perry, so encapsulated the shuffling, childish slouch that the character he played, "Steppin' Fetchit," actually became his Hollywood stage name.

From the 1920s through World War II, grotesque black-faced caricatures with huge red lips and bulging eyes appeared as cannibals and dancing darkies in animated cartoons. They adorned pancake mix packages and tobacco advertisements. Of 100 motion pictures made during this period that had Black themes or characters "of more than passing significance," the great majority were classified as anti-Black, according to one study.[5]

Some enterprising African-Americans started their own film companies, most of which were small and underfinanced. By the 1930s they produced films populated entirely by African-Americans who exercised social power in ways that did not exist in the real world. These movies reached an urban African-American audience, but they failed to draw the great majority of Black moviegoers away from Hollywood movies. It seemed such audiences preferred the higher budgeted and more polished Hollywood star productions over a fantasy of Black power that many found implausible.[6]

When the right kind of music came on the screen, African-American film characters could be counted on to come to life in a bouncy, strutting way. Who can forget (even those of us who want to) the "Who dat?" musical sequence in *A Day At the Races* (1937) with Harpo Marx leading an entourage of shack-dwelling, poor-but-happy darkies in an ensemble number that had everything in it but the watermelon. Such a sequence is memorable not only for its racism but for the implosive, high quality dancing and singing by African-American performers who had to compress their talents into whatever tacky little roles they could get.

Campaigns launched by the NAACP, the African-American press, and show-business groups helped eliminate many of the worst racist images in the media by the mid-1940s. These campaigns were strengthened when the federal government itself entered the fray, attempting to rally the entire citizenry behind the war effort by propagating ideas of racial and religious equality. When the Sambo roles were eliminated, however, nothing better was put in their place, and African-Americans became even less visible than before. They were often systematically excluded from scripts, and when they did appear, it was usually as singers, dancers, and domestics. Even those who excelled in the musical field sometimes had a hard time getting major billing. When the "Nat King Cole Show" was launched by NBC in the late 1950s—the first television show to have an African-American star performer—it failed to attract advertising support and was cancelled early in the season.[7]

The 1950s also gave us the television series "Amos 'n' Andy," originally a radio program created and acted by two White men. The show portrayed almost every character in its all-Black cast as a clown, a conniver, or a dimwit. Black doctors appeared as quacks and Black lawyers as slippery shysters. African-American women were usually shown as bossy shrews, given to hectoring their irresponsible and childish men.[8]

Similar fare could be found in "Beulah," a show about a Black maid who looked like she had come off a package of pancake mix. There was Rochester of the "Jack Benny Show" who deferred to his White boss but in a sly and comically critical way, as did another Black maid in the "The Great Gildersleeve" series. There was Willie, the handyman in "Life with Father" (later the "New Stu Erwin Show") who spent years scratching his head and shuffling around.[9] There was the "amusingly" terror-stricken chauffeur of the Charlie Chan movies—rerun on TV into the 1980s—who reluctantly accompanied his detective boss into dangerous situations, all the while rolling his eyes and babbling: "Oh Missuh Chan, lez get outta dis here place!" Then there was the famous Sam of *Casablanca* (1942), who plays the piano for his boss, Humphrey Bogart. All the White characters call Bogart "Rick," but to Sam he's "Mister Richard." When Mr. Richard is sad, Sam is sad; when Mr. Richard is happy, Sam is happy. Sam experiences Rick's concerns as his own, understandably enough since the script allows him none of his own.

For many years African-Americans in the make-believe media had neither anger, ambition, nor interests of their own. On the rare occasions they did act effectively, displaying initiative and strength, it was most likely in the service of Whites. Hence, when the burly ex-slave in *Gone With the Wind* dispatches two villainous tramps (one White, one Black) who are about to attack Scarlett O'Hara, he is being allowed to commit an act of violence only to defend White womanhood—as might any loyal eunuch. Boys, not men, maids, not women, these African-Americans existed to serve, amuse, protect, and die for their Caucasian superiors. When they were not Uncle Toms, they were Tontos and Gunga Dins.

Not much in the media was designed to give African-Americans a sense of themselves. Like their White counterparts, Black children cheered when Tarzan or some White adventurer obliterated the dark savages in the jungle, when British troops massacred the "blasted fuzzy-wuzzies," and when White cowboys cut down bands of Indians with flawless aim. They had no choice but to find their media heroes among those who ruled over them.

The African-American actress and writer Ellen Holly noted, "I grew up bombarded with movies that depicted Black women almost exclusively as maids or sluts of limited intelligence. . . ."[10] It might be argued that many maids *are* Black, and therefore the media offer a faithful representation of an unfortunate reality. But Holly's complaint is that Black women are not portrayed as human beings. Be they maids or prostitutes, their real stories have never been told. As she goes on to say:

> The irony, of course, is that Hollywood has yet to make a movie that actually deals with a Black maid. . . . I have come to recognize the female Black domestic as perhaps THE great heroine of the Black race. Because that lady was willing to get down on her knees and scrub another woman's floor, clean another woman's house and bring up another woman's children, a whole race survived. But the trauma and the paradox of having to leave your own children in the morning and go out and care for someone else's in order to bring back bread for their table in the evening has yet to be examined on film.[11]

Back in 1943, the actress and singer Lena Horne made a plea regarding media treatment of African-Americans: "All we ask is that the Negro be portrayed as a normal person. Let's see the Negro as a worker at union meetings, as a voter at the polls, as a civil service worker or elected official."[12]

In the media-created world, African-Americans were represented as knowing their place. White audiences and White media owners were made uncomfortable by images of Black anger and assertiveness that might animate the consciousness of African-Americans in troublesome ways. Besides being no threat to White dominance, Steppin' Fetchit, Beulah, and the Kingfish assured Whites that the racial status quo was just fine. These films confirmed the notion that Black folk were neither capable nor desirous of a more elevated station in life. If all that African-Americans could do was shuffle, smile, and serve, then, of course, they deserved their underclass place in society. The entertainment media both reflected and bolstered the racial caste oppression, while ignoring the struggles for survival and for social betterment waged by African-Americans.

On this dreary landscape there appeared a few worthwhile exceptions. Powerfully drawn African-American figures appeared in such far-from-perfect dramas as *The Petrified Forest* (1936) and *Slave Ship* (1937). Movies like *Hallelujah!* (1929) and *The Green Pastures* (1936), despite their stock characters and stereotyped dialect, presented musical interludes that found favor with some Black critics. As might be expected, these films avoided the subject of racial integration.[13]

Clean-Cut and Saintly

After World War II, African-Americans migrated in larger numbers from the rural South to Northern cities and gained a greater measure of political influence. At last, Hollywood tackled the problem of racism, however imperfectly, in *Pinky* (1949) and *Lost Boundaries* (1949). Both dealt with the atypical problems faced by those who pass for White but who are then discovered to be Black. The antiracist position taken in such movies seemed so mild and limited as to be almost itself racist. In so many words: if some people are so Caucasian-looking as to pass for White, then let's not split hairs and cause unnecessary grief; let's be tolerant and accept them as White.

Of more importance were movies like *Intruder in the Dust* (1949) and *Home of the Brave* (1949). Adapted from the Faulkner novel, *Intruder* is about a Black man falsely accused of murder who faces a lynch mob. Events are seen through the eyes of a Caucasian boy who discovers the racial hatred that infects his rural Southern community. *Home of the Brave* deals with the prejudice confronted by a technically skilled African-American soldier who has volunteered to go on a dangerous mission with a White unit in the racially segregated U.S. Army of World War II. The soldier quickly becomes the object of racist jibes from other members of the unit. He quietly endures these insults. It is his White buddy, a former schoolmate, who angrily tells the others to "lay off." When this same buddy is killed in combat, the Black soldier succumbs to a psychogenic paralysis caused—we are asked to believe—by the guilt reaction he suffers at feeling relieved that it was his buddy and not he who was shot. He is cured by an army psychiatrist who moves him to anger by shouting, "Get up and walk, nigger!" He staggers from his hospital bed in a rage, about to strike the doctor with clenched fist, only to crumble in the shrink's arms, tearfully realizing he can walk again.

(In those days, Hollywood endowed the psychiatric profession with miraculously curative powers.)

As with the few other films that dealt with the subject, *Home of the Brave* treated racism solely as a problem of individual prejudice devoid of institutional and class dimensions. The film offers not a word about the racial segregation that was the official policy of the U.S. Army until well into the first year of the Korean war. However, there were moments when the movie seemed to be saying more than it intended. Its climactic scene in the psychiatric ward, for instance, seemed to contain an allegoric message: only when Blacks openly confronted racism with their own anger would they become free of the paralysis imposed upon them.

By the 1950s and 1960s African-Americans were doing just that, militantly mobilizing against oppressive conditions—first in the South, then in the North—demonstrating in the streets, organizing sit-ins and boycotts, and pleading their cases in court and before the general public under the leadership of organizations like the NAACP. The cause of desegregation and civil rights was advanced. The right to vote was made a reality for larger numbers of Blacks. New leaders of the stature of Dr. Martin Luther King, Jr., emerged. It was a period of heroic struggle and sacrifice on the part of civil-rights advocates, as well as violence and murder on the part of racists. Millions of people were affected and a thousand dramas were played out in real life, along with scores of tragedies. At the time, however, Hollywood and television managed to overlook it all. A proud and dramatic page of history was deemed as being of no dramatic merit. (In 1975 there finally appeared a TV movie, *Attack on Terror*, a dramatization of the murder of three freedom riders in Mississippi. This teleplay stuck fairly close to the facts, unlike the 1988 movie *Mississippi Burning*, which is discussed later in the chapter.)

During this period of political fermentation, Hollywood found its ideal Black in the prototype played repeatedly by Sidney Poitier. Whether befriended by nuns in *Lilies of the Field* (1963) or cooperating with a racist Southern sheriff to catch a criminal in *In the Heat of the Night* (1967) or winning the respect of a classroom of adolescent bigots in *To Sir, With Love* (1967) or being invited to meet his prospective White in-laws in *Guess Who's Coming to Dinner* (1967), Poitier was ever on his best behavior. Blessed with limitless supplies of patience, integrity, and self-control, he asserted himself only within limited parameters, never resorting to the harsh tactics of his bigoted adversaries. Here was the kind of African-American male that Whites would find acceptable, a nice, clean-cut, middle-class saint, who would not threaten

Guess Who's Coming to Dinner was one of a number of movies in which Sidney Poitier played a clean-cut, saintly, middle-class African-American who never angered and showed only patience and goodwill toward racists.

White audiences with expressions of Black anger, incapable of doing to them what they were doing to him, never lowering himself to the level of his adversaries.

At the same time, African-Americans began to make occasional appearances on television in minor dramatic parts, rather than just as comics, singers, and tap dancers. In the late 1960s, a weekly adventure series, "I Spy," starring Robert Culp and Bill Cosby, had an African-American actor play a lead character—one who was not involved in a racial situation as such. Lena Horne's plea that Blacks be portrayed as just ordinary normal people had finally come true—except that "normal" for TV meant a gun-toting, fist-swinging, globe-trotting secret agent. Posing as tennis bums, these two U.S. spies traveled from country to country on different assignments. It was Culp, a White man, who got into one romance after another while Cosby remained seemingly free of sexual interests of his own. Cosby also was the more responsible one, coming to Culp's rescue whenever a dangerous predicament arose—as Tonto had often done for the Lone Ranger. Here was a Sidney Poitier with guns and fists, but still safely asexual so as not to evoke White anxieties.

Enter Superhero

Once Blacks qualified for the hero roles previously reserved for White males, they ended up as little more than replicas of a White macho idiocy. In *Sweet Sweetback's Badass Song* (1971), *Shaft* (1971), *Shaft's Big Score* (1972), and *Superfly* (1972), Black males now could be aggressive, violent, ruthless, powerful, and able to outsmart, outtalk, outfight, and outfornicate White males. "Sidney Poitier would no longer have to play the likeable eunuch to a squeamish liberalism still haunted by images of the Black man's threatening masculinity, a central fantasy in the racist mythology."[14] Indeed, in *Sweet Sweetback* and *Superfly* the Black Superhero is a glorified thug with a harem of beauties (both Black and White) but with few mental skills except what is needed to thrive on the streets. Such was the image of hope and betterment that American capitalist culture offered to African-American youth. Loyle Hairston describes it:

> The "supernigger" surfaced as folk hero. Emblazoned in full complement of silk jump suit, fur coat, slack-brimmed hat, alligator boots, a

In films like *Superfly*, a glorification of the successful pimp, hustler, and street gangster, African-American males could now be aggressive, violent, and macho.

marijuana cool, and a custom built Cadillac, "supernigger" glorified the profitable brutalities of the pimp, the drug-pusher, the thug—every scavenger who hustles the Black ghetto.[15]

And as Francis Ward observed: "Only the super-hip, super-slick, super-strong, super-sexed, super-hyped up and inflated Black male could whip and kick around the White boys." A normal Black man with the ordinary mix of strengths and weaknesses would be too real and human and presumably too difficult for Hollywood to handle.[16]

The Black superhero offered African-Americans the escapist illusion of power and wealth. Self-worth was to be measured in terms of money, flashy consumer items, and dominance over others. In addition to keeping Whites in control of the images Blacks had of themselves, these films made enormous profits for their White producers, as African-Americans crowded the inner-city movie houses to view sex-filled, action-packed Black-over-White victories.[17]

The Black superhero made it to television by 1973 but in a sanitized version. Television did not offer the same audience selectivity as neighborhood theaters, and the White public was less likely to respond to macho Blacks winning out over Whites. When Shaft went from films to television series, he was shorn of his power and sensuality, "like they poured a bottle of Listerine over him."[18] Superhero was accompanied by the inner-city "Blaxploitation" horror films of the 1970s, such as *Blacula* (1972) and its equally terrible sequel, *Scream, Blacula, Scream* (1973).

Meanwhile, the few serious, high-quality and deeply engaging films produced during this period, such as Gordon Park's autobiographical *The Learning Tree* (1969), Ozzie Davis's *Black Girl* (1972), *Sounder* (1972), *Sounder, Part 2* (1976), and *Claudine* (1974), were largely left in limbo, given none of the mass promotional hype that bombarded the inner-city neighborhoods on behalf of the trashy superhero and superhorror flicks. Instead, the distribution of quality films was limited to a smaller number of independent theaters and, in subsequent years, to a few college campuses.

One of these quality films, *Sounder*, is an utterly superb drama about a poor, rural African-American family trying to survive and stay human under adverse conditions. For once, the characters are not caricatures but real persons, with attachments, loves, and fears that seem not only credible but deeply moving. The father's victimization by poverty and White authority, the mother's determination to hold the family together, the boy's devotion to both parents and his youthful courage and vulnerability, the story and the characterizations—all make for a great movie that not enough people, of whatever ethnic background, have

Matriarch, Whore—and Underemployed

In a panel discussion, Susan Batson, Cynthia Belgrave, Ruby Dee, Beah Richards and Cicely Tyson made it clear that the new wave of Black [superhero action] movies has little room for actresses like themselves. The impression that these women gave about their careers was of arduous struggle for minimal reward and recognition, at least from the film industry.

Cynthia Belgrave was particularly incensed by the debasement of Black women in theater and film which can occur even in scripts written by Blacks. She pointed out that being a Black female places one in an infuriating bind. If you're strong and stoical you're a matriarch, and if you're weak and sensual you're a whore. . . .

The primary reason that the extremely talented women on the panel and others like them are not being offered parts or are being offered parts incompatible with their own sense of self is that American film is essentially a medium for the promotion of fantasy. Just the visual presence of a Black woman in a film negates illusion because she is not the blue-eyed, blond-haired goddess that Americans have been trained to buy. Films are the vehicles through which all women have been told lies about themselves, lies which they have tried to emulate and believe. . . .

Since the new Black films are the deepest fantasies, serious Black actresses are also excluded from them. As often as not, the Black hero has a White woman instead of, or in addition to, a Black one. These women, Black and White, are dolls, beautiful and unchallenging to anybody's establishment ideas of what a good (passive) woman should be.

Barbara Smith, "Black Women in Film Symposium," *Freedomways* (third quarter, 1974), pp. 266–268.

seen. One measure of the film's quality might be the way its actors feel about it. Cicely Tyson, who like other African-American performers had complained of the dearth of suitable roles, felt that her part in *Sounder* was the one for which she had prepared all her life.

A well-done and entertaining film is *Claudine*, a sympathetic treatment of a welfare mother's struggle to bring up her six kids while carrying on a courtship with a most likeable garbageman. He, in turn, experiences the difficulties of trying to be a breadwinning father while not earning enough money. *Claudine* offers a perspective on the inner-city welfare family that has been accorded almost no currency among middle-class White Americans.

Two Steps Forward, One-and-a-Half Steps Back

The fifties and sixties were decades of struggle for African-American rights. Such struggles created changes in the climate of opinion that were not entirely without effect on the White media. For one thing, the taboo subject of interracial romance was broached. As early as 1957, the beautiful Dorothy Dandridge was cast in one of the first interracial romance roles in *Island in the Sun*. But she was not allowed to kiss her White male leads. Dandridge was also paired romantically with the White actor Curt Jurgens in *Tamango* (1957), though the relationship was hardly between equals since she was a native woman and he, an empowered White male determined to put down a slave mutiny. In the early 1970s Diana Sands had White lovers in *Georgia, Georgia* (1972) and *The Landlord* (1970). Sidney Poitier was matched with a White female lead in *A Patch of Blue* (1965) (but she was blind), *The Lost Man* (1969), and *Guess Who's Coming to Dinner* (1967). In each of these films, the interracial love affair was a key element in the plot. In *One Potato, Two Potato* (1966), a serious effort is made to depict the institutional racism that existed under civil law: a divorced White father wins a court decision to take his daughter away from her White mother because the mother had taken an African-American as her second husband.

By the late seventies and into the eighties, interracial coupling became less frequent. One exception was *Some Kind of Hero* (1982) in which a Vietnam veteran (Richard Pryor), abandoned by his African-American wife and buffeted by hard circumstances, becomes friend and lover to a high-priced White prostitute (Margot Kidder). A Black man gets a White woman but she's a prostitute—that is, a White woman of ill-repute rather than the all-American sweetheart from next door. The film is unusual because despite the interracial coupling, race and racism do not figure prominently in the plot. The couple are just taken as a couple—which itself is something of an achievement. Conflict between the two lovers stems not from their racial backgrounds but from what she does for a living.

Likewise in *The Miss Firecracker Contest* (1989), a worthwhile film, women resist the oppressive sexist expectations of some narrow, ill-spirited locals in a Southern community. The girlfriend of the romantic lead—a part originally written for a White woman—is played by African-American actress Alfre Woodard. Race does not come up as a factor. Woodard merely plays a woman who has a love relation with a man who happens to be Caucasian.

By the early 1970s, Blacks began to appear on television programs as local news announcers, quiz-show participants, and characters in cop shows and situation comedies. But of all the lead roles and major supporting roles in twenty-one new shows in the 1978–79 season, only two were Black and one was Puerto Rican. People of color were more likely than Whites to appear on prime-time shows as crooks, pimps, informers, or persons needing assistance from White professionals. The nine Blacks portrayed in one year of episodes of "Hawaii Five-O," a detective adventure show, consisted of five pimps, two prostitutes, and two students. The eleven Hawaiians and Polynesians on the show that year included two pimps, two assassins, and three mobsters.[19]

During this period, there were also a few outstanding television specials such as "Roots" and "Roots, the Next Generation" and made-for-television movies like *The Autobiography of Miss Jane Pittman* (1974) and *A Woman Called Moses* (1978), the latter about Harriet Tubman, the fugitive slave who helped others make their way north to freedom in the mid-nineteenth century. The popularity of these offerings among Whites and Blacks alike seemed to refute the claim that the public was not interested in quality productions, especially ones about African-Americans.

The African-American experience consists of many compelling real-life stories about confrontations with poverty and police, the struggle for housing, jobs, family, and community, and for a place in the arts, professions, unions, politics, and sports—stories that remained mostly untouched by the entertainment media. Instead, during the 1970s, African-Americans appeared as lead characters mostly in situation comedies like "Sanford and Son" and "The Jeffersons." Glib put-downs, insulting jibes, naïveté, ignorance, and silliness served as the source of humor, as Blacks taunted, derided, and jostled each other in weekly sitcom episodes. When important and relevant issues were touched upon, it was usually in facile, irrelevant ways. No wonder that twenty-three years after the NAACP's criticism of the "Amos 'n' Andy" show, the National Black Feminist Organization issued an almost identical indictment of the way African-Americans were portrayed on television, noting that:

> Black shows are slanted toward the ridiculous with no redeeming counter-images. When Blacks are cast as professional people, the characters they portray generally lack professionalism and give the impression that Black people are incapable and inferior in such positions.
>
> When older persons are featured, Black people are usually cast as shiftless derelicts or nonproductive individuals. Few Black women in TV programs are cast as professionals, paraprofessionals, or even working people.[20]

African-Americans were appearing in new scripts that still tele-graphed some of the old racism. The Black writer Cecil Brown tells how the White producer Steve Krantz thought to work a few jokes into a screenplay Brown was working on. For instance:

> *Kid:* If I eat Wheaties, Uncle Leroy, will I grow up big and strong?
> *Leroy:* Yeah—and a baseball player—and white!

Brown failed to see the humor in a racist exchange that teaches a Black child that being White is the desired thing. Another "joke" in-serted by Krantz:

> *Thelma:* Leroy, don't you get involved with none of this union mess, you hear? Scabbing was good enough for your grandpa. (She motions to a picture on the wall; Leroy looks at the picture.)
> *Leroy:* Mama, that isn't grandpa. That picture was on the wall when we moved in.

The false message is that (1) Blacks are happy as scabs and have no history in the struggle for unionization, and (2) they have no stable family relations and cannot even remember who their parents are. "In short," Brown comments, "what Krantz had done was write coon hu-mor into the script." Brown remembers something James Baldwin once said:

> A Black writer cannot write Black stereotypes the way a White writer can, because he cannot think of himself that way. A Black man cannot see himself as a stereotype. He does not exist the way Whites see him. That's why it's hard for Black writers to write the things Whites want to see.[21]

By the 1980s, African-Americans were appearing regularly in crime shows. When portrayed as criminals, they often had lead roles. When portrayed as cops, they were more often in subsidiary roles. For a while, it seemed that no African-American male could survive to the end of a film. Gregory Hines is eaten in *Wolfen* (1981); Bernie Casey is shot to pieces in *Sharkey's Machine* (1981); Paul Winfield kills himself rather than kill the hero Captain Kirk in *Star Trek II* (1982); Richard Roundtree is devoured by Quetzalcoatl in *Q* (1982); both Howard Rol-lins and Debbie Allen perish in *Ragtime* (1981); Carl Weathers is killed by a Russian pugilist in *Rocky IV* (1985). In the world of make-believe media, the gap between Black and White life expectancy seemed even higher than in real life.[22]

Still missing was any depiction of African-Americans acting with concerted political effort around struggles of real social and class content. By the 1980s, one was lucky to find mainstream productions that even hinted at such themes. One popular film of the early eighties, *Ragtime*, manifests the limited ways that African-American struggle is represented (or misrepresented). The choice this film offers is (1) the individualized Black man defends himself by isolated terroristic action, picking up a gun and suicidally shooting it out with White authorities, or (2) Booker T. Washington takes a subservient, accommodationist role toward racist authority, winning patronizing praise from the same White official who murders the Black insurrectionist. Left out of the picture is reality itself. In fact, during the early twentieth-century period depicted in this film, African-Americans were organizing the NAACP, antilynching campaigns, the Niagara Movement, and other forms of resistance that laid the foundation for the mass democratic protests of subsequent eras.

In keeping with the Reaganite cinema of the 1980s, Blacks began appearing as macho, superpatriotic militarists, best encapsulated in Lou Gossett, Jr.'s performances in films like *Iron Eagle* (1986) and *An Officer and a Gentleman* (1982). In the latter, Gossett won an Academy Award for playing an abusive, fascistic drill instructor whose passion in life is to transform candy-assed recruits into unthinking killing machines forever committed to certain military and class principles: officers and gentlemen, the kind of men who will be addressed as "sir" both in and out of uniform. One remembers in *Gunga Din* how the devoted Indian water boy would snap to attention and announce to British officers, "I want to be a soldier." Gossett plays an updated Gunga Din who made it into uniform, serving the new empire and the new caste system.

In the 1980s, African-Americans appeared with greater frequency in television sitcoms like "Gimme a Break," "Different Strokes," "Benson," and "The New Odd Couple." These shows often featured perky, adorable Black youngsters and broadly drawn adult characters who specialized in smart-mouthing each other as they romped through the shallow, overdone predicaments that are the endlessly recycled stock-in-trade of sitcom humor.

The prime-time hit of the 1980s was "The Cosby Show," a sitcom offering us the "perfect" Black family, the Huxtables. The father, played by one of America's leading and most likeable comedians, Bill Cosby, is a doctor. The young and beautiful mother is a lawyer. The children are sweet and genuine. If "The Cosby Show" does not give us a positive image of African-Americans, then nothing does. But it is a superficial image. Here is that "better class of Negroes" we used to hear about in the 1950s, upper-middle class professionals whom Whites might feel comfortable having as neighbors. "The Cosby Show" falsely implies that this small economic minority within a larger ethnic minority points the way to ending discrimination.

The sitcom world is inhabited mostly by silly little people with silly little problems. "The Cosby Show" is a refreshing exception at least in part. The characters are not silly. Everyone is more or less intelligent; no one is a ridiculous clown. To the show's credit, the confrontations are good-natured and the humor is gentle, devoid of the crude put-downs and aggression that pass for humor on shows like "The Jeffersons." Here are nice people playing idealized roles under ideal social conditions. The Huxtables never worry about money and never seem to need to shop, clean, or even work much at their professions. Unlike most doctors, Cosby spends most of his waking hours hanging around the house. The Huxtables are happy, even when they might get ruffled by the little crises that are resolved within the show's half-hour time frame. Take the episode in which the parents find marijuana in their son's room. It turns out the son is just *holding* it for a friend. Never in his life has he taken a toke. Never. His parents believe him, proving that the show is indeed a comedy.

On rare occasions, an episode will edge toward some serious content as when the Huxtable family reminisces about Martin Luther King, Jr., or when—at Cosby's insistence and over the protests of the show's producers—an "End Apartheid" banner adorned the set. Overall, "The Cosby Show" is a positive representation of African-Americans, but it is still only a sitcom. It represents a giant step up from Steppin' Fetchit, but it still has Black people playing for laughs.

Getting Serious

The 1980s did offer a few quality films and teleplays about African-Americans. Notable among these was the made-for-television movie *Sister, Sister* (1982), a finely cast, moving drama about the relationships of three sisters in a middle-class Black family in North Carolina. The script has a rich Southern Black flavor and was done by the African-American poet-dramatist Maya Angelou. Unfortunately, the film was denied a showing by NBC for more than three years, according to Angelou, because "it was inconceivable to the producers that a whole bunch of Black people could have problems and a life that had nothing to do with Whites."[23] *Sister, Sister* was not the only drama to suffer such restraints. For years, studio and network bosses had shown no interest in serious scripts about African-Americans, preferring action films or comedy shows. They assumed there was no interested public. And, of course, as long as such dramas were not produced, no public materialized to see them.

A rare accomplishment was the PBS television adaptation of James Baldwin's autobiographical novel *Go Tell It on the Mountain* (1985), which manages to capture much of the novel's rich language along with both its warmth and bitterness. Characters are portrayed with depth and in highly nuanced ways. They are shown in all their poverty and despair, yet we do not lose sight of their humanity. The exceptional quality of the script caused one White reviewer to reflect on how little work of this caliber there is for Black actors.[24]

The Color Purple (1985) is a less inspiring example of a serious story about African-Americans in the pre-Depression rural South, seen through the eyes of a poor young woman who is victimized by her unloving husband. One of the movie's finer moments is the touching love scene between the beleaguered underdog heroine and her beautiful female friend. The film caused some controversy among African-American critics because Black males come off as unadulterated and often brutish villains (or minor-role, innocuous, nice guys), while the females are vessels of fortitude, love, and decency. The female predominance, however, hardly comes close to endowing the film with a Black feminist perspective. Under Steven Spielberg's slick Hollywood touch, the movie is saved from any depth or subtlety regarding the plight of poor and mistreated African-American women. Nor is there any recognition of how the oppressive, racist context of the wider society might have contributed to the way some men treated women within the Southern Black community.

John Sayles's *The Brother from Another Planet* (1984), made on a shoestring budget, is a serious science-fiction attempt to deal with racism. The Black fugitive slave from another planet and the outer-space pursuers who come to reclaim him in modern-day New York are an eerie anachronistic reminder of an earlier era in the United States and, at the same time, of contemporary racial injustice.

A film that successfully portrays some of the homicidal horror of lynch-mob racist violence is *Mississippi Burning* (1988). It offers an accurate and shattering account of a real-life atrocity—the 1964 murder of civil-rights workers James Chaney, Michael Schwerner, and Andrew Goodman. Unfortunately, the rest of the story is a monument to Hollywood's audacious ability to omit and distort history. As the movie would have it, the heroes are FBI agents, who crack the case by discarding normal police procedures and resorting to strong-arm tactics against suspects. In reality, as Martin Luther King, Jr., commented at the time, FBI agents in the South were White Southerners who sympathized with the racists, as did the local law enforcement officials. Some of the latter were Klan members who actually participated in the murder of the three young men. One Mississippi summer project volunteer, Harry Nier, who was there at the time and is now a lawyer in Denver, commented: "I am outraged by the portrayal of the FBI as heroes in *Mississippi Burning*. They'd like you to believe the FBI was on our side and they were not. In fact, they were the opposition."[25]

FBI director J. Edgar Hoover was notorious for his unsympathetic attitude toward the civil-rights movement. In the summer of 1964 and in the years before, hundreds of civil-rights advocates endured physical attacks; thousands were terrorized; dozens were killed; scores of meeting places and homes were firebombed. Yet Hoover and the Justice Department repeatedly refused pleas for protection. Only after petitions, vigils, sit-ins, mass rallies, and other vigorous actions did the national media focus on the murder of the three volunteers—and even then it did so principally because two of the victims were White. Only in the face of such public pressure did the FBI finally and reluctantly investigate the case, solving it by paying an informer $30,000.

What is really missing from *Mississippi Burning* is the whole civil-rights movement itself. The struggle against de jure segregation in the South was won because tens of thousands of African-Americans, along with a good number of northern Whites, mobilized and fought for change, electrifying an entire generation around the issue. The movie tells us nothing about the hopes and political commitments of the three victims nor a word about the Mississippi summer project composed of Black and White youth, of which the three were a part. In the film, African-Americans are mostly passive and silent, cowed victims who need to be rescued by Rambo-style White lawmen. Director Alan Parker justified these distortions by arguing in effect that White heroes have more box-office appeal. In response, one witness to the historic struggle wrote: "I can assure the filmmakers that the actual sight of thousands of people daring death for their rights was far more thrilling than any of the scenes in this movie."[26] Be that as it may, Hollywood once again took the artistically shallow and politically safe course, choosing White individual heroics over Black collective action.

A truly superior film that deals with racism in nineteenth-century Australia is the Australian-made *The Chant of Jimmy Blacksmith* (1978). It tells of an Aborigine who is victimized by White society with tragic

and bloody results. Based on a factual account, the movie is a harrow-
ing indictment of a racism that very much resembles what might have
been found in the American South during that same period.

Quality films do not all have to be serious ones. A quality *comedy*
will do—as long as it can entertain us as well as a good drama does.
Robert Townsend's *Hollywood Shuffle* (1987) is a comedy that entertains
while directing satirical salvos against the racism that exists in the
motion-picture industry itself. A young African-American actor trying
to break into films encounters racist stereotypes everywhere he turns.
During one rehearsal, a director tells him to be "more Black" by shuffling around and sticking his ass out when he delivers his lines. The
actor chooses his integrity over his career and walks off the set.

Finally we have Spike Lee's *Do the Right Thing* (1989), an angry film
with a superficial message. An Italian-American, Sal, and his two sons
run a pizzeria in a poor African-American neighborhood in Brooklyn.
Sal's oldest son, Pino, hates the neighborhood and does not hesitate to
voice his low and loathsome opinion of its denizens. They will put a
spear in your back, he warns. Although Sal is quite capable of his own
racial insensitivities, he sees it differently. He tells his son, these are
good people; they "grew up on my food." Sal's deliveryman is Mookie
(Spike Lee), whom he pays $250 a week take-home, if you can believe
that. Mookie is a walking racist stereotype, a goof-off young Black male
who is unable to hold a steady job. He neglects his work in the middle
of a busy day—just as Pino says he would. He neglects his child and his
child's mother, both of whom he never bothers to visit except when his
libido urges him upon the mother. He sponges off his hardworking
sister. He thinks of no one but himself.

After a long, hot day, a fight breaks out at Sal's between the propri-
etor and a neighborhood youth whose function in life is to blast everyone's eardrums with his radio. The police arrive and kill the youth
while supposedly attempting to subdue him. In response to this,
Mookie throws an ash can through the window of Sal's place, thus
setting off a riot that completely destroys the pizzeria. Sal is left sitting
disillusioned in the ashes of his business. The conclusion we might
draw: Sal was wrong; his hate-ridden son was right; untrammeled
ethnic hatred is the order of the day; these people are too dangerous to
be trusted.

In one sequence in quick succession, Mookie shouts anti-Italian
epithets; Pino shouts anti-Black ones; another Black shouts anti-Latino
ones; a Latino shouts anti-Asian ones; and a Korean store owner
shouts anti-Semitic ones. This is about as close as the movie comes to
making a statement.

At the end of *Do the Right Thing*, two quotes come on the screen. The first, by Martin Luther King, Jr., says that violence is no way of achieving racial justice; it "is immoral because it thrives on hatred rather than love." The other, by Malcolm X, notes that along with the many good people in America there are bad ones and the latter seem to have all the power and they use force to keep us from having what we need. We must do what is necessary to change that. "It doesn't mean that I advocate violence, but at the same time I am not against using violence in self-defense. I don't even call it violence when it's used in self-defense. I call it intelligence." The violence in *Do the Right Thing*, however, has no intelligence. It is not directed at the people's enemies about whom Malcolm X was talking nor toward the kinds of actions he envisioned.[27]

A movie that weaves together race, gender, and class in a not very edifying way is *Driving Miss Daisy* (1989). The story, which spans decades, is about a rich, elderly Southern White woman who is driven around by Hoke, her poor Black chauffeur. Hoke endures her bossy arrogance with a long-suffering patience, deferring to her every wish, except on one occasion when he asserts his "manhood" by defying her orders and stopping the car to relieve himself. While firmly in command, Miss Daisy still must rely on Hoke's resourcefulness, just as any pampered superior must rely on a servant. Also, for all her wealth and superior status, she is still "just" a woman. So when left alone in the car for a brief time by the road in the dark of night, she becomes frightened and calls for Hoke, whose protection she needs. The film hints that her vulnerabilities and needs might make her less stern and more friendly toward Hoke.

Indeed, at the end of her life, infirm and hospitalized, she does soften up and recognizes him as her "best friend," thereby overcoming lifelong class and racial barriers—or at least that is what we are invited to conclude. But while she calls him "Hoke," he continues to address her deferentially as "Miss Daisy" in his every utterance. The movie's closing scene of Hoke visiting Miss Daisy in the retirement hospital and feeding her with a spoon is symbolic enough. Their friendship prevails, but it is hardly one of equals. In treating the relationship as an optimal one, the film implicitly endorses its class and racial inequalities. People from different parts of town can be friends—on certain terms. Gunga Din lives.

If we are to believe films like *Driving Miss Daisy*, racism and class power are a matter of personal attitudes that can be overcome in some limited ways only after decades of patient, loving endurance by poor African-Americans, who must wait until more affluent White people divest themselves of their suspicions, fears, and feelings of superiority. The movie provides a few interesting but very fleeting glimpses of Southern Jewish life (Miss Daisy's family is Jewish). But it has not a word about Black anger or institutional racism or structural exploitation. We only get hints of the anti-Semitism and racist tyranny that permeated the South during the Jim Crow era and of the African-American struggle for civil rights. Not surprisingly, *Driving Miss Daisy* was favorably received by White critics and walked off with a load of Oscars. It was the kind of patronizing, unrealistic treatment of race and class relations that Hollywood found "heartwarming."

Films and teleplays such as "Roots," *Sounder, Sounder, Part 2, Go Tell It on the Mountain, The Chant of Jimmy Blacksmith, Glory,* and others mentioned above demonstrate that quality productions about Black themes are not impossible to make. But in noting the existence of such productions, we should also note their relatively scarce numbers. Films of this quality remain mostly beyond the reach, imagination, market considerations, and ideology of Hollywood and prime-time commercial television.

9

Luigi, Tony, and the Family

Throughout the 1960s, social scientists predicted that White ethnic identities were becoming a thing of the past, as various national groups blended into the great American melting pot. No sooner had this opinion become part of the conventional wisdom than there developed in the early seventies a marked resurgence of ethnic consciousness. Sometimes in emulation of the Black struggle and sometimes in competitive response to it, the White ethnics began to make themselves heard.

This resurgence was partly a reaction to a dominant social order that had imposed a program of "Americanization" upon the immigrants and their children. The White ethnics began to resist the homogenization of identity and culture that were the long-standing goals of a society that on other days called itself "pluralistic." In addition, many White ethnic demands, like Black ones, were politico-economic in nature, calling for greater access to political office, improved community services, housing, jobs and job advancement, better schools, and a more equitable tax burden.

By the 1970s, ethnicity was no longer an embarrassment. If anything, it had become a subject of popular interest, enough so to attract the attention of the mass media. Ethnic characters and explicit ethnic references soon became common fare in television situation comedies, cop and crime shows, commercials, and Hollywood films.

To illustrate how the media handle or mishandle the ethnic experience, I will concentrate on Italian-Americans. The screen treatment of this group provides one of the many unfortunate examples of what the make-believe media are capable of doing. In the late 1970s, the Italians were "discovered" by Hollywood. With stars like Al Pacino, Robert De Niro, Sylvester Stallone, and John Travolta shouting, shooting, punching, or dancing their way across the screen, the Italians had become one of Hollywood's favorite ethnic groups. But at what price?[1]

The Stages of Stereotype

How have Italian-Americans been represented in the media? In ways not unlike other ethnic groups:

The Invisible Man. To use the title of Ralph Ellison's book about Blacks, for a long time the Italian, like every other ethnic, was invisible, nonexistent. Be it radio, movies, television dramas, popular literature, or the Dick-and-Jane readers of grade school, the world was inhabited by middle- and upper-middle-class WASPs, creamy-faced suburban youngsters with executive-looking fathers and trim American-beauty mothers, visions of Anglo-Protestant affluence and gentility.

Minor Stock Characters. In the early days of movies and radio when Italians did make an appearance in the Anglo-American world, it was usually as minor stock characters: the cheerful waiter, the talkative barber, the simple pushcart vendor, human scenery on the urban landscape with no lives of their own—or certainly no lives deemed worthy of narrative treatment. As unassimilated oddities, Italians were treated no differently than other ethnic stand-ins, such as the Irish cleaning lady, the Jewish shopkeeper, and the Black domestic.

The Grateful Immigrant. One of the stock characters of the late 1940s and early 1950s became a featured personality in a radio series and subsequently a television series called *Life with Luigi.* Played by an Irish-American actor, J. Carroll Naish, Luigi was the cloyingly sweet immigrant who spent his time gratefully exclaiming, "Mama mia, I'm-a love-a deese-a bootifull-a country, Amerrreeca!" Naish's understanding of an Italian immigrant's looks, accent, and mannerisms, painfully reminiscent of Chico Marx (another caricature), bore little resemblance to the real thing. Luigi was a creature conjured up by the make-believe media as a confirmation of the goodness of the existing American social order. In Luigi and characters like him, we had evidence that the immigrant was not a victim but a joyful, appreciative beneficiary of his adopted country.

The Mafia Gangster. In the fearful imagination of nativistic America, crime was always associated with the big city and the swarthy foreigner. In the 1930s and 1940s, the Italian mobster had to share the Hollywood screen with his Irish and Jewish counterparts. In later years, with television series like "The Untouchables" and movies like *The Godfather,* the Italian was fashioned into the archetypal gangster, so that eventually the

Movies like *The Godfather* repeatedly identify Italian-Americans as gangsters; some are murderous thugs, but the "heroes" are sometimes romanticized as benevolent and empowered patriarchs.

association of Italian-Americans with crime was instantaneous and international. One can travel throughout Europe and most other lands where Hollywood films are shown and encounter the stereotype. While in Lisbon during the revolutionary ferment of 1975, I talked to a Portuguese army lieutenant who, upon discovering I was Italian-American, commented gleefully "Ah, mafioso!" A half-hour later, the exact same response was accorded me by a Portuguese army captain. The lieutenant had right-wing sympathies and the captain was leftist—which demonstrates how Hollywood can cut its swath across the ideological spectrum.

With the help of the media, a few thousand hoodlums in the organized rackets who are of Italian origin, representing a tiny fraction of the Italian-American population, became representative of an entire ethnic group. In one of his stand-up feature films, the comedian Richard Pryor joked: "Not all Italians are in the Mafia. They just all *work* for the Mafia." The Mafia association became one of those respectable forms of bigotry.

There have been Irish, Jewish, Black, Latino, Italian, and even Anglo-Protestant mobsters in our history. None of these hoodlums is representative of the larger ethnic formations from which they happened to originate. Needless to say, none of the movies dealing with such characters has ever provided an authentic rendition of the rich cultural heritages and working-class histories of these groups.

The Respectables. Partly in response to protests launched against the gangland shows, Italian surnames began appearing in movies and television dramas attached to characters other than mobsters and thugs; they were mostly police, criminal lawyers, and private investigators such as Columbo, Baretta, Del Vecchio, D'Angelo, and Petrocelli. The Italian crimebuster, of course, was still closely associated with crime and violence; and like all media lawmen, his operational methods were sometimes difficult to distinguish from those of the criminals against whom he was pitted.

The Jivy Proletarian. In the 1970s, the media discovered commercial success in a new working-class, streetwise Italian who was neither a cop nor a crook, but sometimes a comedy character like Henry Winkler's "the Fonz" or John Travolta's Vinnie Barbarino (unschooled even when going to school), and sometimes a Cinderella as in *Rocky* (I, II, III, IV, V) or in *Saturday Night Fever* (1978). The frequent appearance of this Italian proletariat type, action-prone, noncerebral, at home with sex and violence, was a flashy variation of an older stereotype—not only of Italians but of working-class people in general: loud-mouthed, visceral, nonintellectual, acting on their emotions, living a life worth escaping. The media's ethnic bigotry is also a class bigotry.

The intertwining of class and ethnic bigotry is clearly displayed in the popular film *Saturday Night Fever*. The lead character, Tony Manero (John Travolta), is a working-class Italian-American from Bay Ridge, Brooklyn, whose life, the film seems to say, will—and should—never amount to much. His family is composed of three generations of Italian stereotypes who gather around the dinner table to scold, shout, and whack each other on the head. Tony spends his days working in a neighborhood hardware store and his nights dancing in the local disco. He and his buddies also pass their time ogling women, riding around in an old car, and speaking Hollywood's super-slurry version of Brooklynese. For a change of pace, they do such things as gang-rape a local woman and launch a violent attack on a rival Puerto Rican gang whose members are referred to throughout the film as "spics." "We hit them Italian style—where they live," one of Tony's cohorts proudly exclaims after they almost kill several people by driving a car through the window of the storefront that serves as the Puerto Ricans' clubhouse.

Tony, who is made out to be a shade less Neanderthal than his chums, is finally shaken from his desolate neighborhood life when one member of his group accidentally slips off the Verrazano Bridge during a playful interlude. In the last scene, Tony, rattled by the death of his friend, crosses the bridge, both literally and symbolically, to find his way to the better, finer world: specifically, the middle-class Manhattan apartment of a girlfriend. She herself was originally from a somewhat more respectable part of Bay Ridge, but she knows enough to fix up her place as might any West Village intellectual, complete with bohemian art fixtures and a bare brick wall in the living room. She asks the thoroughly chastised Tony if he is ready to redo his worthless life. With bowed head, he sobbingly announces his desire for personal gentrification. So the movie ends, presumably with our hero preparing himself for voice and diction lessons and evening courses at the New School. Somehow changing one's class is volitional, a mere matter of choosing the right attitude.

The moral is clear: proletariat Bay Ridge is not only a tough place to live, but it offers a morally inferior way of life. The middle-class life is not only economically more secure and comfortable, it is ethically superior.

Five years later, Hollywood inflicted upon us a sequel to *Saturday Night Fever*, entitled *Staying Alive* (1983), with John Travolta still playing Tony Manero, who now is going to dance school after permanently moving to Manhattan. On a visit home, his mother praises him by saying: "You must have something if you could escape from this neighborhood." On another occasion, he excuses his boorish behavior to an upper-crust prospective girlfriend by saying: "The people I lived with didn't know how to be nice." And, "There's a gentleman inside me waiting to come out." So there's hope for the uncouth working-class Italian boy if only he can put enough space between himself and Brooklyn.

The choosing-between-two-worlds theme is explored with somewhat more intelligence in *Bloodbrothers* (1978). Stony De Coco must decide whether he is going to stick with the parochial, male-bonded world of Italian-American construction workers with their pride in their work and barroom camaraderie or become a middle-class professional of sorts, a recreation assistant who deals with children. He really prefers the latter occupation, but his father sees it as "woman's work." Pop says things like: "The blood that runs in your veins—that's De Coco blood. You're ours!" Stony's family turns out to be pathological. Mom is an hysteric who induces anorexia nervosa in his younger brother, and Pop is a macho maniac who beats Mom senselessly because of a suspected infidelity. Once more, working-class Italians are depicted as screaming screwballs. So Stony heads for the kinder, gentler, middle-class Anglo world.[2]

Not so the Italian boy in *The Wanderers* (1979). Engaged to a neighborhood girl, he bolts from his own engagement party when he sees his true love stroll by. Of course, she is a "better-class" lass. He follows her for two blocks, and suddenly he's out of the Bronx and in Greenwich Village, probably not far from where Tony Manero and Stony De Coco have settled down with *their* upper-class women. But some people just don't want to better themselves. He soon realizes he can never fit into his lady's "faintly androgynous, bohemian world. It's back to the trattoria under the wing of his Hawaiian-shirted, mafioso father-in-law."[3]

Sempre Mafia

Of the various Italian stereotypes in the media, the Mafia image is the most enduring. By 1985, *Prizzi's Honor* offered us a new twist in gangster depravity, a romance between a mafioso and a lovely lady who herself turns out to be a gangland hit woman. At one point she refers to her Polish antecedents as "polack," thereby demonstrating Hollywood's inability to recognize the existence of one of America's most defamed ethnic groups in anything but defamatory terms. Prizzi and his Polish-American woman get along swimmingly at first. After a whirlwind romance, they marry. Eventually, however, their relationship comes into conflict with the interests of "the family." It's all resolved when Prizzi beats his wife to the draw, putting a knife through her neck as she is about to blow him away with one of her favorite work tools. The movie actually ends happily after Prizzi stuffs her body in the trunk of a car and returns to an earlier Mafia sweetheart who has all along been plotting to get him back. Done by one of Hollywood's leading directors, John Huston, this comic-book flick was treated as a serious cinematic effort by critics.

Almost forty years after television first featured the Italian mobster in "The Untouchables," Mafia characters continued in abundant supply in films and TV series. As if to demonstrate that nothing changes, in 1990 alone Hollywood gave us *The Freshman, My Blue Heaven, King of New York, Miller's Crossing, Godfather III,* and *GoodFellas.* The first two are comedies. In all of them, Italian mobsters either are the central characters or play important supporting roles. *King of New York* manages to offend women, African-Americans, Chinese, Latinos, and Irish—as well as Italians. *Godfather III* is a dreary imitation of the two previous *Godfather* films, again elevating the don to a kind of admirable patriarchal deity. Distinct among these films was *GoodFellas,* a well-made Martin Scorsese film. Based on a true story, it divests the mobsters

Latino Bad Guys

"Juarez," a new ABC series about a Chicano cop covering an El Paso beat . . . at first appears [to offer more human images of Hispanics] as its opening scenes zoom in on the sights, sounds, moods and folk rhythms of bordertown life. . . . But the plot quickly veers off into Hollywood stereotype territory, with characters degenerating into the old Hispanic predatory villain caricatures. . . .

Sgt. Rosendo Juarez is not at war against a bad or unjust system, but rather pitted against his own people, as well as his "nature" and cultural roots, shown as instinctively criminal and ethnically conspiratorial. Juarez is caught between Anglo "propriety" and a Chicano community infested with stock villains. . . .

In this cynical, glaringly racist world, we see a sad return to the silent-screen "greasers" who were "the most villainous of ethnic screen images," according to Allen Woll, author of *The Latin Image In American Film.* "The only way you could be a good greaser was if you betrayed your people and helped the Anglos." . . .

A recent study by the Center for Media and Public Affairs concluded that Hispanic characters, who rarely appear on TV, commit twice as many crimes as white characters. "We've gone from being Western bandits to urban bandits," notes [University of California professor Carlos] Cortes.

Prairie Miller, "Hispanic Images," *People's Daily World,* June 2, 1988.

of any romantic or glorified aura, revealing them to be the vicious petty hoods, cutthroats, and victimizers they really are.

The image of the Italian as gangster even permeates gangster movies about other groups. *Once Upon a Time in America* (1984), a movie about Jewish mobsters, and *Year of the Dragon* (1985), about Chinese mobsters, were amply offensive to these respective groups. Each also included Italian racketeers as an ethno-criminal element that competes with the Jewish and Chinese mobsters. For an added twist, the hero in *Year of the Dragon* is a slightly crazed Polish-American detective named White, who describes himself repeatedly as a "polack" and even a "dumb polack." On one occasion, he informs an antagonist, "You made one mistake: I'm not an Italian, I'm a polack. I can't be bribed." Detective White refers to the Chinese legacy of a "thousand-year history" of crime—which the Chinese have now brought to this country. He draws feverish comparisons between Vietnam's jungles and Chinatown's streets. "This is Vietnam all over again—nobody wants to win."

The film's Chinese mobsters are in a long line of Asian criminal stereotypes from the old Dr. Fu Manchu movies down to the James Bond flicks and "Hawaii Five-O" television series. The only Asian female of note in this movie is the Chinese-American newscaster who, of course, becomes a compliant appendage to Supercop White once the action moves from the streets to the bed.[4] *Year of the Dragon* offers some intriguing glimpses into life in New York's Chinatown, leaving one to wonder what interesting movies could be made about the Chinese-American experience were the make-believe media ever to pay attention to Chinese who don't shoot people in the face.

In comedy films, too, Italians have often appeared as mobsters, as in *The Ritz* (1976), in which a Mafia-related son-in-law goes to a gay bathhouse to avoid extermination by his family. Similarly, in *Some Like It Hot* (1959), *Broadway Danny Rose* (1984), and *The Freshman* (1990) the protagonists have scary and humorous encounters with Italian mobsters.

Italian-American women are almost nonexistent as central characters in the entertainment media, portrayed mostly as homebound acolytes. A typical representation was offered on "Wiseguy," a CBS weekly serial running in the late 1980s, featuring a Federal agent named Vinnie Terranova along with assorted mob figures, some of whom happen to be his relatives. In the final episode of the 1988–89 season, Vinnie's mother, who talks with what is supposed to be an Italian accent, rushes from her vacation in Italy because she senses correctly that her Vinnie has a "girl-a." "Oh, he looks-a awful. I shudden-a left-a him alone," the protective mama says when she reunites with him. Sounding like

The Chinese who appear in *Year of the Dragon* are mostly killers and mobsters, and the hero is a White detective who describes himself as "a dumb polack." The film manages to be offensive to more than one ethnic group.

Luigi in drag, she asks anxiously if Vinnie's new girlfriend, Amber, is Italian. "No? well-a is-a she Catholeec?" Thank goodness, yes. A third of a loaf is better than none. But Vinnie's mom is offended when she pops over to Vinnie's apartment unannounced and finds him in bed with Amber. "And they-a no yet-a married." Later she comes around and kisses Amber when their engagement is announced. "You-a are engaged and-a I am-a happy." Mama herself married a reformed Mafia don who had renounced his life of crime.

A seemingly refreshing departure from this kind of mama-mia stereotype was the 1986 NBC autobiographical film about Antoinette Giancana, a young woman who loves her father but rebels against his domination and seeks to be herself in a male-ruled household. Here is one of those rare instances where the struggles of an Italian-American woman are given respectful treatment. There is one catch, however: Papa Giancana is a notorious Mafia don and the title of the film is *Mafia Princess*. To the extent that the media can explore new and worthwhile themes, it seems they must still be packaged in an old casement.

After being fed enough of this fare, we need to remind ourselves that not all Italians are gangsters and not all gangsters are Italian. As with other ethnic groups, in the last several decades Italians have moved in noticeable numbers into government service, political life, the professions, and the arts. It can be argued that these people usually do less sensationally horrifying things than mobsters and are therefore less likely to win the attention of an image industry that specializes in violence and other forms of sensationalism. Still, noncriminal characters do appear in films and television shows; it would not be unrealistic to portray ethnics more frequently engaged in normal social activities and in positions of responsibility and empowerment. And the introduction of ethnic themes into story lines other than those occupied by Hollywood stereotypes might represent a refreshing and appealing departure from the usual fare. To prove the point, one need only recall *Marty* (1955), originally a television drama and later an Oscar-winning Hollywood film that portrayed a love affair involving a lonely Italian-American butcher. Marty is a likeable, hardworking guy, who lives with his mother and hangs out with his buddies, cruising the neighborhood dance halls in the evenings. Doubting that he is very lovable, he nevertheless wins the heart of a local lass, who is intelligent, sensitive, and supposedly of plain appearance. Marty's mother is a first-generation Italian immigrant, who struggles to remain active and useful in her old age. She is concerned about the Americanizing influences that might induce her son "to give up the house" and move into an apartment. The characterizations are touching and readily recognizable without being stereotypic or slighting.

Moonstruck (1987) is another example of that rare genre: a movie about Italians who are not gangsters. The humor is sometimes overly slick in that silly, heavy-handed TV sitcom way. The characters are broadly drawn; occasionally overdrawn. For instance, the grandfather—played by an actor with an odd Eastern European accent—is predictably quaint as he herds his dogs into the park so that they might bay at the moon. The mother oozes familial integrity. The daughter—and heroine of the story—falls in love with the brooding brother of her fiancé, a love consummated to the wonderful music of *La Boheme*. Whatever its flaws, *Moonstruck* is an entertaining film that portrays Brooklyn working-class and petty bourgeois ethnics as warm, engaging—and law-abiding—human beings.

A film done with more intelligence and realism is *Dominic and Eugene* (1988), which tells the story of fraternal twins who plan on sharing a house together. One brother is being helped through medical school by the other, who is a sanitation worker. The story focuses on how they resolve the contradictions that face them while managing to remain close and stay committed to each other. *Dominic and Eugene* is well-acted; it is touching but not oversentimentalized or overdone. The Italian-American identities of the brothers and some neighbors are established early and easily and do not figure in the plot in any prominent way, except to leave us with an impression that Italian working-class people are human and decent, capable of living lives that are worthy of narrative treatment—without the assistance of a single mafioso thug.

Free of Mafia thugs but not of other threadbare ethnic stereotypes is "The Fanelli Boys," an NBC 1990 television situation comedy series about four working-class, Italian-American brothers who are trying to get their lives into shape. Lucky for them, their mama decides not to move to Florida. Instead she stays in Brooklyn to help them through their difficulties. The show's sitcom humor is abrasive and overdone and the Italian working-class characters are loud and harsh. Having discovered an ethnic group, NBC demonstrates it has nothing better to offer us than the same old hackneyed standbys.

Spaghetti Benders for Madison Avenue

Once ethnicity became an acceptable media topic, it was not long before ethnic types were worked into television ads. The TV commercial is the quintessential propaganda message: single-minded, brief, simple, slick, and repetitive. Ethnic stereotypes offer their own instant image recognition: Parsimonious Scots offer us wise counsel regarding bargain-priced gasoline; elegant and snobbish French recommend the best wines, perfumes, and mustards; sweaty, robust Irishmen endorse the right deodor-

Italian—Madison Avenue Style

The setting is a rather attractive middle-class kitchen somewhere in America. It is Sunday. We know this because there is some commotion over whether or not the dinner guest, a skeptic in all things, is going to like the sauce. It is an Italian home. We know this because the people really care whether or not the skeptic is going to like the sauce. The object of everyone's attention—the sauce—is bubbling thick and red in a large, overworked pot.

The skeptic stands over the sauce uneasily. The cook (we know she's the cook because her hair is up, she's fat, and she's wearing an apron) looks at him pleadingly. His face tells everyone around him that he thinks the idea of a good tomato sauce coming out of a jar is absurd. He reaches for the wooden spoon by the side of the stove. Dipping it into the hot red liquid, he brings it up to his lips. As he tastes the sauce, his eyes explode with pleasure. "That's Italian!" he exclaims. "Now, that's Italian!"

No, that's Madison Avenue hype.

Marco Ciolli, "Exploiting the Italian Image," *Attenzione*, September 1979.

ant soap; rotund Germans offer up the best beer; while Japanese prove their love for the extra light beer in the way they supposedly know best—by smashing a barroom table in half with a karate blow.

The Italian has appeared in a variety of advertising roles. There is the Latin lover who wins his lady, less with his amorous overtures than with his right choice of beverage; the Mafia don ready to start a gangland massacre if the lasagna isn't *magnifico;* the nearly inarticulate disco dimwit who can barely say "Trident" as he twirls his partners around the dance floor.[5] The ethnic characters in commercials are literally caricatures of caricatures.

In the world of commercials, Italians tend to be simple-minded oral creatures. They taste, sip, eat, chew, and offer exclamations such as "Mama mia! Datza spicy meatball!" The stereotypic linking of Italians with food so predominates as to preclude this ethnic group's association with other realms (except crime, of course). Thus, a 1986 PBS documentary mini-series on the English language, narrated by Robert MacNeil, noted how various foreign languages have enriched the English language. However, Italian was something of an exception, MacNeil said, since the Italian words that have passed into English "all relate to

food." (Overlooked were such inedibles as cognoscenti, literati, illumi-
nati, ghetto, crescendo, aggiornamento, gambado, inamorata, vendetta,
virtuoso, paparazzi, impresario, rotunda, chiaroscuro, buffo, brio, bravo,
bravado, divertimento, and imbroglio, along with musical terms like
contralto, soprano, fortissimo, basso, pizzicato, piano, and viola.)

Their days taken up with runs to and from the kitchen, Italians, no
doubt, would be a poor choice when it comes to chairing a board
meeting, offering medical advice, or conducting a scientific experiment,
notes Marco Ciolli. "Certainly, no commercial has ever shown an
Italian-American involved in any professional activity."[6] A leader of the
National Italian-American Foundation complained that "commercials
are outdated and subconsciously give a negative image to people who
have never had any personal contacts with Italians."[7] One advertising
executive concedes the point: "What the hell do I know about Italians?
I mean, outside the fact that they like to eat spaghetti, drink wine, and
the men chase after women. What more am I supposed to know?"[8]

To say that the media merely reflect reality (after all, there *are*
Italian gangsters and Italians *do* drink wine and eat spaghetti) is to
overlook the distorted dimension of the "reality" presented. The media's tactic, finding its highest (or lowest) articulation in television ads,
is to move *with* the cheap, facile notions about one group or another,
rather than against them. If there are misconceptions that can easily be
made plausible, amusing, or sensational, then the media will use them.
Madison Avenue's goal is to manipulate rather than educate, to reach
as many people as quickly as possible with readily evocative images. So
the media merchandisers pander to the crudest impressions of ethnics
held by the public, encouraging each group to embrace the prefabricated images of other groups—and even of its own.

Internalizing the False Image

The make-believe media's treatment of Italian-Americans provides dramatic illustration of how commercially produced stereotypes become
accepted by the entire society, including many members of the ethnic
group itself. "The ethnic becomes part of the world that is stigmatizing
his very self," notes the writer Joseph Papaleo.[9] More than once, on
strolls through Italian neighborhoods in New York, I have spotted cars
with bumper stickers that read, "Mafia Staff Car, Keepa You Hands
Off." While in Philadelphia, my attention was directed to a musical rock
group of Italian-American youths who billed themselves as "The Godfa-
thers." In 1981 at the feast of St. Anthony of Padua in New York, the

neighborhood band played as its opening number the theme from *The Godfather*. As of the early 1990s, there even existed a "Godfather's" chain of pizzerias.

While many Italians find the association with crime offensive, some are finding a kind of group recognition in it—especially when the movies in question tell us nothing about the mob's role in union-busting, extortion, and shakedowns, and nothing about its victimization of workers, consumers, women (as wives or prostitutes), and small-business owners—including many Italians. Instead, hoodlums are transformed into folk heroes, loveable patriarchs who want nothing more than a decent life for their families and a steady income from their often unspecified "business" ventures.

Just as many African-Americans avidly watched "Amos 'n' Andy," so Mafia movies "play to audiences just as large in the theaters of Italian-American neighborhoods as they do elsewhere."[10] Like other ethnic groups, Italians have been starved for acknowledgment from the dominant culture, from that prosperous, powerful Other World. The feeling of being shut out, a stranger in one's own land, is part of what makes many ethnics so responsive to any kind of media representation, even a derogatory one.

The ethnics are always looking for signs that they count for something, that they *exist*—in a society that usually ignores their existence. A starving person will eat junk food. Better to be represented as a buffoon or even a murderous thug than not to exist at all. Like other ethnics, the Italians are still fighting the "invisible man" burden.

Mafia movies also offer the appeal of empowerment; they portray Italians in positions of strength and dominance, able to get things done as they want, in direct and forceful ways, not unlike the frontier cowboy hero. For powerless people, the Mafia don, with his army of hit men and network of lawyers, obliging politicians, and big-business friends, becomes an appealing figure. For these same reasons, I suspect, did some Chinese-Americans enjoy *Year of the Dragon*. That Chinese were being portrayed as thugs, extortionists, narcotic smugglers, and murderers weighed less than that they were finally being portrayed at all. No longer quaint and comic laundrymen and waiters, they were conducting serious conversations with each other in Chinese in the middle of an American movie, displaying shrewdness and resourcefulness (as well as homicidal ruthlessness)—and occupying positions of power and leadership.

The above observations might also help explain the popularity of ethnic mobster films to the public in general. Here are a breed of people who live outside the law with a powerful law of their own, who kowtow

Sometimes Our Stereotypes Are All We Have

"The Goldbergs" [was] a family sitcom that had begun as a radio serial in 1929 [and played on television in the late forties and fifties]. The Goldbergs and their friends and neighbors served as an extended family to their fans, made up to a great extent of Jewish immigrants and children of immigrants. . . .

It never occurred to me in those days or even later to be embarrassed by Molly's exaggerated accent and gestures or uncomfortable with Uncle David's self-effacing shrug and timid manner. Never, that is, until recently, when I watched a Jewish audience view some clips of early "Goldberg" TV shows during a discussion about the image of Jews on television.

Some viewers squirmed with discomfort, others expressed outrage at what they considered blatant stereotyping: Molly, the inevitable Jewish mother, butting into everybody's business; her Jewish neighbors speaking in loud Bronx-accented voices, her Irish friends all with rolling brogues. "It's so demeaning," one young woman said. "How could you have tolerated such stereotyping?"

How indeed? . . . the popularity of "The Goldbergs" rested on its magnification of specifically Jewish characteristics. . . , In all of Molly's encounters with the non-Jewish establishment, WASPs appear as soft-spoken and perfectly mannered, and she appears ill at ease and out of place. . . .

Jewish audiences cherished the Goldberg clan precisely because it did mirror our unease in American society. . . . We can't, I imagine, expect to see reruns of "The Goldbergs" in seasons to come any more than we would hear replays of the "Amos 'n' Andy" radio show. Such programs have slipped into history.

But at a time when Jews—like Uncle David—saw themselves as "alsos" in America, "The Goldbergs" helped make us feel like somebodies.

Francine Klagsbrun, "The Goldbergs—Stereotypes Loved by Americans," *New York Times*, August 8, 1988.

to no one, who are powerful and effective, who show cruelty to competitors and kindness to family and friends—except when family and friends become competitors. Here are the real urban cowboys, Jesse James with a machine gun, the Sicilian Robin Hoods—all as American as pizza pie. The Mafia has achieved a kind of folklore status, "rooted in a foreignness that makes it so much more mysteriously titillating than the same activities of organized crime by old-line American thugs might be."[11]

Finally, it must be noted that the media deny the seriousness of the ethnic experience and thereby evade the larger, more taboo question of class struggle. The ethnics' attention is directed toward irrelevant caricatures of themselves that serve as objects of either emulation or insult or both. The ethnics—of whom the Italians are only a more obvious example—are told what to think of themselves by the make-believe media. Controversies about ethnic "identity," group "dignity," and "assimilation" continue endlessly. Ignored by the make-believe media are the pressing problems of working-class ethnics: the demoralizing hardships of underemployment, layoffs, low wages, high taxes, job-connected disabilities, and staggering living costs.

Having their identities suppressed or falsified is but one manifestation of a larger violation that ethnics are made to suffer. What has been stolen from many of them is their labor, their health, their communities, and their ability to live with a sufficient measure of ease and security. So the ethnics are distracted from their own struggle and their own experience by the daily psychological muggings of Hollywood and television, by fabricated images of the world and of themselves. The medium is the message, and the media are the Mafia.

10

Child Abuse

By the time a child graduates from high school, she or he will have spent some 20,000 hours watching television. To put it another way, she or he will have spent an average of twenty-seven hours a week—or almost four hours a day—in front of the tube. In contrast, the "average middle-school child in the United States spends four minutes a day reading for pleasure."[1] During those years of televiewing, the high-school graduate will have witnessed about 13,000 killings and many times that number of beatings, muggings, fistfights, robberies, shootouts, knifings, rapes and attempted rapes, and verbal threats. What effect does this have on juvenile viewers?

Zapping Young Minds

Most of us think that what children are exposed to in school affects them and is a matter of some importance. So too, then, should we consider television to be a significant influence upon young minds, especially since children spend more time with the TV than with their lesson books. One study finds that, except for friends, the media are the primary influence in shaping children's sense of sex roles and future aspirations.[2] Other studies show that children learn both constructive and antisocial values and behavior from television. A report prepared under the direction of the National Institute of Mental Health surveys a decade of research and finds "overwhelming" evidence that excessive violence on TV causes aggressiveness in the children who watch it.[3] In addition, it has been found that:

 1. The level of generalized fear among children increases with heavy television viewing.

2. Children select their heroes and emulation roles more frequently from television programs than from family, school, government, or church. Thus, while relatively few preschoolers might be able to identify their national leaders, "90 percent of all American three-year-olds recognize Fred Flintstone," a television cartoon character.[4]

3. Children, especially toddlers who watch the same programs as older kids, sometimes have trouble distinguishing between televised fantasy and reality. Unable to grasp the motives behind the violence, they see everyone involved in a generalized brutality.

4. Among children, heavy TV viewers are generally more conventional in their views of life than light viewers; they adhere more to the cultural and social stereotypes fostered by television, or at least find more reinforcement for such stereotypes.[5]

5. Films and cartoons containing violent acts can instigate aggressive and violent behavior in children during subsequent playtimes.[6] Furthermore, children, as well as adult criminals, have utilized ideas and techniques from television shows when performing actual crimes.

Regarding that last point, television violence may not be able to transform an emotionally healthy child into a serial killer, but it can have a "copycat" or "trigger" effect on more troubled youngsters. Disturbing examples are occasionally reported in the press. A twelve-year-old boy in Arkansas stabbed his playmate to death. When questioned by police, he told them about a movie he had recently seen, *Friday the 13th*, which contained graphic scenes of slashings and slayings.[7] A nine-year-old girl was sexually assaulted with a beer bottle by four other children on a beach in San Francisco. This happened a few days after NBC televised a show depicting a teenage girl in a detention center being gang-raped with a broom handle by other inmates. The youngsters involved in the real-life assault said they had watched the episode.[8]

Additional evidence suggests that televiewing hurts academic performance, lowers reading levels, erodes linguistic powers, diminishes ability to handle abstract symbols, and shortens the attention span of the young.[9] The average shot on a network show lasts about three seconds, and on a commercial about two-and-a-half seconds—thereby conditioning the mind to an endless flicker of changing pictures rather than developing its ability to give protracted attention to one thing. Television is not the medium for conveying sophisticated ideas or devel-

Captain Kangaroo
Tells It Like It Is

When you are spending time in front of the television, you are not doing other things. The young child of three or four years old is in the stage of the greatest emotional development that human beings undergo. And we only develop when we experience things, real-life things: a conversation with Mother, touching Father, going places, doing things, relating to others. This kind of experience is critical to a young child, and when the child spends thirty-five hours per week in front of the TV set, it is impossible to have the full range of real-life experience that a young child must have. Even if we had an overabundance of good television programs, it wouldn't solve the problem.

Robert Keeshan, the actor who played Captain Kangaroo, quoted in Jerry Mander, *Four Arguments for the Elimination of Television* (New York: Quill, 1978), p. 265.

oping the cognitive habits and intellectual discipline that print medium is potentially capable of promoting. Rather, it encourages passivity in the viewer and a kind of unthinking receptivity to quick images. Today, the child who enters grade school ostensibly to begin reading and learning has already been subjected to four or five years of the tube's own mind-pulverizing curriculum.

In response to protests regarding the quality of children's programs, the Public Broadcasting System and, to a lesser extent, the networks, began offering age-graded and somewhat better quality shows in the 1960s and 1970s. For instance, PBS introduced "Sesame Street" for younger children and "Electric Company" for older ones. Interesting and informative programs about science, nature, and animal life appeared during "children's prime time," specifically, Saturday mornings and weekday afternoons. Some of the informational shows were a mixed blessing, subject to the usual ideological distortions of corporate American culture. Thus, segments of NBC's "In the News," sandwiched between the Saturday-morning kid shows, informed its young viewers that Colombian peasants were getting rich from the rise in coffee prices and that U.S. corporations moved to Puerto Rico to encourage the island's economic development.

The advent of the Reagan administration in 1981 brought a decline in the already dubious quality of children's television. The networks got the nod from the Federal Communications Commission (FCC) to let market forces decide programming. Commercial television is a matter of selling audiences to advertisers. The thinking of profit-conscious network executives went something like this: Children will watch anything on Saturday morning and weekday afternoons, so why bother spending millions of dollars putting out an original and creative program for them when some inexpensive cartoons will do.

By the end of 1982, more than half of the nation's television stations had no children's programming on weekday afternoons. The best and brightest shows began to disappear. CBS cut back on "Captain Kangaroo" and abolished "30 Minutes." The latter was the only national current-affairs program for young audiences. NBC's "Special Treat" and ABC's "Animals Animals Animals," two long-running, award-winning children's series, were taken off the air. Advertisements targeting a younger audience, however, continued unabated and even increased substantially on the remaining children's shows. The FCC's admonition in 1974 that "broadcasters have a special obligation to serve children" was replaced with a new rule: "Let profits prevail."[10]

The children's programs that did survive in the early 1980s often had little to recommend them. Some were scaled-down replicas of adult quiz shows, encouraging young contestants to compete like shrieking, greedy little maniacs for flashy prizes. New additions included such gems as ABC's "Goldie Gold and Action Jack," a cartoon about "the world's richest girl" and the reporter who worked for her newspaper, the "Gold Street Journal." Their adventures included the usual mysterious haunts and mad scientists. Throughout these escapades, Goldie's limitless wealth was flaunted before the eyes of young viewers. Following Goldie was "The Richie Rich/Scooby Doo Show," featuring an impossibly rich little blond boy. He had a dog named Dollar, a "Dollarmation," whose coat was spotted with dollar signs. A screen full of dollar signs was also used to mark transitions between scenes. The Goldie-Richie message was clear enough: kids, there's nothing wrong—and a lot right—with wallowing in wealth and being filthy rich.

According to one psychologist, "The lesson of most TV series is that the rich, the powerful and the conniving are the most successful."[11] In a sense, such a lesson is accurate. Rich, powerful, and conniving individuals *are* usually the more successful ones in a society like ours. What is left out is any vision of alternative modes of behavior and alternative dimensions of social reality.

Children's programs most often cast White male figures in dominant roles. People of Third World origin (African, Latino, Asian, Native

American) compose about 25 percent of the U.S. population but only 7½ percent of 1,145 television characters surveyed in one study of children's shows. African-Americans were more often sympathetic characters than villainous ones, but this positive point was partially offset by the infrequency of their appearances and the relatively minor quality of their roles. Characters with foreign accents and odd appearances tended to be portrayed negatively. Native American Indians were represented solely by Tonto in the "Lone Ranger" cartoons.[12]

One study found that only 16 percent of all major dramatic television characters were female. They were generally portrayed as younger than males, more likely to be married, less active, and with lower self-esteem. The family usually had a competent housewife-mother, who was obligated to manipulate a dominant but often bungling father.[13] In both children's and adults' television, female characters usually are supportive of male heroes and fit the "feminine" stereotype of beauty and behavior that seems required to qualify them as acolytes to the good guys.[14] A study of 200 episodes of network TV programs found that teenage girls are represented as obsessed with shopping, grooming, and dating; looks count more than brains and bright girls are social misfits. Week after week, the adolescent girls display no visible skills, no real interest in school subjects, and no vocational plans.[15]

By the mid-1980s, in response to public pressure, the networks cut back a little on the violence and began putting more people of color into their children's shows. This did not mean they were making any attempt to explore ethnic themes or teach tolerance and brotherhood. The most popular show of this period was "Mr. T," an animated spinoff from the popular prime-time series "The A-Team." It was also the most violent show on children's television. Perhaps through repeated and early exposure, children develop a taste for viewing violence. In any case, the networks do not offer the kind of imaginative, creative, violence-free programming that would engage the attention of youngsters the way smash-'em-up shows do.

In the 1980s, interested groups, such as Action for Children's Television (ACT), were angered by the cancellation of quality shows, the increase in commercialism, and the persistence of violent themes. Public pressure induced Congress to pass the Children's Television Act of 1988 by a 328-to-78 bipartisan majority in the House and unanimous voice vote in the Senate. In its final compromised version, the bill even gained the lukewarm support of the National Association of Broadcasters. A Reagan-dominated FCC had abolished all limitations on the number of commercials. The bill restored them, restricting advertising in children's programs to ten-and-a-half minutes per hour on week-

ends and twelve minutes on weekdays. The stations were given a full
year to comply. The bill also required stations to provide some educational and informational programs for children, with the FCC evaluat-
ing those efforts when stations sought to renew their licenses. But
President Reagan pocket-vetoed the legislation, claiming it was an un-
constitutional infringement on the freedom of expression. He was referring to the freedom of broadcasters to offer whatever they wanted on
the airwaves, without having their commercial interests and money-
making abilities limited—even in the mildest way—by government
regulations.

The Saturday Morning Massacre

Whatever changes have come to children's programming over the
years, one genre has endured as a staple: the "animal chase" cartoon. It
continues to impose its idiocy on kids today as on the earlier generations
of youngsters who patronized Saturday matinee movies in the days
before television. On weekday mornings and afternoons (usually on
local television stations) and on Saturday mornings, one can encounter
the hyperkinetic creatures of the "Bugs Bunny" and "Woody Wood-
pecker" set. These cartoons rely on a simple formula: the taunting,
audacious rabbit or defiant mouse incites an adversary. The larger creature plans strategies of entrapment in order to hunt down, flatten, swal-
low, or pulverize the troublesome smaller one. However, the latter usually outsmarts or outsteps his infuriated foe, causing the hunter to be
victimized by his own hunt amidst an abundance of "playful" violence.

Along with the animal chase, children's television offers more "sophisticated" cartoon shows. Known as the "Saturday morning massacre," these programs have been roundly criticized for their violence.
Equally disturbing is their thematic context and political and social
orthodoxies. In one of the more popular series, "Superfriends," various
comic-book heroes such as Batman, Robin, Wonder Woman, and, of
course, Superman remain on call at the "Hall of Justice," ready to do
battle with alien invaders who, in episode after episode, try to attack
and destroy the earth or some portion of it. Sometimes the menace
assumes the form of snarling "Wild Beasts from Another World," who
tear people to shreds, driven by no apparent objective other than a
wanton lust for killing. Sometimes the invaders are disembodied "Giant
Alien Brains." Flying about in outer space like cerebral spaceships,
emitting mind-paralyzing rays, the Brains turn people into helpless
automatons. Why? Because that's what Giant Alien Brains like to do.

"Roadrunner" is just one of an enduring genre of "animal chase" children's cartoons, in which one hyperkinetic creature tries to do violence to another— only to be outsmarted and outdone by its own tactics.

If not always extraterrestrial, the threat is inevitably alien, taking the form of slimy creatures from within the earth or beneath the sea or killer bees that attack peaceful African villages. In each instance, the formula is the same: the embattled people beg for help from the Hall of Justice. An offscreen stentorian male voice in the Hall of Justice sends out a call to one or more of the Superfriends to come to the rescue. A speedy flight to the scene of the danger, a cascade of punches, kicks, and tricky ploys, and our superheroes have quickly dispatched the alien menace. Through it all, the ordinary folk in these episodes remain incapable of defending themselves against the alien intruders. They depend upon the force and violence of the fearless paladins.

Other shows offer much the same. "Thundarr the Barbarian" uses his "sun sword" to battle "forces of evil" twenty centuries in the future. By the 1980s, "Star Wars" high-tech, with its lasers, blasters, and dissolving rays, had become a major mode of cartoon violence. Raised on such fare, the coming generation of young voters should have little trouble

Creating Cretins

Washed by the cathode-ray glow, the Saturday morning children of the '80s watch TV in their "Star Wars" pajamas with catatonic eyes. They are the children of budget cut schools without school lunch programs—the children likely to be abused because of rising unemployment and [poverty]. They are getting what the market forces give them to watch: rich boys on mega-buck capers, brutal barbarians, scantily clad she-heroes, muscular he-heroes and incessant canned laughter. . . .

What are the kids learning? Captain Kangaroo likes to tell the story of a musician who came up to him once and said: "I'm a concert pianist today because of your program."

That may be a bit of an overstatement about what a little exposure to classical music will do. Yet after a few droning hours of video comics, you can imagine these children walking up to producers and saying: "I'm a sadist today because of your show." Or, "I'm a moron today. . . . " With role models like Thundarr the Barbarian and his grisly band of wonder-thugs, or Pac Man (and Ms. Pac Man and Pac-Baby) cavorting through Pacland protecting power pellets for the Paclanders, what can we expect?

Saturday television not only feeds sexism and violence, it is the Skinner-box of paranoia. Evil is everywhere. From nasty sheiks trying to take over oil fields (that's right) to sinister aliens (that's right) trying to capture magic pyramids, the plots are reduced to a simplistic good-guys, bad-guys context. Scripts call for the star of the show to kill, wound, vaporize, jail, scare away or otherwise remove the evil.

Paul Choitz, "Reruns and Cheap Shots," *In These Times*, October 27–November 2, 1982.

accepting the idea of a large defense establishment with its arsenals of high-tech weaponry ready for use against foreign adversaries.

A 1989 study of the images of the enemy and the ideological messages in the most watched children's cartoon shows ("He-Man," "She-Ra," "Rambo," "G.I. Joe," "Transformers," "Gobots," "Voltron," and "Defenders of the Earth") reveals a pattern. Every episode tends to have one main enemy or evil leader who is accompanied by dangerous ferocious animals, foreigners (with accents), and dubious-looking people who are capable of violent acts, including sadistic Russian scientists and Asian assassins. The enemy wants money, absolute power, war, and global conquest. He is violent and dictatorial, enforcing his rule by inflicting severe punishment even on his own subordinates. The heroes are almost always American and they are totally virtuous.[16]

The message of these shows is that the world is filled with evil forces that cannot be controlled except by violent countermeasures. "Children learn to expect . . . that their country has to remain in a state of military readiness. . . . Heroes and enemies never get together to negotiate. They only meet to fight. As a result, children are socialized to believe in peace through strength."[17]

The themes found in these cartoons parallel the more adult Rambo-type movies and science-fiction films discussed earlier. We are menaced by evil foreigners, Communists, and alien space invaders, who are endowed with formidable technology and limitless supplies of lethal energy. We are rescued from catastrophe by individual heroics or state authorities, rather than by our own concerted actions. It is never explained why evil forces want to conquer us. It is just supposedly part of their nature.

The ultimate Reagan-era creation, managing to wrap a science-fiction outer-space menace, anticommunism, and missile-war militarism into one package, was the Atari video game marketed in 1983 entitled "Communist Mutants from Space." According to a sales catalogue description: "The communist mutants are invading and you must save the planet. Watch the mutants change form before your eyes. You have four defense options, shields, time warp, penetrating missiles, and guided missiles."

By 1987, as relations between the United States and the USSR showed signs of thawing, an occasionally more benign image of the Soviets was allowed to creep into the cartoons. Thus, one show called "GI Joe, A Real American Hero" has GI Joe and his buddies fighting "Cobra," an "international ring of terrorists" bent upon dominating the world. This sounds familiar enough. But our heroes also encounter what Joe himself identifies as "the Russian version of GI Joe, an elite combat unit." "Thar's nothing ah hate more than a Russkie," says one of GI Joe's sidekicks, Gung Ho. He then punches a Russian who has made a derisive remark about his corpulent appearance. But Cobra attacks both Moscow and Washington. So after some initial conflicts, GI Joe's group and the Russians settle their differences and join together to fight off the mutual menace.

The Little Consumers

Along with the many acts of murder and mayhem, a child entering kindergarten will have seen 75,000 thirty-second TV commercials. The average young person views upwards of a million television ads by the age of twenty, at a rate of about a thousand a week.[18] Some 80 to 90 percent of the commercials push junk toys and junk foods. Not surprisingly, boys appear in ads for cars, guns, planes, and other mechanical devices, whereas girls are shown with traditional female products such as dolls.[19] The efficacy of television commercials is known to any parent who has ever been pulled down an aisle in a supermarket or toy store by a pleading child in hot pursuit of the sugary snacks or expensive toys hawked on kiddie shows. "I spent $50 on toys for Jesse's last birthday, and he doesn't use them," complained Joni Colburn, a single parent and student nurse, with a $100 weekly income and a six-year-old son who thought he wanted the toys advertised on children's TV shows. "Toys are a kid's world," she added, "and the ads manipulate that [world] and my relationship with my children."[20]

A former Federal Trade Commission chairman, Michael Pertschuk, observed: "To the small child it is as if a trusted friend is urging the consumption of a particular product. Advertisers seize on the child's trust and exploit it as a weakness for their own gain."[21] Laboratories devoted to child research regularly conduct experiments to develop commercials calculated to make children desire the advertised brands. The television industry has kept a tight lid on these experiments, fearing that they will be criticized for manipulating children's behavior. "Child research is so important because if you get them young, you keep them," confided one researcher.[22]

Along with selling particular products, many of them worthless, some harmful, all overpriced, these advertisements help implant the consumeristic mentality at an early age, not only teaching children to get their parents to spend more but preparing them for the day they themselves will have income of their own to buy the right car, designer jeans, or seductive after-shave lotion.

Television is also a source of nutritional information for youngsters. A barrage of ads invite the child to dietary and dental disaster, pushing color and sweetness over real food value, with an endless succession of sugar-ridden candies, cereals, pies, cakes, ice creams, soft drinks, and fast foods. Children of low-income families are the worst hit by the junk-food blitz, being especially dependent on television for information and entertainment, while often denied access to regular dental and health care. The food commercials depict children as hyped-up little gluttons who devour Twinkies, Hostess Cupcakes, Sugar Frosties, and M&M candies with a greedy enthusiasm seldom displayed for regular meals, all under the approving gaze of mother, a junk-food pusher who knows how to keep her little ones happy.

Television's Contribution to Child Development

Kids who watch TV may not develop flabby minds, but they run the risk of flabby bodies. Analyzing data from the National Center for Health Statistics, William Dietz of New England Medical Center Hospital in Boston found that childhood obesity has risen sharply in the past twenty years—about the time the television set became America's most reliable babysitter. Chubbiness increased 39 percent for teens and 54 percent for six-to-eleven-year-olds. In the six-to-eleven group, 30 percent of the boys and 25 percent of the girls were overweight.

These findings tie in with earlier studies at the University of Montana. Boys were found to be more susceptible to TV junk-food ads than girls were. American kids . . . [are] bombarded with commercials for high-calorie, low-nutrition snacks. What kids are losing in outdoor playtime, they're gaining in extra pounds.

Psychology Today, November 1988, p. 12.

The kind of corporate commercialism found on television has penetrated the classrooms of our country. More than half of all classroom teachers in the United States are using the slick, attractively packaged teaching aids produced by industry. They are promoted at teachers' conventions, advertised in educational publications, and distributed without cost. The result is that sugar companies furnish information on nutrition; utilities push a brand of energy education that often includes nuclear power; and other corporations preach the virtues of private enterprise.[23]

The most obvious problem with industry-produced instructional material is that it allows for influence-peddling in an environment—the public schools—that must be free from profit-making and private interests. The image of McDonald's arches printed on each page of the nutrition action packs means that the subliminal sell has gone to school. Many of these corporations are the same companies that have long utilized the prime advertising medium of television.[24]

The make-believe media produce more than entertainment. For instance, Walt Disney Productions has an Educational Media Company that turns out "educational" filmstrips about the free enterprise system, featuring old television and comic-book favorites. The company notes that these filmstrips "introduce students, grades 4 through 6, to the private enterprise system. . . . Common economic principles like supply and demand and product development are demonstrated and explained by [cartoon characters] as they run their own business."[25]

During the 1980s, the distinction between program and product became increasingly difficult to draw, as children's cartoon shows devolved into program-length commercials of sorts. The shows featured heroes and villains drawn directly from the toy store or developed in conjunction with the marketing of toys. Previously banned by federal regulation, such programs enjoyed a boom in the Reagan "free-market" era, achieving high ratings and huge merchandising profits. Thus, the Mattel Toy Co.'s "He-Man and Masters of the Universe" line of toys, fortified by its own TV series, brought in $350 million in 1985. By 1986, six of the seven animated shows broadcasting weekdays between 3 and 5 P.M. in the New York metropolitan area, including such epics as "GI Joe" and "He-Man," were based on toys. Aided by forty-three hours a week of TV war cartoons, war-toy sales climbed 700 percent between 1982 and 1987.[26] In 1990 the new craze was the Teenage Mutant Ninja Turtles. Incongruously endowed with classically artistic names like "Michelangelo" and "Donatello," these ugly killing-machine monster heroes have a TV show, an extensive line of toys, and even a couple of movies. "A toy featured in its own show gains not only publicity, but also a valuable sales gimmick: a story line that can enhance the toy's appeal."[27]

The confluence of toys and television was disturbingly evident to media critic Elayne Rapping, who visited Children's Palace, one of several "supermarket-style toy chains," during Christmas season:

> The complete penetration of consumer values and images into the world of fun, and even education, is awesome. Every item bears the mark of a current movie or TV show. . . . Every "learning" cassette is based on single-fact, out-of-context answers. The point is always to win, not to understand things. And the video games themselves are just another variation on that theme. Whether it's Warlords, Space Wars, Missile Command, or Donkey Kong, the idea is to "win" by annihilating your opponent.
>
> The obsession with war and destruction is another seemingly obvious aspect of Christmas shopping, which, when experienced in total, can be overwhelming. . . . Macho is definitely back in style.
>
> And in the next aisle, there's still a lot of little homemaker stuff around too. But . . . "women's work" has been transformed into

Ever in search of aberrant gimmicks, the entertainment media gave children and adults the Teenage Mutant Ninja Turtles, monster heroes irreverently named after Renaissance artists.

what can only be called "Total Consumerism." Dishes are by
Corning. Shelves are stocked with prepackaged brand-name foods
and cooked in General Electric microwaves. . . .

"There must be somewhere else to buy toys," you're thinking.
Well, there is. You can go to the more posh emporia where the
bourgeoisie browse and charge things. There, in well-appointed sur-
roundings, full of attentive salespeople, you'll find what the market
offers in class merchandise. The building sets and models are attractive, strong, and geared to stimulate the imagination rather than
block and halt it. . . . All these are free of trademark logos, of course,
and include natural objects—animals, trees, etc.—which are obsolete at Children's Palace. They run from $40–$80 and up. . . .

There's [also] the outrageous Public Assistance Game, sold
mostly at these "classier" stores, which uses racism, sexism, and
more, to degrade and slander the poor. A typical card reads, "You
are up for promotion but a disadvantaged, minority, Buddhist, homo-
sexual female is promoted over you. Go back three squares."[28]

Finally, it should be recalled that "kid shows" are only part of a
child's television experience. Every night at midnight as many as
750,000 children in the nation watch *adult* television. A study of suburban Connecticut school districts found that one-fourth of the students
from kindergarten to the second grade and one-third from grades three
to five were likely to be in front of the television set until 11 P.M.[29] Not
only kiddie shows, but adult shoot-'em-ups, sitcoms, horror mysteries,
and the like are shaping the consciousness of children. To put it another
way, the psychological and propagandistic influence which television
exercises over adults begins in early childhood. Passive spectatorism,
individual isolation, militarism, superpatriotism, sexism and conventional gender roles, Anglo-White predominance, limitless consumerism, and money-grabbing greed—all the virtues of an advanced capitalist society—are there in abundance throughout the day, for children of
all ages.

11

Preemption, Profits, and Censors

As we have seen, the media are filled with themes and images that are decidedly political, drawn mostly from the mainstream spectrum, ranging from pale liberal to brute conservative. What the British musician and pop-star Billy Bragg said about music could hold for entertainment in general: "What people mean when they say music and politics don't mix is that music and left-wing politics don't mix. Right-wing politics go right through all our music: materialistic, racist and sexist imagery and the dwelling on exploiting people's feelings."[1]

Retarding Our Capacities

I have tried to show that there is an ideological content to Hollywood and television productions. Some offerings are more importantly or more blatantly political than others. But just about all of them, from the old cowboy-and-Indian flicks to the latest prime-time television cop-and-crime show, offer characters and themes that generally reinforce established ideological values.

Though it has become the fashion in some circles to accuse the media of being the sinister cause of all of society's ills, I have not argued as such. The media are not the sole manipulators of mass consciousness. But they certainly do their share.

TV critic Les Brown argues that television not only misrepresents particular ethnic groups, it is "guilty of an unrealistic portrayal of the whole human race."[2] As already noted, these portrayals are taken for the real thing by large numbers of people, by *all of us* at one time or another. The make-believe media's impact is experienced daily. Children fashion their play and fantasy life around media characters and television-marketed toys. Adults draw upon media themes for verification of their life experiences. Many of our social misconceptions have their origin or find verification in the entertainment world. For many people, the last chapter of history or political reality is the Hollywood film or teledrama they saw. This is true not just of ordinary viewers but of political leaders. During a terrorist crisis, President Ronald Reagan remarked: "After seeing *Rambo* last night, I know what to do next time this happens." Not such a joke when coming from a president who often drew upon cinema to verify his understanding of real life.

Syndicated columnist Richard Cohen offered these observations about an acquaintance who found "reality" in the film *Mississippi Burning:*

> It was not the FBI that desegregated the South. It was a handful of Black and White students who did, and they were joined by literally thousands of southern Blacks whose courage, even now, seems incredible. . . .
>
> One of those with whom I saw the movie was a young physician. . . . He bought the story in its entirety. When I told him how the FBI solved the case [by bribing an informer], he found it hard to believe me. After all, he had just seen otherwise. Did he know the FBI had not a single Black agent at the time? How could he? He had just seen one in [the] film. Did he know that the struggle to desegregate the South did not come down to a cops-and-robbers fight between the FBI and the Ku Klux Klan but amounted to an uprising by many southern Blacks allied with some northern Whites? No. And now he might never know.[3]

Other examples of how people use the entertainment media as a source of misinformation about real life can be found throughout this book.

It is sometimes said that people are better informed today because of the media. Neal Postman argues the contrary. He maintains that earlier in U.S. history, when the printed word was dominant, reading was a prevailing source of both recreation and information. The taste for books was widespread. Even greater was the demand for newspapers and pamphlets. Tom Paine's *Common Sense* sold 400,000 copies to a population of three million. To do proportionately as well today, a publication would have to sell 32 million copies. Noah Webster's *American Spelling Book* sold 24 million copies between 1783 and 1843. *Uncle Tom's Cabin* sold 305,000 in its first year, equivalent to selling four million in one year nowadays. Between 1836 and 1890, the *McGuffey Reader* sold

107 million copies. Foreign observers noted how Americans of all social classes seemed to be immersed in printed matter. They also remarked on how lecture halls were well-attended throughout the land.[4]

Reading was a form of both recreation and learning at a time when there were fewer leisure-time distractions than at present. Through most of the nineteenth century, the printed word had a monopoly on mass communication. With the advent of the yellow press and the dime novel, the print medium began to serve more decisively as an instrument of mass amusement, divorced from information and learning.

The media's baneful effects on public discourse are today readily apparent. One need only compare the Lincoln-Douglas debates of 1854, in which ideas and arguments were given prolonged and complex treatment, with the televised presidential debates of today in which well-coached, image-conscious candidates are given two minutes to respond to contextless questions presented by journalists who specialize in superficial presentations of the news. News shows themselves have become forms of entertainment. Reports are given little or no background or context and are kept brief and upbeat. With the advent of modern electronic media, Postman suggests, Americans have probably become the best entertained and the least informed people in the Western world.[5] (In recent times, other peoples have undergone the same sort of cultural maldevelopment. American movies and prime-time television shows are almost as widely distributed in Europe, Asia, and Latin America as in the United States.)

Actually, the recitations, readings, debates, and storytelling of an earlier preelectronic era seem to have been far more engrossing than today's average television show. We are not really better entertained, only *more* entertained—and in a less imaginative but more sensationalistic way, with more glitter but less content, more distraction but less engagement, more sugar and spice but less nourishment, more goofiness but less wit, and even more information of a sort but less meaning.

By eating up our leisure time, fragmenting our attention, and keeping us from reading, the entertainment media retard our capacity and willingness to handle complicated ideas and engage in serious discourse. What passes for political discussion today often consists of "shows" featuring panel guests and sometimes audience participants who often must outshout each other in order to finish a sentence.

It has been argued that the printed word has not been displaced. Americans buy more books and magazines today than ever. Yet most of those publications are devoted to life-style activities, consumerism, recreation, romance, tabloid sensationalism, and the like. A large number of books and magazines focus on entertainment media figures. In any

Two-thirds of the U.S. public cannot name a single member of the Supreme Court, but a majority can identify Judge Wapner of "The People's Court" TV program. Television entertainment has a greater command on our consciousness than political reality.

given week, the best-seller list will contain several titles that feature the lives and loves of Hollywood and television personalities along with adventure and cold-war potboilers that read like the movie scripts they are destined to become. The printed word is increasingly at the service of the electronic image. Rather than being obliterated, it has been co-opted.

According to a 1989 *Washington Post* survey, more than two-thirds of all Americans cannot name a Supreme Court justice. The best known by far was the only woman on the Court, Sandra Day O'Connor, who was identified by 23 percent. Over 90 percent could not name another justice. Yet a majority of these same respondents, 54 percent, could identify Joseph Wapner, the judge on "The People's Court" television show.[6] In sum, the make-believe media not only distort reality, they preempt it. Little reason exists to ban books when so few persons want to read them. Little reason exists to ban critical films when they are accessible to so few. Censorship and restrictions on distribution are real problems in this allegedly free and open society. But equally dangerous is the way criticism is buried under the avalanche of entertainment distractions. In time, dissident ideas are not treated as dangerous, they are just not treated.

Even when the truth is not totally suppressed and parts of it get out to the public in an occasionally dissident book or film, it no longer seems all that important to a public conditioned to mass-market glitz and glamor. Thus books and films that tell us something of the truth about our history and our social and political life pose only a marginal challenge to the dominant ideology, if even that. They are crowded to the edges of the communication universe by the crush of mainstream offerings. Rather than being completely interdicted, truth is submerged in a sea of irrelevance. Silly amusement, contrived distraction, and endless hype become the foremost means of social control.[7] Preemption is the most effective form of social control. Rather than being politically repressed, people are made apolitical.

The Money Media

It is not enough to bemoan the biases of the make-believe media; we need also try to explain why they exist in the form they do. What is called "mass culture" today is a communication universe largely owned and controlled by transnational corporations. These corporations are highly concentrated capital formations whose primary functions are (1) *capital accumulation:* making a profit for their owners and investors; and (2) *ideological legitimation:* supporting an opinion climate that is favorable, or at least not hostile, to the continuation of profit-making and corporate economic dominance.

From the earliest days of the talkies, some of the largest corporations and banks in America have had a stake in the movie industry. By 1936, all the major studios had come under the suzerainty of either the Morgan or Rockefeller financial empires. The studios were in Hollywood, but the money was in New York. For several decades, an oligopoly of five majors, Paramount, MGM, RKO, Warner Brothers, and Twentieth Century Fox, dominated cinematic production, distribution, and exhibition, producing almost 90 percent of the films and owning over 70 percent of the first-run theaters in large metropolitan areas. By giving preferential distribution to their own films, they closed off the market to independent producers. At the same time, they could dictate terms to independent exhibitors who wanted access to popular and profitable movies.[8]

Such arrangements were deemed by the Justice Department to be a violation of the antitrust laws. In *United States v. Paramount Pictures* (1948), the Supreme Court agreed, ruling that the majors had to divest themselves of all their theaters in the United States. About that same time, television began taking a serious toll on movie attendance. By 1960, weekly patronage had declined by half; the number of movie houses also diminished. The studios attempted to lure audiences back with elaborate productions and cinematic techniques of a kind that television could not offer, such as Cinemascope and 3-D. Movies were now far fewer in number and more costly to make. The big-budget film had to be highly saleable in order to recoup its investment and make a profit. More than ever, the tendency was to rely on big-name stars, flashy scripts, and safe themes that would not divide audiences.[9]

Making a movie increasingly became a matter of assembling a "package," consisting of script, director, actors, and investors. Such deals were still initiated by studios, but independent producers, including actors and directors like Robert Redford, Clint Eastwood, Jane Fonda, and Francis Ford Coppola, started production companies with their own money. Movies could now be made without the studios. The advent of cable television and videocassettes offered new outlets and new investors. The independents became the prime source of politically aware, quality films like *Missing, Sounder, Executive Action, Matewan, Silkwood, Norma Rae, The China Syndrome, Reds,* and *The Milagro Beanfield War.*[10]

Still, independent production does not guarantee support for independent ideas. Filmmaking remains an enterprise available only to a select few. In 1988, the average cost of producing a movie in the United States was $18.1 million, not counting advertising expenses—which can equal production costs. In earlier days, when the majors produced hundreds of low-budget films yearly, they were able to swallow the costs of an occasional flop. For the independent company, however, one or two box-office failures can spell doom.

Investment support for almost all films, including independent ones, still comes from the major studios and from the entertainment divisions of parent business firms. (By 1982, the majors had all become subsidiaries of other large corporations.) The major studios also have revolving credit with the big banks. While they no longer manufacture films, they finance and distribute them. The independent producer of an iconoclastic film, who might not be able to get studio financing, has to

Who Presides?

If there be any doubt as to who presides over the communication world, a glance at this incomplete listing of people who sat on the board of directors of Capital Cities/ABC, as of 1987, is revealing:

Robert P. Bauman was also chairman and executive director of Textron and a director of Avco Financial Services, top contractors for the Pentagon.

William I. Spencer was also on the board of directors of United Technologies, a large military contractor.

M. Cabell Woodward, Jr. was also vice chairman, chief financial officer and a director of ITT, a major Pentagon contractor and multinational communications corporation.

Frank T. Cary was also a board member of IBM and Morgan Guaranty Trust; IBM is a major Pentagon contractor; Morgan is the primary bank for a large number of corporations.

Alan Greenspan also sat on the board of Alcoa, a major producer of aluminum and a military supplier.

Norma T. Pace was also a director of Sperry Corporation, a contractor for the Pentagon.

The late CIA director William Casey was a board member of Capital Cities before the merger with ABC and a former director of the Export-Import Bank and former head of the Securities Exchange Commission.

Persons of this background are not likely to support the funding of movies and teleplays that expose the interests behind the U.S. military build-up and U.S. intervention in the Third World.

Dolores Dwyer, " 'Amerika': The Corporate, Military, Star Wars Connection," *People's Daily World*, February 12, 1987.

rely on personal funds and sympathetic individual investors. Sufficient backing may take years to procure, as was the case with John Sayles's *Matewan*, the story of class warfare in the West Virginia coal mines.

Furthermore, the majors control all distribution. An independent usually has no way of gaining access to a national audience without dealing with the studios. Hundreds of films are made that never see the light of day. They may be fully financed, but they fail to get distribution because the studios decide they lack "commercial viability," or less often because of a film's controversial political content. Sometimes it is a combination of both, as studios tend to equate political controversy with lack of commercial appeal. The big distributors manifest "a reluctance to support films that deal with controversial subjects, owing to preconceived ideas about what kind of subject matter makes profits."[11]

In short, the film industry is still a major corporate enterprise whose financing, production, and distribution are controlled by rich companies and banks. Consider the Music Corporation of America (MCA). Originally a talent agency with links to organized crime, MCA controlled hundreds of performing artists and exercised a highly profitable grip on much of the entertainment world. Today, MCA is a billion-dollar firm in control of Universal Pictures and Universal Television, respectively the largest companies in cinema and television. Universal Pictures rakes in about 20 percent of the total revenues of Hollywood's film releases at home and abroad, and Universal Television controls a large chunk of weekly prime-time TV hours.[12] In 1990, MCA was bought by Matsushita, a Japanese multinational corporation.

As the MCA empire indicates, corporate concentration is found in both the film industry and television. To be sure, the growth of new networks such as Fox, along with cable and satellite systems and videocassette recorders (VCRs), has cut into the market enjoyed by CBS, ABC, and NBC. The big three's audience share had shrunk from 90 percent to a little over 70 percent by 1988. Still, the three networks enjoy a dominant position, selling over 86 percent of all TV advertising intended for a national audience, with total annual sales of up to $9 billion in recent years. In contrast, advertising sales for all cable networks remain around $1 billion. Profits for the three networks and the television stations they own were estimated at over a *trillion* dollars yearly in the late 1980s.[13]

Furthermore, the networks have been getting into the cable act, picking up millions of subscribers with their own cable shows. Other big corporations like Warner Amex, Times Mirror, and Viacom have won local franchises and bought up many smaller cable operators.[14] This trend toward concentration is likely to continue, especially since the Federal Communications Commission relaxed ownership restrictions in the mid-1980s. As with newspapers, so with television; more and more mergers have concentrated outlets in fewer and fewer hands, bringing a continual decline in independently owned broadcasting stations.[15]

In sum, our "free and independent media" are really huge business conglomerates that are able to control most of the communication universe. In the grip of a few rich interests, the mass media are really class media.

Product Control

Big corporations may own the film and television industries, but do they determine the media's ideological content? Isn't that done by producers, directors, scriptwriters, and actors, some of whom are on the left of the political spectrum? An investigation of the hundreds of films and television shows offered each year suggests that a truly leftist movie or teleplay, offering *a class analysis of power and wealth*, is something not to be expected from the mainstream media. While many progressive people work for the entertainment industry, they do not control the product any more than they control their own jobs. A right-wing media critic asserts that leftists were highly successful in infiltrating Hollywood during the 1930s and 1940s: "Hollywood, because of its wealth and influence, was one of the prime targets for subversion."[16] If trying to inject your political views into movies is "subversion," then the Hollywood leftists were remarkably unsuccessful. To be sure, they raised funds for popular front groups and signed numerous petitions but, as noted earlier, they were able to insert very little if any of their politics into the movies on which they worked. Even the more overtly political films seldom went beyond a bland New Deal liberalism and an affirmation of democracy over dictatorship.[17]

The most radical film of the 1930s, *Our Daily Bread* (1934), a story about itinerant unemployed workers who form a cooperative and work collectively, was denied funding by the studios and banks. The film's producer and director King Vidor received some financial help from Charles Chaplin but went deeply into debt on this limited-budget production.[18] A modest success at the box office, the film might have done even better with better financed promotion and distribution.

The situation today is not too different from what it was almost six decades ago when *Our Daily Bread* was made. Films that deviate from the mainstream political credo can be produced if there is a promise of profit, but they usually have to be toned down, rewritten, and larded with stars in order to get funded, as was the case with *Missing* (1982). Once made, they are usually accorded limited publicity and distribution, as was true of *1900* (1977) and *Reds* (1981). The dissident film *Romero* (1989)—the story of the Salvadoran archbishop who is murdered by a death squad because he sided with the oppressed people of his country—was denied funding by major studios and networks. It saw the light of day only because funds were forthcoming from sympathetic Catholic agencies. Such films can afford only limited publicity and distribution, depending on reviews and word of mouth for audiences.

Sometimes the distribution works in a mysterious way. As noted earlier, the remarkably revealing anti-imperialist *Burn!* (1969) was given a limited distribution and then taken off the screen after a day or two in some theaters that normally had weekly runs of movies. In other places *Burn!* was cancelled without a showing. More recently, there was

Rude Awakening (1989), about two sixties radicals who return to the United States from exile in Central America to alert people to a CIA plot. They confront former comrades who are now the self-involved, materialistic yuppies of the 1980s, and they are pursued by a crazed FBI agent because "they're much worse than terrorists; they're idealists." In Washington, D.C., this film was shown for merely four days, Monday through Thursday, only at 5 P.M. in one theater and only at 11 P.M. in another, making it too early or too late for most patrons.

Television shows undergo "product control," usually by network bosses and advertisers. Scripts that deal with the role played by U.S. government and multinational corporations in fostering class oppression at home and abroad seldom see the light of day. Far milder but still "sensitive" subjects experience difficulty. For years, TV's biggest advertiser, Procter and Gamble, imposed an editorial policy on its shows that read in part:

> There will be no material that may give offense either directly or by inference to any commercial organization of any sort. There will be no material on any of our programs which could in any way further the concept of business as cold, ruthless and lacking all sentimental or spiritual motivation. . . . Members of the armed forces must not be cast as villains. If there is any attack on American customs, it must be rebutted completely on the same show.[19]

Specific instances of censorship might be noted:

1. Westinghouse and its ad agency, McCann-Erickson, demanded a rewrite of a teleplay that did not portray the army in the best possible light. Westinghouse has a lot of contracts with the Defense Department.[20]

2. One ad agency denied sponsorship to the teleplay *Street Scene* because of its "lower class social level." Preferring to avoid any association of its products with "squalor," the agency noted: "The American consuming public as presented by the advertising industry today is middle class, not lower class; happy in general, not miserable and frustrated."[21]

3. Television writer David Rintels offered to write an episode for "The FBI" television series; it was to be a fictionalized version of the 1963 terror bombing of a Birmingham church in which four African-American girls were killed. The proposal had to pass four censors: the producing company, QM; the network, ABC; the sponsor, Ford Motor Company; and the FBI, any one of which could veto it without having to give a reason. Instead, Rintels relates:

[They] reported back that they would be delighted to have me write about a church bombing subject only to these stipulations: the church must be in the North, there could be no Negroes involved, and the bombing could have nothing at all to do with civil rights.

After I said I wouldn't write that program, I asked if I could do a show on police brutality, also in the news at that time. Certainly, the answer came back, as long as the charge was trumped up, the policeman vindicated, and the man who brought the specious charge prosecuted.[22]

4. Sometimes it is not a matter of censoring a particular script but of cancelling an entire show. "The Smothers Brothers" show, which touched on peace and antiwar themes occasionally, was taken off the air in 1969 because they did not submit their programs sufficiently ahead of time to CBS's Standards and Practices department for censorship.[23] (All the networks have such censorship departments.)

5. In 1982, "Lou Grant," a series about a crusading newspaper editor that touched on liberal themes, was cancelled under pressure from right-wing groups. Kimberly-Clark Corporation announced it would no longer sponsor the show because its star, Ed Asner, had announced plans to raise $1 million in medical aid for liberation forces in El Salvador. The cancellation caused a public furor among civil-liberties advocates and devoted viewers of the show.

6. A television movie about an African-American family, *Sister, Sister* (1982), discussed in Chapter Eight, was denounced as anti-Christian by right-wing religious groups because of its allegedly unfavorable portrayal of a pastor. The denunciation came before any of the groups actually had seen the movie. Five advertisers, General Electric, Colgate-Palmolive, Eastman Kodak, American Home Products, and Johnson & Johnson, quickly withdrew their sponsorship. They were replaced in time by five other sponsors with no loss to NBC.[24]

7. One of the world's largest advertisers, General Motors, reportedly talked about pulling all its advertising from Time-Warner magazines because that company distributed *Roger and Me* (1989), a scathing documentary that attacks GM for closing down its automobile plants in Flint, Michigan. The film included some telling digs at GM's CEO Roger Smith.[25] The GM ads were never actually withdrawn, but the threat was probably enough to make Time-Warner think twice about giving mainstream distribution to another mildly dissident film.

8. In 1990, Neighbor to Neighbor, a peace group, launched a boycott of Salvadoran coffee that included a thirty-second television spot

The CBS television series "Lou Grant" was canceled after coming under fire from right-wing groups and conservative corporate sponsors, who disapproved of its liberal themes and the progressive political activities of its star, Ed Asner.

with actor Ed Asner saying: "The murderous civil war in El Salvador has been supported by billions of American tax dollars and by the sale of Salvadoran coffee." The picture on the screen is of a coffee mug decorated with a Salvadoran flag and stuffed with U.S. dollars. Asner calls for an end to U.S. military aid to El Salvador and urges viewers to boycott Folgers because it imports Salvadoran coffee. "What [Folgers] brews is misery and death." The last shot is of the cup overturned with blood pouring out from it. Folgers is a subsidiary of Procter and Gamble, which responded furiously, announcing it would no longer advertise any of its many products on WHDH, a CBS affiliate in Boston. One of only two stations out of thirty that was willing to run the political ad, WHDH thereby suffered $1 million in revenue losses. (The other station carried no Procter and Gamble spots.) Procter and Gamble, the largest packaged-goods advertiser in the United States, warned its ad agencies that it would pull its commercials from any station that aired the controversial advertisement.[26]

Television shows are often prescreened by advertisers. Eastman Kodak noted: "In programs we sponsor on a regular basis, we do preview all scripts before the airing of the program. If we find a script is offensive, we will withdraw our commercials from the program."[27] A growing number of corporations along with their ad agencies have issued "hit lists" of shows they refuse to sponsor, because they contained "unacceptable materials." Among the programs were those that did not meet "family viewing standards," as well as "Saturday Night Live" with its occasionally liberally oriented political satire and "20/20" with its investigative journalism.[28]

A 1988 television movie about the Korean Air passenger plane that was shot down over the Soviet Union was subjected to politically motivated cuts and rewrites by NBC censors. The movie, *Shootdown*, based on R. W. Johnson's superb book by that title, argued that KAL 007 did not "stray" or "drift" into Soviet airspace but had been intentionally sent that way to test Soviet defense responses and spy on Soviet installations.[29] According to the show's producer Leonard Hill, NBC censors "played the role of grand inquisitor. It was quite a relentless interrogation and it turned into a war of attrition."[30] Dialogue criticizing the U.S. government for using the incident for its own political purposes was deleted. Specific criticisms of the Reagan administration were blunted. A lot of damning information was left out. Thus, the film did not mention that the U.S. Air Force destroyed all radar tapes after the incident or that the Korean pilot, Captain Chun, took out a lot of insurance the night before the flight. The network also insisted that Seymour Hersh's view be inserted. Hersh had written a book that simply assumed without evidence or argument that the plane had drifted innocently into Soviet airspace, a nearly impossible feat in an air corridor so heavily monitored by U.S. radar stations and U.S. planes. Referring to the struggle over this film, the *New York Times* noted that although network censorship departments have cut back drastically in their policing of sexual and other cultural taboos, "the network censors continue to be vigilant when it comes to overseeing the *political* content of television films."[31]

Vigilant is also what they are in regard to another taboo subject: abortion. As media critic Elayne Rapping noted in 1989, with the exception of the sitcom character Maude, nobody on prime-time or daytime television ever had an abortion. One "Cagney and Lacey" episode planned to have Cagney get an abortion, but the network scotched the story. A breakthrough came when NBC aired *Roe vs. Wade* (1989), a well-done film about the struggle for safe, legal abortions. The script was subjected to seventeen rewrites because network censors did not want the final product appearing too prochoice.[32] Scriptwriter Alison Cross said she was forced to tone down the character of the prochoice lawyer and make a stronger case for the advocates of compulsory pregnancy. A scene that showed some of the blood and filth of an illegal abortion mill was cut by NBC as being too unpleasant—a curious concern, considering the blood and gore that drenches prime-time TV.

Even before *Roe vs. Wade* was shown, compulsory-pregnancy advocates pressured at least ten sponsors to ask NBC to keep their ads off the show. To NBC's credit, network officials announced their determination to air (the watered-down) *Roe* regardless of how many sponsors they got.

One would hope for something better from public broadcasting. But censorial control and class bias are evident in what the Public Broadcasting System (PBS) offers. Nature films, concerts, and drawing-room dramas are the standard fare. News interviews on PBS focus predominately on representatives from government or establishment think tanks. What is missing from public television is the public, the wage and salary employees who compose 80 percent of the work force.

Made in USA Productions, an independent film organization, has struggled for some fifteen years to get a dramatic series about American labor on PBS. PBS officials turned down the series because part of the project's financing came from labor unions. They argued that interested parties could not be allowed to underwrite programs intended for public television. Others pointed out that a series on the history of labor hardly "promotes the specific financial interests" of labor unions. Furthermore, these same PBS officials allow corporations like General Motors, General Mills, Pepsico, Mobil, Dow Chemical, LTV Corporation, Conoco, and Merrill Lynch to finance pro-business shows like "Wall Street Week," "American Enterprise," "Adam Smith's Money World," Milton Friedman's "Free to Choose," and "Nightly Business Report," along with right-wing, pro-business commentators like William Buckley and John McLaughlin.

It was not until 1984 that a pilot script, *The Killing Floor*, the superb drama about the struggle to organize the meatpackers in Chicago in 1919, was aired by PBS's "American Playhouse," after much pressure and controversy. Labor unions provided only about 30 percent of the funding and were not allowed a peek at the script. But PBS ran *The Killing Floor* only once and did not again touch a labor history production. In 1990, PBS's "American Playhouse" refused to back a Made in USA screenplay entitled *Lost Eden*, which portrayed the struggles of female mill workers in Lowell, Massachusetts, in the 1840s. This decision came after "American Playhouse" initially had committed itself to the production.[33]

In 1990, a study by the City University of New York Committee for Cultural Studies found that PBS devoted nearly twice as many prime-time hours to business and social elites as to all other social strata combined. Programs about workers make up less than half of 1 percent of PBS prime time and most of that is about British rather than American workers. Programming about unions is practically nonexistent.[34] Along with PBS's underrepresentation of women and people of color, is its almost total exclusion of workers and labor.

Censorship is far more widespread than the publicized incidents suggest. According to a poll conducted by the Writers Guild of America, 86 percent of the writers who responded found from personal experience that censorship exists in television. Many claim that every script they have written, no matter how mild, has been censored. And 81 percent believe that "television is presenting a distorted picture of what is happening in this country today—politically, economically and racially."[35]

Even more common is what might be called "precensorship," a control over the image agenda that precludes the need for actual censorship. In the early 1980s, the word was out in Hollywood that politically controversial film and television scripts were not welcomed.[36] Corporate advertisers, Hollywood studio bosses, and TV network presidents are almost all politically conservative, as are their boards of directors and financial backers. Film and television creators develop a finely tuned sense of what is and is not acceptable to the people who own and control the industry. If they are not censored more often, it is because they censor themselves.[37] By defining beforehand what are the saleable subjects, the media bosses predetermine the kind of scripts they will get. "If you know which ideas have very little chance of passing the initial network-screening procedure, which is predetermined, you will bury those story ideas, often subconsciously, before they ever find their way onto a piece of paper."[38]

Other conservative censors are at work. As noted in Chapter Two, the military exercises an influence over many cinematic and television scripts, as do the FBI and the White House. Congressional inquisitions of the kind that the House Un-American Activities Committee made infamous (see Chapter Three) have effected an ideological control over what appears and who is allowed to write, direct, or act for the media. Additional censorial pressure has come from right-wing ideological pressure groups and self-appointed watchdog censors, such as the Moral Majority and the Coalition for Better Television, groups that have often exercised an influence far out of proportion to their numbers because they have greater support from leading advertisers than from the general population.[39]

For years, Hollywood policed itself, setting up the Hays Office and a "Production Code" that not only imposed limits on such things as sex and nudity, but also issued instructions "cautioning against criticisms of capitalism or glorification of 'the collective' or 'the common man.' "[40]

The dissident views that manage—in one form or another—to survive the maulings perpetrated by producers, investors, studio moguls, insurance underwriters, government officials, right-wing watchdogs, corporate advertisers, and network bosses must then face another group of ideological gatekeepers: the critics who review films and television shows. If they treat progressive story lines too favorably, their employers may charge them with diverging from their roles as balanced, detached cultural evaluators. Generally, little need exists to call them on these things since they already have been preselected and are not likely to take positions much beyond acceptable ideological molds.

The mainstream critic's definition of a political film is itself political. The dissident political film is readily and disparagingly identified as "ideological," "agitprop," "propagandistic," "leftist," or "preachy." In contrast, films and teleplays ladened with political values and images that are within acceptable parameters are less likely to be perceived as ideologically inspired.

Reviewers like *New York Times* TV critic John Corry openly assault politically dissident programs. Throughout the 1980s, Corry searched out shows that were insufficiently militant in their anticommunism or seemed favorably disposed toward nuclear disarmament, Third World liberation struggles, Cuba, Nicaragua, or peaceful cooperation with the Soviet Union. He would then write as a review what amounted to a polemical tract on the subject. Right-wing themes, however, would win his undiluted praise. Thus, Corry once cooed over a documentary telecast by PBS about the Miskito Indians of Nicaragua that painted the Sandinistas as ruthless oppressors. He neglected to tell his readers that the film was funded by the reactionary Moonies' Unification Church.

(PBS itself repeatedly noted the Moonie funding when the film was shown.)

New York Times movie reviewer Walter Goodman discards the appearance of neutral critic and gets into substantive political polemics when dealing with a leftist film. In his review of *Salvador,* he questions the film's "interpretation of history" that lays "blame on conservative forces in the United States for abetting the horrors in El Salvador." Goodman finds this to be "an arguable position." Is he suggesting that conservative administrations in the United States have not been involved in financing, training, equipping, advising, and directly abetting the repressive regime in El Salvador, even using U.S. military personnel, the CIA, and the Green Berets to do so? Are we hallucinating the billions of dollars in U.S. aid sent to a right-wing Salvadoran government that regularly unleashes its death squads and helicopter gunships upon the civilian population? Supremely unaware of his own centrist political biases, Goodman criticizes the film for failing to acknowledge that there "is any position between the murderers on the right and the Marxist-led" guerrillas. The persons occupying this mysterious middle ground in El Salvador are the ones supported by U.S. policymakers— and Goodman. They supposedly are unable to rein in the murderers on the right. Goodman also never tells us what is wrong with Marxists and what makes someone a Marxist in the Third World.[41]

During the 1980s, *Washington Post* TV critic Tom Shales, normally flaccid in his political postures, would stiffen visibly when confronted with something that leaned too far left or failed to toe the prevailing Soviet-bashing line of the Reagan years, such as Ted Turner's relatively friendly documentary on the USSR that CNN aired in 1987. On one occasion, Shales praised a TV movie for not being concerned about "a single chic social issue" and for being so firmly apolitical and entertainingly "escapist."[42] There is nothing inherently wrong with escapist entertainment; most of us need it now and then, but we might question why Shales finds it necessary to *praise* a movie for being empty of social content while dismissing social issues as "chic." Other *Post* reviewers, such as Rita Kempley, resort to snide, dismissive comments when confronted with films that contain any class-conscious politics, such as *Matewan* and *The Good Fight.*

Sometimes critics hide their political prejudices behind a cloak of artistic judgment. Gary Arnold, erstwhile movie critic for the *Washington Post* and later for the right-wing *Washington Times,* has been a regular practitioner of this technique. He pans any film that contains anti-militarist, anti-imperialist, feminist, or progressive themes, such as *Gandhi, Reds, Gaijin, Missing, Yol, The China Syndrome,* and *Tootsie,* faulting them because the plot is "unresolved," the characters "not developed," and the story line "weak." The films that rub against Arnold's conservative biases are judged as "tedious," "boring," "poorly made," and not worth seeing. Films that feed his sexism and conservatism, including junky war flicks like *The Big Red One* (1980) and the misogynistic *The Adventures of Ford Fairlane* (1990), are hailed as "well done" and "highly entertaining."

By focusing on form, the cultural gatekeepers can fault a movie without being too explicit about its politics—or their own. There are other reasons why critics favor form over content. The honesty and accuracy of the film's content are of less import than something called the "film experience." The film's crafting is accorded more attention than its relation to history or the real life it misrepresents. This approach is most evident among the high-toned, self-aggrandizing critics whose objective in writing reviews is not to give us new insight into the work under question but to impress us with their own brilliance. They operate from the questionable premise that the more complicated the form of the film, the more superior it is as a work of art. Content becomes less important than textures, visual effects, musical scores, and motif structure. Above all, *technique* preoccupies the highbrow and even middlebrow critics who are capable of writing sentences such as the following (gleaned from four different movie reviews that appeared in an "alternative" newspaper distributed in one metropolitan area)[43]:

"Intriguingly pantheistic, from the primal screeching of its musical
    score to its almost ceremonial elementality, the film suggests a
    bond between man and earth. . . . "

And: "For once, the director's over-the-top conceits are anchored in
    a fairly humdrum horror story, and allowed to flourish mainly at
    privileged moments of hallucinatory delirium. For the rest of the
    time, the story-telling is serviceable if occasionally lumpy. . . . "

And: "She has mainly abandoned the lightness that sparked her ear-
    lier work for a tic-ridden arsenal of pile driver techniques."

And: "This film looks out on utter devastation, but gathers the
    threads of its narrative—the visual and aural motifs, the sublime
    camera movements—to weave a final image of affirmation, tran-
    scendence, and eternity."

If readers do not know what "a final image of affirmation, transcendence, and eternity" looks like, they can be forgiven, for neither does the author of those inflated lines.

Giving attention to form while ignoring essence is a habit that carries over into both news commentary and academic scholarship. In their treatment of political affairs, news commentators and political scientists downplay content and tend to concentrate respectively on the image management and process of politics (what the media pundits call "spin analysis"). By focusing on style, strategy, and process and ignoring the substance of actual issues, news pundits and academics alike manage to avoid controversial substance and thereby maintain the appearance of neutral but very knowing observers. In fact, instead of neutralizing themselves as observers, they only succeed in neutralizing their subject matter. In their elaborate but essentially vapid offerings and in their primary dedication to displaying their own smarts, they come to resemble the culture critics. Instead of advancing our political understanding, they do their part to retard it.

Bourgeois media critics generally treat personalized experience as a deeper, more meaningful subject than experience or events derived from larger social issues. In Europe in 1931, unemployment was taking a heavy toll; fascism was gathering strength; Hitler was coming close to gaining power in Germany; and, in Paris, a leading artistic figure, Jean Cocteau, brought forth *Sang d'un Poete,* a film that gave serious—albeit not very edifying—attention to the subject of masturbation. It goes without saying that *Sang d'un Poete* was widely acclaimed by critics in the bourgeois press and art world and discussed at length by persons of culture. There is probably nothing inherently wrong with making a film about masturbation, even in troubled political times. What *is* wrong is when the make-believe media as a whole seem like one perpetual masturbation session, seizing upon any fanciful stimulant to keep us distracted from the social realities of our world.

12

The Myth of Cultural Democracy

Some people defend rather than deplore the censorship exercised within the entertainment industry. They maintain that media owners, investors, and advertisers have a right to do what they want with the product they market since it is they who put up the money. This contention at least avoids the usual cant about how the media are devoted to serving the public interest. It claims that those who pay the piper have every right to call the tune. In response, the following arguments might be raised:

First, the media are not just like any other business. As a *cultural* industry, they produce images and ideas. Their commodities are not just ordinary consumer items. The media exercise an influence upon public consciousness. In that respect they are more akin to education than to industry, and their offerings should be as much a matter of public concern as the quality of our education.

Second, even the goods and services of ordinary industry are not supposed to be marketed without regard to their effect upon consumers (although they often are). There supposedly exist safety and quality standards to protect consumers when they buy automobiles, toys, soaps, foods, and medicines. In short, producers have no absolute right over their product. They are not free from obligations toward the public.

Third, if it is true that those who pay the piper should call the tune, then the public itself ought to have a greater say, since the money they put up for their movie tickets is what keeps the whole industry going. Even with the "free entertainment" of television, consumers pay twice over. Billions of dollars in TV advertising costs annually are passed on to the public in the form of higher prices for goods and services. In addition, these billions are written off by sponsors as business expenses, allowing them to pay less taxes—and thereby shifting still more of the tax burden onto the rest of us.

Fourth, in the case of television, the airwaves do not belong to the networks or to any station owner. The airwaves are the property of the people of the United States, part of the public domain. Rich owners and sponsors therefore have no right to use them in ways that limit our access to ideological diversity.

Giving the People What They Want

It is also argued that the public already decides what is going to be shown. Supposedly the entertainment industry is in the business of making money for its owners, advertisers, and investors. To do that, it must reach the largest possible markets. Popular culture, therefore, is a product of popular demand. If the entertainment media produce trashy films and television programs, they do so because that's what the people want. People prefer to be entertained and distracted rather than informed and uplifted. If some reform-minded intellectuals do not like what is produced, too bad for them. While claiming to speak for the masses, the leftist critics are really opposed to what the masses want. So the argument goes.

There is certainly truth in the assertion that the entertainment media are primarily a money-making industry interested in reaching mass audiences. It is also true that the largest audiences are those that watch prime-time TV and flock to the Hollywood movies. Millions saw the *Rambo* films—each of which opened in over 2,000 theaters. Only a few thousand saw *Salt of the Earth*—which managed a brief run with only eleven small exhibitors, subjected to all sorts of coercions in its production and distribution.[1] Was it just a matter of public taste or was it the power of private distribution that determined the respective audience sizes of these films?

Another example is *Salvador* (1986), a searing drama about the U.S.-supported, counterrevolutionary, terrorist repression in El Salvador. This film was rejected by every major Hollywood studio and described by one of them as "a hateful piece of work."[2] Such a vehement rejection has less to do with market considerations than with political convictions. The film was eventually financed by British and Mexican investors and granted a very limited distribution. Was it really the public that was not interested in seeing *Salvador* or was it the studios that were not interested in showing it because of ideological reasons? The film was gripping, action-packed, and suspenseful, just the things that

A gripping, action-packed drama critical of U.S.-supported political repression and military terrorism in Central America, *Salvador* was rejected by every major Hollywood studio and gained only a limited distribution.

the public supposedly wants. But it did not have the right politics, so it got a cold shoulder from the studios. This suggests that the entertainment industry does not merely "give the people what they want"; it also is busy shaping those wants.

It is misleading to say that dissident films fail to reach a mass audience when in fact they are kept from mass audiences by the minimal distribution and limited publicity they receive. They have to rely on word of mouth and on reviews—which are often politically hostile. This is in sharp contrast to the multimillion-dollar publicity campaigns that help *create* the mass markets for the supposedly inherently "mass-market films." If a Rambo film has a "natural" mass market, why is it necessary to spend $20 million on a publicity hype that is intended to *create* a mass audience?

In sum, it is not simply a matter of demand creating supply. Often it is the other way around: supply creates demand. The first necessary condition for all consumption is accessibility to the product. Be it movies, television shows, or soft drinks, consumption will depend in large part on how well-distributed the product is. Prime-time TV shows, along with movies that open in every shopping mall in America, win large audiences not because there is a spontaneous wave of popular demand carrying them to the top, but because there is "a lot of conscious pulling *from* the top."[3]

Television audience size is to some degree predetermined by how available a show is to viewers, that is, by its viewing time. Change the time slot from 8 P.M. to 10 A.M. or midnight, and you will have changed the size and composition of the audience, even if the show itself remains exactly the same. This is why we can speak of a "prime time" that provides accessibility to the largest possible audience, regardless of the content of particular shows.

This argument should not be overstated. The public is not infinitely malleable. Supply does not always create demand. Some media offerings flop despite vigorous publicity and wide distribution. But even these instances in their own way illustrate how the cultural democracy of "giving people what they want" is too simple an explanation of what the media do. The media industry foists upon us what it thinks we want, often promoting films and television shows that we never asked for and do not particularly like. With enough publicity and distribution, even these flops are destined to reach more people than the financially starved dissident films.

Films and teleplays that are ideologically conservative will sometimes get vigorous support no matter what their box-office draw. We already noted that in the wake of the House Un-American Activities Committee investigations of Hollywood from 1947 to 1954 the film industry made more than fifty anticommunist movies that the public never asked for. These pictures were box-office flops—but Hollywood kept making them, for the industry was out to please the right-wing Red-bashers in Congress, not the viewing public. It was not financial gain and popular demand that motivated production but considerations of ideological orthodoxy.

The Pentagon—John Wayne production of *The Green Berets*, a movie filled with militaristic violence and superpatriotic hype designed to boost the U.S. war effort in Vietnam, appeared at the height of the antiwar protests when the Vietnam war was more unpopular than ever. There was no great public demand for this kind of motion picture. It flopped. Yet *The Green Berets* maintained massive distribution, playing to sparsely attended theaters in just about every mainstream movie chain in America.

The most expensive anticommunist movie ever made, *Inchon* (1982) cost $48 million plus another $10 million to $20 million for publicity and a million-dollar audience "sweepstakes" to boost attendance. This Korean war epic produced by the right-wing Reverend Sun Myung Moon, had everything the public supposedly craves: a star-studded cast, a spectacular production, a love angle, blood-filled battle scenes, militaristic superpatriotism, a simplistic rewrite of political history, and

an empty-headed plot about Communist aggressors who murder innocent civilians and are themselves then wiped out by a right-wing war
hero. Yet it was a box-office disaster. The film was mercilessly panned
even by normally anticommunist critics, one of whom described it as
"the worst movie ever made." But this did not prevent it from opening
in 1,250 theaters across the United States. The fact that people did not
want *Inchon* did not keep the multimillionaire Moon from trying to
make them want it.

Americans are not terribly excited about the U.S. space program nor
are they particularly happy about seeing billions of their tax dollars
appropriated for it. Yet great effort and money were spent in producing
and promoting *The Right Stuff* (1983), a film that glorified America's
space ventures. It, too, was a box-office flop.

Likewise, the television mini-series "Amerika," about an imaginary
Soviet invasion of the United States, attracted a good deal of attention
because of public protests against its inflammatory, cold-war mon-
gering. It got a big audience the first night then dropped drastically in
ratings for the rest of the week—despite its publicity, its sensationalistic
anticommunism, and a $44 million production tab.

Films such as *Cobra* (1986), *Rambo III* (1988), and *The Dead Pool*
(1988) were box-office disappointments. Given their multimillion-
dollar publicity campaigns, these motion pictures all had fairly strong
opening weekends, but they then flopped. This may indicate either that
people's tastes are changing or they are getting jaded and need a different stimulation. Even people who have been conditioned to respond to
junk begin to tire of consuming the same old junk.

It might be noted again: if these films are just what the public
wants, one wonders why it is necessary to spend $10 million to $20
million on each of them in massive publicity campaigns in order to
convince the public to go see them. Those who claim to give us what
we like presume to know what we like. Then they do everything they
can to *make* us like what they serve up.

What Does the Public Want?

Despite all the claims about "giving the public what it wants," audience
preferences can be difficult to divine. In the early 1980s, the network
brass thought the public was in a "conservative mood" and "moving to
the right." Having so decided, they produced a number of law-and-
order television series like "Walking Tall," "Today's FBI," and "Strike
Force," all of which suffered dismal ratings and died early deaths.[4]

The media production process involves a lot more than just satisfying the public. In fact, the public is not the first audience a producer has in mind. If something is to be shown, it must first please its financial backers, its would-be sponsors, the studios, and the networks. It is with these interests that the producer has the most direct interaction. Audience influence is indirect. All films and most television series are completed before they are shown to the public; hence they cannot be altered to reflect audience feedback. Public reactions that come in the form of individual letters are usually not given much weight, being considered unrepresentative of a large heterogeneous audience. Market research and rating services are also not that helpful, since they seldom tell anything about reactions to specific content. The only direct feedback is from network representatives who preside over the productive process and from the producer's family and friends who are usually no more representative of the public than the media bosses themselves.[5]

Sometimes "what the public likes" is really what the producers like. Les Brown observes that golf has a very limited audience, yet, in defiance of the usual market criteria, it receives more television exposure than other more popular sports. He speculates that this is due to its being a favorite recreation of media executives, agency men, and corporate sponsors. Since golf matters to them and to nearly everyone with whom they associate, the game is regularly televised. "This recalls the possibly apocryphal story of the sponsor who, in the early days of television, berated his advertising agency for buying Sunday afternoon programs. 'No one watches television on Sundays,' he argued. 'They're all at the polo matches.' "[6]

On the relatively infrequent occasions the public does exercise direct input, it is usually of a censorial nature, a protest against a particular film or show. Given their own ideological proclivities, studios, networks, and sponsors are more responsive to pressures from the right than from the left. It is hard to believe that Procter and Gamble—concerned that its shows not utter a critical word about business, the military, or any other conservative interest—would respond very favorably to grievances expressed by leftist protest groups.

This should remind us that there is not *one* public but *many* publics. The advertising community has a strong preference for a youngish, middle-class audience as opposed to low-income rural or urban publics with less buying power. Because of the relative shortage of telephones in the poorer households, low-income audiences are also underrepresented in the telephone polls and surveys that measure audience preferences—just as they are underrepresented in polls that measure political opinions.[7]

A World of Their Own

The much-wooed audience doesn't make "demands." Groups don't fire off telegrams asking for a sitcom about waitresses working for a gruff diner owner; people don't tell pollsters they're pining for intelligent comedy about irreverent army doctors in Korea. . . . Public opinion, such as it is, speaks with a vast silence, or with a background yammer that is incessant, indecipherable, contradictory. What kind of guidance is this for cultural suppliers?

The yammer guarantees, though, that executives, producers, and writers are going to turn their antennae to the murmurs of public concern that come home to them, to the preoccupations that seep into their private worlds. They do not often go looking for issues; it would be more true to say that issues go looking for them. If an issue makes headlines in the *New York Times* for months and years, if it makes the cover of *Time* or *Newsweek*, if one starts hearing about it at the tennis courts, if the neighbors' kids are into it, if one's wife hears about it at the hairdresser's in Beverly Hills, if one's daughter comes home from Berkeley for Thanksgiving and is talking about it, then no mystery about it: The issue is going to seep into the common lore, fairly begging to be concocted into the stuff of entertainment. And so it happens that the networks are often developing shows on similar themes, even with similar approaches. During his incarnation as a top supplier, Grant Tinker said, "There are always these coincidences. I mean, you just try to do a show about [something] and you are stunned to read in the trades that somebody else is doing that. I never understand how it happens but it happens a lot." It happens routinely in a small, dense world; the themes come out of the same cultural air.

Todd Gitlin, *Inside Prime Time* (New York: Pantheon, 1983), p. 226.

When media bosses make the effort to ascertain what the public really wants, the outcome can be surprising. In April 1983, *Variety* published the results of a confidential National Association of Broadcasters (NAB) study of audience attitudes toward television, based on five hundred in-depth interviews and one thousand telephone interviews. The survey findings were overwhelmingly negative. Respondents complained that television was less entertaining than ever; about half of them said they were watching less TV than in earlier years. More than half wanted "more relevant" programs that gave audiences the chance to participate "in discussion or [ask] questions of political figures."[8] Not surprisingly, the NAB refused to release the study. Five years later in October 1988, when I asked an NAB representative if nonrelease was due to the fact that the report's findings were so unfavorable, she refused to comment. Nor would she give out any further information about the survey.

An earlier 1970s Roper poll revealed that though people watched a lot of television, they rated it poorly. Like other addictions such as drugs or cigarettes, TV programs "have a built-in failure to satisfy that provides only enough pleasure to bring viewers back for more."[9] Rating services like the Nielsen Company have documented a steady erosion of prime-time network audiences since 1980.[10] A 1985 Roper poll reported that only 8 percent of viewers rated themselves as "very satisfied" with television entertainment shows, and 43 percent only "moderately satisfied." Nearly half registered some degree of dissatisfaction.[11]

A survey in Great Britain yielded similar results. Coverage of the doings of the royal family and other such "royal events"—thought to be close to the hearts of most British viewers—held an attraction for only 22 percent. Over 55 percent of the British public wanted serious news and documentaries and only 35 percent preferred game shows.[12]

Shows or films that are commercially viable and win an interested audience may nevertheless be canceled because of ideological concerns. As noted in the previous chapter, in 1982 the series "Lou Grant" came under right-wing pressure because of its consistently liberal themes and the outspokenly progressive political activities of its star, Ed Asner. Supporters of the program launched letter-writing campaigns and public rallies. Thousands picketed CBS headquarters to keep the show on the air. More significantly, by September of that year "Lou Grant" was sixth from the top among some ninety shows. Nevertheless, the network ignored this popular support and bowed to rightist pressure by cancelling the series, replacing it with a show that had a lower rating. The make-believe media will give us what we want as long as what we want is not politically troublesome.

It is assumed by media manufacturers that most people want to escape reality, not confront it. But as we have just seen, there are high-powered escapist productions that are flops. And there are large and interested publics who respond positively to quality dramas that contain real-life relevance. The mini-series "Roots" lacked all the usual glamor and glitz yet it reached record audiences, including many people who normally do not watch television.[13] Other quality made-for-television movies with socially relevant messages have won impressive viewing audiences, including *The Autobiography of Miss Jane Pittman* (1974), *A Woman Called Moses* (1978), *A Matter of Sex* (1984), *The Burn-*

The TV mini-series "Roots" dealt with some of the history of slavery in America. It lacked all the usual promotional hype yet it played to record audiences, demonstrating that the public will respond to serious quality drama.

ing Bed (1984), and *Shootdown* (1989). Christensen notes: "Contrary to conventional wisdom, audiences do not ignore political films. Although message movies hardly ever rank as blockbusters, many have actually turned a handsome profit."[14] He also notes that "sixties films" like *Easy Rider* (1969), *Medium Cool* (1969), and the highly political French-made *Z* (1969) "were sufficiently profitable to make the studios take notice, while big productions like *Hello Dolly* and *Ryan's Daughter* lost more money than most of the political films cost. . . . "[15]

Other quality political films that dealt with controversial issues in a critically progressive way have been box-office successes, such as *Julia* (1977), winner of three Oscars, *Coming Home* (1978), *Norma Rae* (1979), *The China Syndrome* (1979), and *Missing* (1982). Political films, dealing with U.S. imperialism in Latin America, have played to enthusiastic but—given their limited distribution—relatively small audiences: *El Norte* (1983), *Latino* (1985), *Salvador* (1986), and *Romero* (1989).

The public may not always know what it likes until it sees what is offered and until it can get attuned to the new offerings. Most people have little exposure to alternative social and political views. They tend to "know" what has been fed to them. Yet, when introduced to new realities, they sometimes respond with surprising alacrity in ways that the mass-market hucksters never anticipated. We usually do not have much opportunity to ascertain what the potentials of public taste might be, since the media industry has no interest in exploring such potentials and instead offers us a prefabricated, precensored, diluted product that seldom ventures onto politically taboo ground.

Given the often indeterminate nature of audience preferences, there is substantial opportunity to influence and even create public tastes. The entire advertising industry is predicated on the notion that people do not automatically know what they want and public consumption can be preconditioned by publicity and product availability. Again, it is a matter of supply creating demand.

Karl Marx wrote: "Not only the object of consumption, but also the manner of consumption is produced by production; that is to say, consumption is created by production not only objectively, but also subjectively. Production thus creates the consumer."[16] As applied to the realm of culture, this production creates what Antonio Gramsci called the ideological hegemonic process.[17] Alternative views are preempted and pushed to the margins of society, rather than censored outright. Censorship is, of course, necesssary and useful, but it becomes counterproductive if relied upon too heavily. Hegemony is more effective when oppositional themes are seen as so lacking in validity as to be unworthy of exposure or rebuttal. Thus, the bulk of the public remains unaware and untouched by dissident understandings of past and present political reality.

In time, people become conditioned to accepting slick, shallow, mediocre, and politically truncated media. Production indeed creates the consumer. The standardized images become the only digestible ones. With enough conditioning, consumers will consume even that which does not evoke their great enthusiasm. It is like living in one of the many places in America that specialize in mediocre restaurants: customers settle for the dismal fare that is served them, having access to nothing better. Likewise with entertainment: people end up watching movies or TV programs they might have never considered had there been something better to choose from. If they were never exposed to anything else to begin with, they are all the more inclined to seek diversion in whatever is offered. This preconditioned consumption is then treated as evidence that the public is getting what it wants.

This is not to say that everyone is waiting for more brilliant anti-imperialist movies like *Burn!* or revolutionary ones like *Reds* or great television mini-series like "Roots." Some viewers may always prefer junk products. They may find that nothing can compare to contrived plots, instant stimulation, fast and violent action, authoritarian characters, and superficially conventional themes. Even in Pericles' Athens there must have been people who would have preferred the spectacle of Rome's blood-soaked arena. What is remarkable is the converse: despite all their exposure to trash, many people are still keenly interested in quality productions dealing with themes that go beyond apolitical idiocy or mainstream orthodoxies.

Pseudorelevance
and Pseudochoice

The public is not a purely dependent variable in all this. New concerns are generated by particular publics in response to changing social conditions. Committed to marketing timely products, the entertainment industry must give attention to newly emerging sentiments. Therefore, even while trying to mold popular feelings, the media respond to them to some extent. Of course, there is no guarantee this will always happen. The abortion issue was kept completely out of teleplays and soap operas for decades after becoming a public issue, because it was considered too divisive of audiences and therefore potentially harmful to ratings. Generally, however, the entertainment media have been somewhat more willing to tap into controversial themes, especially since the late 1960s.

What should not be overlooked, however, is the entertainment industry's capacity to handle burning issues in ways that mute their impact and reduce their significance. Oppositional realities are incorporated into the mainstream media but in a predigested form. Racism is portrayed as little more than the rantings of individual bigots, with no recognition given to its institutional and economic dimensions. Poverty becomes just one of those unfortunate and unavoidable accidents of life. Official injustice and corruption become the doings of a few bad apples. The Vietnam war becomes nothing more than a tough, bitter experience for the soldiers involved. Young radicals are just spoiled malcontents with personal grievances against authority. Political leaders face hard choices about integrity and fair play but rarely take a stand on real economic issues. Resistance to injustice is expressed through gutsy individual defiance rather than collective action. Through its own special packaging process, the make-believe media can appear topical and socially relevant, without having to deal with the real dimensions of social conflict.

What we usually get is pseudorelevance. Tribute is paid both to popular feelings and to the concerns of the rich and powerful. Irreconcilable forces are smoothed over. The media reinforce the hegemonic ideology while giving the appearance of challenging it. Oppositional opinion is articulated but contained; it is contoured to the dominant ideology. "Suppression proceeds alongside accommodation: sometimes one predominates, sometimes the other. The blandness of television entertainment in the 1950s . . . was displaced in the 1970s by a style of entertainment that takes account of social conflict and works to domesticate it—to individualize its solutions, if not its causes."[18]

The view of the world that most films and television shows deliver is apolitical or antipolitical, "but its consequences are not. The debased prime-time product doesn't just occupy space, it prevents other 'more intelligent, complicated, true, beautiful, or public-spirited' forms of popular culture from emerging."[19] The choices remaining open to us are limited ones. They contribute to the illusion that we have a cultural democracy, a culture of our own choice. What we actually have is a narrow range of pseudochoices. Jeffrey Schrank puts it well:

A pseudo-choice should not be confused with the absence of choice. A pseudo-choice is a real choice exercised by a person using what is commonly recognized as free will, but the choice has carefully controlled boundaries that often exclude what the person choosing really wants. . . . In pseudo-choice, the world is a multiple-choice test. We are free to answer questions only in terms of the options presented. . . . The factors shaping the choices are invisible to most people. . . .

Pseudo-choices are often supported by advertising or public relations efforts which invariably attempt to make them appear far more significant than they are.

They are preselected, controlled choices that tend to prevent people from asking the basic question: "What do I really want?" By so doing, they contribute to the state of general detachment and help create large numbers of people who simply don't know what they want. And those who don't know what they want are the most easily satisfied with pseudo-choice.[20]

The independent production of films and the proliferation of cable television stations does not guarantee better entertainment, only *more* entertainment, more of the same with slightly different packaging, "more choices and more variations in style and format on what are still pretty basic pop culture themes and perspectives."[21]

It is time to summarize some of the points made in this book: The entertainment media do more than entertain us. For many people they create social and historical images that are embraced as reality. The media have a twofold purpose. First, they make money for their corporate owners. The entertainment industry is big business, manifesting the same symptoms of high profits, hostility toward labor unions, and increasing concentration of ownership found in other big businesses.

Second, the media help legitimate the hegemonic ideological system with images and themes that propagate private enterprise, personal affluence, individual acquisitiveness, consumerism, superpatriotism, imperialism, racial stereotyping, and sexism. The make-believe media also do their part in bolstering negative views about working-class people and labor unions. They sensationalize crime and crime-fighting, helping to activate a crime phobia in the public mind and a desire for authoritarian and vigilante solutions. For decades the media have created sinister images of Communists and revolutionaries, while glorifying the all-American superheroes who protect hearth and home from foreign Red-Menace terrorists and domestic subversives.

The media rely mostly on violent, shallow, contrived, formularistic plots and characters. The viewing public is bombarded with banalities, trivialities, imbecilities—but also with sociopolitical orthodoxies.

Themes that raise questions about the existing arrangements of wealth and power are, with rare exception, kept out of sight and sound. The broader systemic causes of social problems must not be dwelled upon, although the symptoms may be bemoaned—but not too much. The injustices and inequities of the modern capitalist social order at home and in the Third World are glossed over or ignored entirely. In the fictional world of film and television, adversities are caused by happenstance or by ill-willed individuals rather than by economic and social forces. Problems are solved by individual efforts within the system rather than collective effort against it.

Above all, the existing class structure and prevailing distribution of economic wealth are either ignored or accepted as the best of all possible social arrangements. The media rarely attack the established institutions of wealth and power. The economic class structure must not be challenged in its fundaments.

Far from being the free and independent media of a cultural democracy, the entertainment industry is the centralized domain of a rich oligarchy. The media regularly undergo a rigorous political censorship from their financial backers, producers, and studio and network officials. A leftist perspective is about as rare in the entertainment media as it is in news reportage and commentary.[22] Media productions that present a critical reading of social reality and history seldom find sufficient financial backing or mainstream distribution. With some notable exceptions, they are usually denied mass-market visibility.

The make-believe media's existing fare is justified as being the product of "popular culture," of a cultural democracy that gives people what they want. It is supposedly not the media's fault if people prefer the trashy or conventional stuff. It is said that people robbing banks makes for more inherently interesting entertainment than banks robbing people. In fact, the public may be getting bored with the car-chase, shoot-'em-up, cops-and-robbers, hackneyed "thrillers," with their police-helicopter, freeze-or-I'll-shoot showdowns. In fact, a story about banks robbing people can make for much more compelling drama than people robbing banks, as *A Matter of Sex* (1984) demonstrated.

What are we to make of popular culture? The word "popular" is an adjective for "populace," meaning "of the people." But as it exists today in the United States and much of the world, popular culture is anything but that. It does not arise from the people. Authentic popular culture—as manifested in a folk culture, including dances, songs, music, crafts, storytelling, reading groups, book circles, street theater, community drama clubs, children's play culture, and even ordinary primary group sociability and conversation—are preempted or at least greatly diminished by cinema and much more so by television. Real popular culture has been replaced by a marketed mass culture, an electronic image culture, in which a few highly centralized production units feed messages and images to millions of consumers.

Doing It Right

There is no going back to a pretechnological age when people entertained themselves by telling stories around the fireplace—although one can still spend some enjoyable evenings doing just that. We face multibillion-dollar, mass-media conglomerates that reach millions of people, filling their minds with authoritative images and beliefs about the world and dulling their sensibilities and imaginations. What can we do about this?

First, there are the obvious things. We need to exercise the limited consumer sovereignty available to us by voting with our pocketbooks and refusing to attend slick, superficial, Hollywood movies. Also we need to stop sacrificing large portions of our lives to the unsatisfying but addictive television set.[23] We need to rediscover, or discover for the first time, the gratifying nourishments of reading and of engagement in community activities with other humans. There is much talk today about people taking control of their own lives. One way to start is by dropping out of the mass-media culture as much as possible and reclaiming our own brains and sensibilities.

Second, when progressive themes find their way into films and teleplays, such offerings deserve our patronage, assuming they are well done. Sometimes it takes a good deal of special effort to locate the poorly distributed, underpublicized dissident offerings. But it is worth doing, if one wants to be truly entertained rather than momentarily distracted. This is not to say that we must never indulge ourselves with light, distracting, and genuinely amusing entertainment—especially of a kind that does not insult our intelligence.

Third, we need to organize politically to pressure the media into creating better and more politically diverse offerings. "Talking back to our television sets" is something we have to do through organized action. Women's groups, labor unions, ethnic and environmental organizations, and politically dissident groups must exert direct pressure upon the media, not just to protest the trash but to demand something better and to voice support and encouragement when superior films and programs do appear. Public pressure is immediately seen by some as an infringement on the media's right to free speech. But protestors also have the right to exercise their free speech and should do it in a more organized and vigorous fashion, their goal being not to censor programs but to broaden and deepen the choices.

Fourth, in regard to television, we need a growth in alternative public-access TV. The airwaves of America are the property of the people of the United States. We need noncommercial, publicly funded television, featuring documentaries, docudramas, and movies that are open to all political perspectives, including those on the left, including the concerns of labor, women, people of color, environmentalists, and peace groups—interests that normally do not enjoy access to national television and do not have sufficient funding to distribute their messages to a mass audience. All public television today is corporate-financed. If this political system is truly dedicated to pluralism, it must make special provision by law and public funding to provide a platform for the democratic and reformist voices in news and entertainment that seldom reach mass audiences for want of money.

Fifth, in regard to movies, the money-dominated film industry should be supplemented—and challenged—by a publicly funded film corporation that is free to venture on its own into forbidden political realms. The Australian "film renaissance" of the 1970s that brought us such fine productions as *The Chant of Jimmy Blacksmith* (1978) and *My Brilliant Career* (1979) owed its existence, in large part, to the Australian Labor government's willingness to augment public financing of film-making. So in the United States, if there is money and distribution to encourage better things, more creative and critical talents are likely to come forth.

Finally, political struggle in the larger social realm helps create a climate of opinion that allows the mainstream media opportunity to treat somewhat more controversial and less mendacious images. For instance, a discerning television viewer might have noted that not long after the Iran-Contra scandal rocked the Reagan administration and people began talking about a liberal resurgence, more liberal themes started appearing in prime-time television scripts. By creating larger and stronger realms of political protest, we create more legitimacy for representations of realities that are so often suppressed.

This is the least we owe ourselves and our society: the chance to move away from a lobotomizing, propagandizing mass culture and toward media that offer a more faithful engagement with life in all its beautiful, intriguing, amusing, awesome—and sometimes dreadful—realities.

The make-believe media are no less free from conservative political bias and ideological control than the news media. Of this we should become aware if we are going to resist indoctrination and mind-manipulation. And resist we must. The struggle against corporate cultural hegemony is an important part of the struggle for political democracy itself.

Notes

Chapter 1 Political Entertainment

1. Robert Cirino, *We're Being More Than Entertained* (Honolulu: Lighthouse Press, 1977).
2. George Gerbner, Larry Gross, and William Meldoy, eds., *Communications Technology and Social Policy* (New York: Wiley, 1973).
3. Hal Himmelstein, *Television Myth and the American Mind* (New York: Praeger, 1984), p. 3.
4. Herbert Schiller, *The Mind Managers* (Boston: Beacon Press, 1973), pp. 79–80.
5. Erik Barnouw, "Television as a Medium," *Performance*, July/August 1972, cited in Schiller, *The Mind Managers*, p. 80.
6. Ralph Arthur Johnson, "World without Workers: Prime Time's Presentation of Labor," *Labor Studies Journal*, 5, Winter 1981, p. 200.
7. Schiller, *The Mind Managers*, p. 11.
8. For a critical study of the news media, see Michael Parenti, *Inventing Reality: The Politics of the Mass Media* (New York: St. Martin's Press, 1986).
9. Jack G. Shaheen, *The TV Arab* (Bowling Green, Ohio: Bowling Green State University Popular Press, 1984).
10. Walter Lippmann, *Public Opinion* (New York: Macmillan, 1922), pp. 88–89.
11. Ellen Holly, "The Role of Media in Programming of an Underclass," *Black Scholar*, January/February 1979, pp. 34–35. For a fuller discussion of African-Americans in the media, see Chapter Eight.
12. Jeffrey Schrank, *Snap, Crackle, and Popular Taste* (New York: Delta, 1977), p. 84.
13. Jerry Mander, *Four Arguments for the Elimination of Television* (New York: Quill, 1978), pp. 250–52.
14. Ibid., p. 257; and passim; also Martin Large, *Who's Bringing Them Up? Television and Child Development* (Gloucester, U.K.: MHC Large, 1980).
15. See the reports by David P. Phillips in *Science*, 196, June 24, 1977, pp. 1464–65; and in *Science*, 210, August 25, 1978, pp. 748–50.
16. The example of *The Deer Hunter* is from Tim Lahaye, *The Hidden Censors* (Old Tappan, N.J.: Revell, 1984); all the other examples are from Schrank, *Snap, Crackle*, p. 29. For other instances of the relationship of trigger effect to violence, see the discussion in chapter ten: "Child Abuse."
17. Schrank, *Snap, Crackle*, p. 154.
18. George Gerbner and Larry Gross, "The Scary World of TV's Heavy Viewer," *Psychology Today*, April 1976, p. 45.
19. Catherine Larza and Michael Jacobson, eds., *Food for People Not for Profits* (New York: Ballantine, 1975), p. 165.
20. *Washington Post*, February 1, 1983.
21. *City Paper* (Washington D.C.), May 10, 1985.
22. Leslie Goodman-Malamuth, "Hollywood Hucksters," *Public Citizen*, April 1986, p. 11; *New York Times*, January 13, 1989.

23. Eli Rubinstein, George Comstock, and John Murray, eds., *Television in Day to Day Life: Patterns of Use* (Washington, D.C.: National Institute of Mental Health, n.d., circa 1975).

24. Gerbner and Gross, "TV's Heavy Viewer," p. 42.

25. Richard Adler, "A Context for Criticism" in Richard Adler, ed., *Television as a Cultural Force* (New York: Praeger, 1976), p. 6.

26. *Washington Post*, July 27, 1980; UPI report in the *Bennington Banner* (Vermont), April 27, 1985.

27. Schrank, *Snap, Crackle*, p. 27.

28. Barbara Ehrenreich, "Life After Spudding Out," *Washington Post*, April 5, 1988.

29. Newsletter of the International Organization of Journalists, March 1987, p. 4.

30. T. H. Guback, "Film as International Business," *Journal of Communication*, 24, Winter 1974, pp. 94–95.

Chapter 2   Swarthy Hordes and Other Aliens

1. Paul Jacobs and Saul Landau, with Eva Pell, *To Serve the Devil*, vol. 1 (New York: Vintage, 1971) for documentary evidence on the mistreatment of Native American Indians. For a discussion of the relationship of imperialism to racism, see Michael Parenti, *The Sword and the Dollar: Imperialism, Revolution, and the Arms Race* (New York: St. Martin's Press, 1989), Chapter Eight.

2. Tom Engelhardt, "Ambush at Kamikaze Pass," *Bulletin of Concerned Asian Scholars*, Winter–Spring 1971, p. 28.

3. Ibid.

4. Ibid.

5. Ibid.

6. Ralph Willett, "The Nation in Crisis: Hollywood's Response to the 1940s" in Philip Davies and Brian Neve, eds., *Cinema, Politics and Society in America* (New York: St. Martin's Press, 1981), p. 62.

7. Engelhardt, "Ambush at Kamikaze Pass," pp. 34–35.

8. J. Fred MacDonald, *Television and the Red Menace* (New York: Praeger, 1985), p. 135.

9. Both the Gene Autry and Lone Ranger statements are in MacDonald, *Television and the Red Menace*, p. 136.

10. Ibid.

11. Engelhardt, "Ambush at Kamikaze Pass."

12. Robert Hart, "Hollywood's African Safari," *Daily World*, May 8, 1985.

13. Hanna Lassinger's discussion of *Gandhi*, *Guardian*, February 2, 1983.

14. Jennifer Stone, *Mind Over Media* (Berkeley, Calif.: Cayuse Press, 1988), p. 104. Italics in the original.

15. Pat Aufderheide, "Mr. Machismo and the Boys," *In These Times*, June 30–July 13, 1982, p. 21.

16. Peter Biskind, *Seeing Is Believing* (New York: Pantheon, 1983), p. 83n; also Nora Sayre, *Running Time: Films of the Cold War* (New York: Dial Press, 1982), pp. 184–85.

17. MacDonald, *Television and the Red Menace*, pp. 117–18.

18. Franz Miller, "Violence as Entertainment," *Democratic Journalist* (Prague), July/August 1988, p. 22.
19. William Claiborne, "Hollywood's Mideast Policy," *Washington Post*, July 14, 1986.
20. Ibid.
21. *New York Times*, February 23, 1986.
22. Biskind, *Seeing Is Believing*, pp. 107–108. On the link between Cold-War anti-communism and science-fiction films see Eric Smoodin, "Watching the Skies: Hollywood, the 1950s, and the Soviet Threat," *Journal of American Culture*, summer 1988, pp. 35–39.
23. Ibid., p. 129.
24. Sayre, *Running Time*, p. 201; also Biskind, *Seeing Is Believing*, pp. 137–144.
25. MacDonald, *Television and the Red Menace*, p. 125.
26. Ibid.
27. Ibid.
28. Hal Himmelstein, *Television Myth and the American Mind* (New York: Praeger, 1984), p. 177.
29. Elayne Rapping, in the *Guardian*, October 7, 1981.

Chapter 3   The Media Fight the Red Menace

1. Terry Christensen, *Reel Politics* (New York: Basil Blackwell, 1987), p. 22; also the examples in Kevin Brownlow, *Behind the Mask of Innocence* (New York: Knopf, 1990).
2. Christensen, *Reel Politics*, p. 67.
3. Ibid., p. 88; also Richard Maltby, "Made for Each Other: The Melodrama of Hollywood and the House Committee on Un-American Activities, 1947," in Philip Davies and Brian Neve, (eds.), *Cinema, Politics and Society in America* (New York: St. Martin's Press, 1981), pp. 76–96.
4. Nora Sayre, *Running Time: Films of the Cold War* (New York: Dial Press, 1978), p. 79.
5. Ibid., p. 80.
6. Ibid., p. 81 and pp. 82–99; J. Fred MacDonald, *Television and the Red Menace* (New York: Praeger, 1985), pp. 103–111.
7. MacDonald, *Television and the Red Menace*, p. 119.
8. Ibid., p. 107.
9. Sayre, *Running Time*, p. 207.
10. MacDonald, *Television and the Red Menace*, p. 127. For an analysis of how television is used by the televangelists, see Hal Himmelstein, *Television Myth and the American Mind* (New York: Praeger, 1984), pp. 253–277.
11. *Wall Street Journal*, June 3, 1980; *Washington Post*, January 27–30, 1981.
12. Prairie Miller, review of *Rocky IV, Daily World*, December 26, 1985.
13. For a fuller discussion and documentation of this see Michael Parenti, *The Sword and the Dollar: Imperialism, Revolution, and the Arms Race* (New York: St. Martin's Press, 1989).
14. Christensen, *Reel Politics*, p. 203.

15. Dave Kindred in *Washington Post*, January 31, 1983.
16. For a treatment of U.S. militarism in the Third World see Parenti, *The Sword and the Dollar: Imperialism, Revolution, and the Arms Race.*

Chapter 4   Make-believe History

1. William Blum, *The CIA, A Forgotten History* (London: Zed Books, 1986), p. 11.
2. Nina Leibman, "Mini-Series/Maxi-Messages: Ideology and the Interaction Between 'Peter the Great,' Aetna, AT&T and Ford," *Journal of Film and Video,* 39, Spring 1987, pp. 5–18.
3. Terry Christensen, *Reel Politics* (Basil Blackwell: New York, 1987), pp. 18–19.
4. Norman Markowitz, "Reviving Conservative Notions of the Civil War," *Daily World,* December 10, 1985.
5. Anne Rizzo quoting Herman Wouk's *The Winds of War* in her "Historical Facts Corrupted for Your Viewing Pleasure," *Daily World,* February 25, 1983.
6. Anne Rizzo, "More About Winds of War," *Daily World,* February 26, 1983.
7. Benjamin Ferencz, *Less Than Slaves* (Cambridge, Mass.: Harvard University Press, 1979); and Roman Rosdolsky, "A Memoir of Auschwitz and Birkenau," *Monthly Review,* January 1988, pp. 33–38.
8. Norman Markowitz, "Springtime for Benito," *Daily World,* December 13, 1985.

Chapter 5   Blue-Collar Blues

1. See the comments by Studs Terkel and historians Philip Foner and Herbert Gutman in the *New York Times,* September 8, 1981.
2. On the history of workers' struggles, see Richard Boyer and Herbert Morais, *Labor's Untold Story* (New York: United Electrical, Radio and Machine Workers, 1972); and Philip Foner, *History of the Labor Movement in the United States* (New York: International Publishers, various volumes, 1947, 1955, 1964, 1965, 1980, 1981).
3. "Television Entertainment Report Part II: Conclusions and National Summary of Occupational Frequency in Network Primetime Entertainment for February 1980," International Association of Machinists and Aerospace Workers, June 12, 1980; also Mil Lieberthal, "TV Images of Workers—Reinforcing the Stereotypes," *Labor Studies Journal,* 1, Fall 1976.
4. Ralph Arthur Johnson, "World Without Workers: Prime Time's Presentation of Labor," *Labor Studies Journal,* 5, winter 1981, p. 203. The same conclusion is drawn in the IAM study. See also Nick Trujillo and Leah Ekdom, "A 40-year Portrait of the Portrayal of Industry on Prime-Time Television," *Journalism Quarterly,* 64 summer/autumn 1987, p. 374; and G. Gerbner, L. Gross, M. Morgan, and N. Signorielli, "Charting the Mainstream: Television's Contribution to Political Orientations," in Donald Lazere (ed.), *American Media and Mass Culture* (Berkeley: University of California Press, 1987), p. 444.

5. Johnson, "World Without Workers"; and Gerbner et al., "Charting the Mainstream."

6. "Television Entertainment Report" (IAM study).

7. Hal Himmelstein, *Television Myth and the American Mind* (New York: Praeger, 1984), p. 123.

8. Todd Gitlin, *Inside Primetime* (New York: Pantheon, 1983), p. 213. For a study supporting this point, see Neil Vidmar and Milton Rokeach, "Archie Bunker's Bigotry: A Study in Selective Perception and Exposure," *Journal of Communication*, 24, winter 1974, pp. 36–47.

9. The *Focus* editorial is quoted in *Time*, April 24, 1972, p. 86.

10. "Television Entertainment Report" (IAM study).

11. Gina Marchetti, "Class, Ideology and Commercial Television: An Analysis of 'The A-Team'," *Journal of Film and Video*, 39, spring 1987, pp. 19–28.

12. See the excellent review by Lydia Sargent, *Z Magazine*, April 1990, pp. 43–45.

13. Ibid.

14. Eric Smoodin, "Watching the Skies: Hollywood, the 1950s and the Soviet Threat," *Journal of American Culture*, Summer 1988, p. 39.

15. Philip Davies and Brian Neve (eds.), *Cinema, Politics and Society in America* (New York: St. Martin's Press, 1981), pp. 102–103.

16. Prairie Miller, "Images of Workers in U.S. Films," *Political Affairs*, May 1988, p. 36.

17. Richard Freeman and James Medoff, *What Do Unions Do?* (New York: Basic Books, 1984).

18. On news media treatment of labor unions, see Michael Parenti, *Inventing Reality: The Politics of the Mass Media* (New York: St. Martin's Press, 1986), pp. 79–87.

19. Leonard Quart and Albert Auster, "The Working Class Goes to Hollywood," in Davies and Neve (eds.), *Cinema, Politics and Society in America*, pp. 169–170.

20. Miller, "Images of Workers" p. 36.

21. " 'Skag': TV's Steel Soap a Factual Wipe-Out," *Steel Labor*, February 1980, p. 7.

22. Dan Cohen, "Workers Slandered—When They Appear at All," *Guardian*, August 31, 1988.

23. Terry Christensen, *Reel Politics* (New York: Basil Blackwell, 1987), p. 52.

24. Christensen, *Reel Politics*, pp. 94–95; Nora Sayre, *Running Time: Films of the Cold War* (New York: Dial Press, 1978), pp. 173–175; *New York Times*, April 10, 1986. *Salt of the Earth* is available on videocassette from Voyager company in West Los Angeles.

Chapter 6   Affluent Class and Corporate Brass

1. P. H. Melling, "The Mind of the Mob: Hollywood and Popular Culture in the 1930s," in Philip Davies and Brian Neve (eds.), *Cinema, Politics and Society in America* (New York: St. Martin's Press, 1981), p. 24.

2. Leonard Quart, "Frank Capra and the Popular Front," in Donald Lazere (ed.)

American Media and Mass Culture (Berkeley: University of California Press, 1987), pp. 178–79.

3. Charles Eckert, "Shirley Temple and the House of Rockefeller," in Lazere, *American Media*, p. 172 and p. 177.

4. Ralph Willett, "The Nation in Crisis: Hollywood's Response to the 1940s," in Davies and Neve (eds.), *Cinema, Politics and Society*, pp. 72–73.

5. Bradley Greenberg, et al., "The Soaps: What's On and Who Cares?" *Journal of Broadcasting*, 26, spring 1982, pp. 519–35.

6. Michael Intintoli, *Taking Soaps Seriously* (New York: Praeger, 1986).

7. Rose Rubin Rivera, "The World of Afternoon Soap Operas," *World Magazine*, February 17, 1983, pp. 12–13.

8. Adapted from Nancy Reichardt's weekly "Soap" synopsis, *Washington Post*, May 28, 1989.

9. Fred Blair, "Soap Watchers Beware," *Daily World*, October 8, 1983.

10. Elayne Rapping, "Soap Operas Lead the Way as Pop Culture Tackles AIDS," *Guardian*, April 6, 1988, p. 17.

11. Elayne Rapping, "Looking Inside Soap Operas' Bubbles," *Guardian*, August 22, 1984, p. 21.

12. Elayne Rapping, " 'Dallas': Capitalism's Heroes," *Guardian*, February 11, 1981.

13. Paul Wilcox, "Three Jeers for the Ruling Class," *Workers World*, February 6, 1981.

14. Les Brown, *Television, The Business behind the Box* (New York: Harcourt, Brace, Jovanovich, 1971), p. 309.

15. Ford is mentioned once in a neutral context.

16. Gerbner's report is referred to in Todd Gitlin, *Inside Prime Time* (New York: Pantheon, 1983), p. 268.

17. Terry Christensen, *Reel Politics* (New York: Basil Blackwell, 1987), p. 58.

18. Gitlin, *Inside Prime Time*, p. 59.

Chapter 7   Superdocs and Shoot-'em-ups

1. Tania Modleski, "The Search for Tomorrow in Today's Soap Operas," in Donald Lazere (ed.), *American Media and Mass Culture* (Berkeley: University of California Press, 1987), p. 273.

2. Robert Alley, "Media Medicine and Morality," in Richard Adler, (ed.), *Television as a Cultural Force* (New York: Praeger, 1976), p. 100; Hal Himmelstein, *Television Myth and the American Mind* (New York: Praeger, 1984), p. 180; Michael Real, *Mass Mediated Culture* (Englewood Cliffs, N.J.: Prentice-Hall, 1977), p. 241.

3. George Gerbner and Larry Gross, "Living with Television: The Violence Profile," *Journal of Communications*, 26, spring 1976, p. 178.

4. Himmelstein, *Television Myth and the American Mind*, p. 172.

5. Ibid., p. 59.

6. Harvey Rosenfield, "Fraudulent Billing Costs," *Public Citizen*, February 1986, pp. 19–20; Marcia Millman, *The Unkindest Cut: Life in the Backrooms of Medicine* (New York: Murrow, 1976).

7. Robert Alford, *Health Care Politics* (Chicago: University of Chicago Press, 1975); Stanley Wohl, M.D., *The Medical-Industrial Complex* (New York: Harmony Books, 1984).

8. J. R. Dominick, "Children's Viewing of Crime Shows and Attitudes on Law Enforcement," *Journalism Quarterly*, 51, 1974, pp. 5–12; Gerbner and Gross, "Living with Television" pp. 172–200. For other statistics on the prevalence of television crime and violence, see Chapter Ten, "Child Abuse."

9. Stephen Arons and Ethan Katsh, "How TV Cops Flout the Law," *Saturday Review*, March 19, 1977, pp. 11–18.

10. Dominick, "Children's Viewing of Crime Shows."

11. Arons and Katsh, "How TV Cops Flout the Law."

12. Robert Reiner, "Keystone to Kojak: the Hollywood Cop," in Philip Davies and Brian Neve (eds.), *Cinema, Politics and Society in America* (New York: St. Martin's Press, 1981), p. 212.

13. Ibid.

14. Ibid., p. 202.

15. " 'Kojak' Attacks El Comite on CBS," *New American Movement*, February 1975.

16. George Gerbner and Larry Gross as reported in *Psychology Today*, April 1976; Gerbner and Gross, "Living with Television"; Linda Heath and John Petraitis, "Television Viewing and Fear of Crime," *Basic and Applied Social Psychology*, 8, 1987, pp. 97–123.

17. Richard Saltus, "The Research Shows Cop Shows Make Us Violent," *Leisure*, February 21, 1976, p. 22; Heath and Petraitis, "Television Viewing and Fear"; Judith Stoll, "TV's Message Creates Fear to Bolster Cop Repression vs. Poor," *Workers World*, April 8, 1977.

18. Elayne Rapping in the *Guardian*, October 21, 1981.

19. Les Brown, *Television, The Business behind the Box*, (New York: Harcourt, Brace, Jovanovich, 1971), pp. 307–308.

20. Elayne Rapping, "Balm for Liberal 'Walking Wounded,' " *Guardian*, November 25, 1981.

21. Paul Buhle, "Dragnet to Miami Vice," *Guardian*, May 18, 1988; also *City Paper* (Washington, D.C.), September 29, 1989.

22. For one of many examples of grossly deficient police work in detecting a serial killer, see Tim Cahill, *Buried Dreams* (New York: Bantam, 1988), pp. 176–184. For the sloppy work done on a multiple murder, see Loretta Schwartz-Nobel, *Engaged to Murder* (New York: Jove Books, 1987), pp. 27–28.

23. Frank Donner, "The Theory and Practice of American Political Intelligence," *New York Review of Books*, April 22, 1971, p. 28*fn*. Police "Red squad" surveillance enjoyed a revival in the 1980s under the encouragement of the Reagan administration. On the racial, gender, class, and antilabor bias of law and law enforcers, see Michael Parenti, *Democracy for the Few*, 5th edition (New York: St. Martin's Press, 1987), Chapter Eight.

24. Robert Elias, *The Politics of Victimization* (New York: Oxford University Press, 1985). For instances of how the police entrapped Blacks who tried to organize community resistance to the narcotics trade, see the cases of Martin Sostre, *New York Times*, December 25, 1975; Frank Shuford, *Guardian*, September 24, 1975; also the arrests on trumped-up charges of three members of the Black

Men's Movement Against Crack in New York, *Guardian,* August 3, 1988. See this same issue of the *Guardian* for a report on police repression of two Native Americans who opposed police-backed drug dealings.

25. Elias, *The Politics of Victimization;* also Mark Green and John Berry, "White Collar Crime as Big Business," *Nation,* June 8, 1985, pp. 704–707; Marshall Clinard and Peter Yeager, *Corporate Crime* (New York: Free Press, 1986).

Chapter 8   Black Images in White Media

1. "SAG Documents Use of Women and Minorities in Prime-Time Television," Screen Actors Guild news release, October 31, 1974, cited in *Window Dressing on the Set,* A Report of the United States Commission on Civil Rights, August 1977, p. 2.
2. Isabel Wilkerson, "Blacks in Films," *Washington Post,* August 15, 1982.
3. Charles Trueheart, "In Hollywood, the Question of Racism," *Washington Post,* February 14, 1989; Jacqueline Trescott, "Minority Coverage Faulted," *Washington Post,* April 12, 1985; Nick Kotz, "The Minority Struggle for a Place in the Newsroom," *Columbia Journalism Review,* March/April 1979, pp. 23–31.
4. Joseph Boskin, *Sambo: The Rise and Demise of an American Jester* (New York: Oxford University Press, 1986), pp. 149–158.
5. C. Reddick's study in *Journal of Negro Education,* Summer 1944, cited in Royal Colle, "Negro Images in the Mass Media," *Journalism Quarterly,* 45, spring 1968, p. 56. Reddick finds 75 percent of the films were "anti-Negro," 13 percent neutral and 12 percent "pro-Negro." For a full-length study, see Donald Bogle, *Toms, Coons, Mulattoes, Mammies and Bucks: An Interpretive History of Blacks in American Films* (New York: Crossroad Continuum, 1973, 1988).
6. Thomas Cripps, "Black Stereotypes on Film," in Randall Miller (ed.), *Ethnic Images in American Film and Television* (Philadelphia: The Balch Institute, 1978), p. 7.
7. Colle, "Negro Images in the Mass Media," pp. 56–57.
8. Erik Barnouw, *The Golden Web: A History of Broadcasting in the United States 1933–1953,* vol. 2 (New York: Oxford University Press, 1970), p. 297. See the critique by the NAACP quoted in George Simpson and J. Milton Yinger, *Racial and Cultural Minorities,* rev. ed. (New York: Harper and Bros., 1958), p. 716.
9. Bob Ray Sanders, "25 Years of Amos 'n Andy," *New American Movement,* February 1975, p. 9. For a full-length study, see J. Fred MacDonald, *Black and White on TV: Afro-Americans in Television Since 1948* (Chicago, Nelson-Hall, 1983).
10. Ellen Holly, "The Role of Media in the Programming of an Underclass," *Black Scholar,* 10, January/February 1979, p. 31.
11. Ibid.
12. Mary Ellison, "Blacks in American Film," in Philip Davies and Brian Neve (eds.), *Cinema, Politics and Society in America* (New York: St. Martin's Press, 1981), p. 181.
13. Cripps, "Black Stereotypes on Film," p. 8.
14. Loyle Hairston, "The Black Film—'Supernigger' as Folk Hero," *Freedomway*

(third quarter, 1974), p. 218; Francis Ward, "Black Male Images in Films," ibid., pp. 225–226.

15. Hairston, "The Black Film," p. 220.
16. Ward, "Black Male Images," p. 226.
17. One survey in Chicago found that Black-oriented films accounted for about 40 percent of the box-office grosses in the Loop, although they represented only about 27 percent of the films shown. *Chicago Sun-Times*, January 8, 1975.
18. Donald Bogle quoted in Joel Dreyfuss, "Blacks and Television," *Washington Post*, September 1, 1974.
19. NFBO statement quoted in *Window Dressing on the Set*, pp. 21–22.
20. Dreyfuss, "Blacks and Television"; Eugenia Collier, " 'Black' Shows for White Viewers," *Freedomway* (third quarter 1974), pp. 212–213; also Ellen Holly, "The Role of Media," p. 33.
21. Cecil Brown, "Blues for Blacks in Hollywood," *Mother Jones*, January 1981, p. 23.
22. Ronald Tyson, "Worthless Film Provokes Worthwhile Observation," *Daily World*, October 23, 1982.
23. Interview with Pele de Lappe in *Daily World*, June 24, 1982.
24. Christopher Swan, *Christian Science Monitor*, January 8, 1985.
25. Nier is quoted in *Denver Post*, January 16, 1989.
26. Dorothy Zellner, letter to the *New York Times*, January 13, 1989.
27. In an interview after his film appeared, Lee readily noted that he knew nothing about literature, poetry, film history, or politics; he had no idea who C. L. R. James was (the noted Black historian who had just died); nor did he seem to care. Lee is, however, an admirer of Louis Farrakhan, the Black Muslim separatist. His message is about as unidimensional as Farrakhan's. See Herb Boyd, "Does Lee 'Do Right Thing?' " *Guardian*, July 5, 1989.

Chapter 9   Luigi, Tony, and the Family

1. For an earlier, shorter version of this treatment of Italian Americans see Michael Parenti, "The Media Are the Mafia," *Monthly Review*, March 1979, pp. 20–26.
2. Peter Biskind and Barbara Ehrenreich, "Machismo and Hollywood's Working Class," in Donald Lazere (ed.), *American Media and Mass Culture* (Berkeley: University of California Press, 1987), pp. 208–209.
3. Ibid.
4. Eric Dittus, "A Review of 'Year of the Dragon,' " *Hawaii Herald*, September 20, 1985, pp. 1–2.
5. Marco Ciolli, "Exploring the Italian Image," *Attenzione*, September 1979, p. 16.
6. Ibid.
7. Frank Rotondaro, quoted in ibid.
8. Ibid.
9. Joseph Papaleo, "Ethnic Pictures and Ethnic Fate," in Randall Miller (ed.), *Ethnic Images in American Film and Television* (Philadelphia: Balch Institute, 1978), p. 94.

10. Richard Juliani, "The Image of the Italian in American Film and Television," in Miller, *Ethnic Images*, p. 102.

11. Television critic Richard Shepard in the *New York Times*, January 18, 1986.

Chapter 10   Child Abuse

1. *Washington Post*, December 15, 1986; Harvard Medical School Newsletter, December 1988, for the statistics in that paragraph.

2. Study of 380 Denver children by psychologist Phyllis Katz, reported in *USA Today*, January 25, 1983.

3. David Pearl, *Television and Behavior: Ten Years of Scientific Progress and Implications for the 1980s* (Washington, D.C.: National Institute of Mental Health, 1982); *Television and Growing Up: The Impact of Televised Violence*, Report to the Surgeon General, U.S. Public Health Service (Washington, D.C.: Government Printing Office, 1972).

4. Natalie Rothstein, "The Third Grade Has Been Brought to You by . . . " *react*, fall/winter 1980, p. 15.

5. Robert Liebert and Neala Schwartzberg, "Effects of Mass Media," *Annual Review of Psychology*, 28, 1977, p. 149.

6. F. B. Steuer et al., "Televised Aggression and the Interpersonal Aggression of Preschool Children," *Journal of Experimental Child Psychology*, 11, 1971, pp. 442–447.; M.A. Hanratty, et al., "Imitation of Film-Mediated Aggression Against Live and Inanimate Victims," cited in Liebert and Schwartzberg, op. cit.; G. A. Comstock and E. A. Rubinstein, (eds.), *Television and Social Behavior*, vol. 1 (Washington, D.C.: Government Printing Office, 1972).

7. *Washington Post*, August 23, 1982.

8. *Washington Post*, February 5, 1982; also the related Supreme Court decision, *NBC vs. Niemi* (1978), which dismissed the case brought by the victim against the network.

9. Tim Patterson, "The Deadly Impact of TV on Kids," *Guardian*, March 23, 1977, and the study by the Foundation for Child Development cited therein; also "TV's 'Disastrous' Impact on Children," *US News and World Report*, January 19, 1981, pp. 43–45, and the California Department of Education study cited therein.

10. Kim Hays, "Washington Welches on Children," *react*, spring/summer 1982, p. 9; Judy Mann, "Kangaroocide," *Washington Post*, March 18, 1983.

11. Robert Liebert quoted in Patterson, "The Deadly Impact."

12. F. Earle Barcus, *Images of Life on Children's Television: Sex Roles, Minorities and Families* (New York: Praeger, 1983).

13. Ibid.; Joyce Sprafkin and Robert Liebert, "Sex-Typing and Children's Television Preferences," in Gaye Tuchman et al., *Hearth and Home* (New York: Oxford University Press, 1978), pp. 228–239.

14. Rose Rubin Rivera, "TV and Kids," *World Magazine*, April 5, 1984, p. 14.

15. Sally Steeland, *Growing Up in Prime Time* (Washington, D.C.: National Commission on Working Women, 1988).

16. Petra Hesse and Ted Stimpson, "Images of the Enemy on Children's Television," *Propaganda Review*, summer 1989, pp. 22–25.
17. Ibid., p. 25.
18. Rothstein, "The Third Grade Has Been Brought to You by . . . "; estimates by Neil Postman, New York University professor of communication arts in *U.S. News and World Report*, January 19, 1981, p. 44.
19. F. Earle Barcus, *Saturday Children's Television* (Newtonville, Mass.: Action for Children's Television, 1971).
20. Quoted in Jim Jordan, "TV Ads Exploit Children," *Guardian*, October 1, 1980.
21. Ibid.
22. See *Guardian*, October 19, 1977.
23. Rothstein, "The Third Grade Has Been Brought to You by . . . "
24. Ibid.
25. Quoted in *Dollars and Sense*, September 1979, p. 11.
26. *People's Daily World*, December 24, 1987.
27. Peter Bayer, "Toy-Based TV: Effects on Children Debated," *New York Times*, February 3, 1986.
28. Elayne Rapping, "'Tis the Season to Warp the Children," *Guardian*, December 8, 1982.
29. Tim Patterson, "Profit Picture Bright for Kids' TV," *Guardian*, March 30, 1977.

Chapter 11 Preemption, Profits, and Censors

1. Quoted in *World Magazine*, June 16, 1988.
2. Les Brown, *Television: The Business behind the Box* (New York: Harcourt, Brace, Jovanovich, 1971), p. 296.
3. Richard Cohen, "Hollywood's Civil Wrongs," *Washington Post Magazine*, January 8, 1989. *Mississippi Burning* is discussed in more detail in Chapter Eight.
4. Neal Postman, *Amusing Ourselves to Death* (New York: Penguin Books, 1986), pp. 34–41.
5. Ibid., pp. 97 and 106; also Postman's comments on the Lincoln-Douglas debates, pp. 44–47.
6. Richard Morin, "Wapner v. Rehnquist: No Contest," *Washington Post*, June 23, 1989.
7. See the discussion in Postman, *Amusing Ourselves to Death*, p. vii.
8. Richard Maltby, "The Political Economy of Hollywood," in Philip Davies and Brian Neve (eds.), *Cinema, Politics and Society in America* (New York: St. Martin's Press, 1981), pp. 43 and 47; Tina Balio, "A Mature Oligopoly," in Tina Balio (ed.), *The American Film Industry* (University of Wisconsin Press: Madison, 1976), p. 213.
9. Philip Davies, "A Growing Independence," in Davies and Neve (eds.), *Cinema, Politics*, pp. 122–123.
10. Terry Christensen, *Reel Politics* (New York: Basil Blackwell, 1987), p. 157.
11. Philip Davies, "A Growing Independence," in Davies and Neve (eds.), *Cinema, Politics*, p. 132.

12. Dan Moldea, *Dark Victory: Ronald Reagan, MCA, and the Mob* (New York: Penguin, 1986), pp. 310–311.

13. Danny Schechter, "Will It Play in Peoria?" *Z Magazine*, April 1988, p. 27; Jack Valenti, "Network Monopoly" (Hollywood, Calif.: Motion Picture Association of America, March 1989).

14. Todd Gitlin, *Inside Prime Time* (New York: Pantheon, 1983), pp. 327–328.

15. Walter Powell, "The Blockbuster Decades: The Media as Big Business," in Donald Lazere (ed.), *American Media and Mass Culture* (Berkeley: University of California Press, 1987), p. 53*fn*.

16. Joseph Farah, "The Real Blacklist," *National Review*, October 27, 1989, p. 43.

17. See Chapter Three; also Leonard Quart, "Frank Capra and the Popular Front," in Lazere (ed.), *American Media*, p. 181.

18. Christensen, *Reel Politics*, pp. 36–37.

19. Quoted in *Alternative Media*, spring 1981, p. 21; Murray Schumach, *The Face on the Cutting Room Floor* (New York: Da Capo, 1964); Erik Barnouw, *The Sponsor* (New York: Oxford University Press, 1979).

20. J. Fred MacDonald, *Television and the Red Menace* (New York: Praeger, 1985), p. 132.

21. Quoted in Erik Barnouw, *The Sponsor* (New York: Oxford University Press, 1978).

22. David Rintels quoted in Todd Gitlin, "Television's Screens; Hegemony in Transition," in Lazere (ed.), *American Media*, p. 250.

23. Gitlin, *Inside Prime Time*, p. 206.

24. Perle de Lappe, review of *Sister, Sister, Daily World*, June 24, 1982.

25. *Newsweek*, February 26, 1990.

26. Jack Colhoun, "P&G Yanks Ads" *Guardian*, May 30, 1990; Zachery Schiller and Mark Landler's commentary in *Business Week*, June 4, 1990.

27. Jeffrey Schrank, *Snap, Crackle, and Popular Taste* (New York: Delta, 1977), p. 36.

28. B. H. Lawrence, "Advertisers' 'Hit Lists' of Network Shows Grow Longer," *Washington Post*, June 22, 1989.

29. For the best book on this subject see R. W. Johnson, *Shootdown: Flight 007 and the American Connection* (New York: Viking Penguin, 1986).

30. Stephen Farber, "Why Sparks Flew in Retelling the Tale of Flight 007," *New York Times*, November 27, 1988.

31. Ibid.; italics added.

32. Elayne Rapping, "Prime Time for Prochoice Film," *Guardian*, May 17, 1989.

33. See Thomas Collins in *New York Newsday*, July 8, 1990; and Les Brown in *New York Times*, February 13, 1980.

34. Committee for Cultural Studies, CUNY, "PBS and the American Worker," unpublished study, June 1990.

35. Guild President David Rintels, quoted in Claus Mueller, "Class as the Determinant of Political Communication," in Lazere (ed.), *American Media*, p. 437.

36. Gitlin, *Inside Prime Time*, p. 10.

37. Muriel Cantor, *The Hollywood TV Producer* (New York: Basic Books, 1971).

38. Hal Himmelstein, *Television Myth and the American Mind* (New York: Praeger, 1984), p. 31.

39. Gitlin, *Inside Prime Time*, p. 31; Alice Sunshine, "AFTRA Convention Renews

Commitment to Oppose Entertainment Industry Blacklist," *People's Daily World,* August 25, 1989.
40. Christensen, *Reel Politics,* p. 75.
41. *New York Times,* March 5, 1986.
42. *Washington Post,* November 20, 1989.
43. *City Paper* (Washington, D.C.), November 25, 1988.

Chapter 12   The Myth of Cultural Democracy

1. See the discussion of *Salt of the Earth* in Chapter Four.
2. Prairie Miller, review of *Salvador* in *Daily World,* March 18, 1986.
3. John Stevenson and Jeremy Turner (eds.), *The Shattering Screen,* no. 1, 1984 (Chicago).
4. Todd Gitlin, *Inside Prime Time* (New York: Pantheon, 1985), pp. 221–223.
5. Muriel Cantor, "Producing Television for Children," in Gaye Tuchman (ed.), *The TV Establishment* (Englewood Cliffs, N.J.: Prentice-Hall, 1974), p. 116.
6. Les Brown, *Television: The Business behind the Box* (New York: Harcourt, Brace, Jovanovich, 1971), p. 64.
7. Ibid., pp. 59–60.
8. *Variety*'s report of the NAB survey is summarized in Hal Himmelstein, *Television Myth and the American Mind* (New York: Praeger, 1984), p. 316.
9. Jeffrey Schrank, *Snap, Crackle, and Popular Taste* (New York: Dell, 1977), p. 38. The quotation is Schrank's, not from the Roper poll he cites.
10. Douglas Davis, "Zapping the Myth of TV's Power," *New York Times,* May 20, 1988.
11. As reported in *U.S. News & World Report,* May 31, 1985, pp. 67–68.
12. John Pilger, *Heroes* (London: Pam Books, 1986), p. 506.
13. Todd Gitlin, "Television's Screens: Hegemony in Transition," in Donald Lazere (ed.), *American Media and Mass Culture* (Berkeley: University of California Press, 1987), p. 259.
14. Terry Christensen, *Reel Politics* (New York: Basil Blackwell, 1987), p. 2.
15. Ibid., p. 125.
16. Karl Marx, *A Contribution to the Critique of Political Economy.*
17. Antonio Gramsci, *Selections from the Prison Notebooks* (New York: International Publishers, 1971).
18. Gitlin, "Television Screens," p. 242.
19. Pat Aufderheide, "The Banality of Banality," *Village Voice,* October 25, 1983, p. 51.
20. Schrank, *Snap, Crackle,* pp. 11–13.
21. Elayne Rapping, " 'Concept,' 'Topspin,' 'Traction,' and Trash," *Guardian,* October 12, 1983, p. 20.
22. For political bias and censorship in the news media, see Michael Parenti, *Inventing Reality* (New York: St. Martin's Press, 1988).
23. On the addictive nature of television, see Marie Winn, *The Plug-In Drug* (New York: Viking Press, 1977).

Suggested Readings

Here are some works on subjects that have been treated insufficiently or not at all in this book.

On women and sexism, one might look at Gaye Tuchman et al. (eds.), *Hearth and Home: Images of Women in the Mass Media* (New York: Oxford University Press, 1978); Helen Baehr and Gillian Dyer, *Boxed In: Women and Television* (New York: Pantheon, 1987); and the writings of Tanya Modleski, Judith Williamson, and Lillian Robinson.

For a collection of essays on some of our larger ethnic groups, see Randall Miller (ed.), *Ethnic Images in American Film and Television* (Philadelphia: Balch Institute, 1978). On Latinos, see Allen Woll, *The Latin Image in American Film* (Los Angeles: University of California Press, 1977). See also, Arthur Pettit, *Images of the Mexican-American in Fiction and Film* (College Station: Texas A&M University Press, 1980).

One of the most media-mauled groups is the Arabs. See Jack Shaheen, *The TV Arab* (Bowling Green, Ohio: Bowling Green State University Popular Press, 1984) and Lawrence Michalak, "The Arab Image in American Film and TV," special supplement to *Cineaste,* vol. 17, no. 1.

Volumes could be written on how Asians have been mistreated by the media, but, as far as I know, volumes have not been written. I hope someone will inform me that I am wrong. I included nothing in this book on how elderly people are mercilessly stereotyped in the media. I have not researched the subject nor, I suspect, have many other people.

There are some worthwhile studies on how gays and lesbians have been represented: Vito Russo, *The Celluloid Closet, Homosexuality in the Movies,* rev. ed. (New York: Harper & Row, 1987); and Richard Dyer (ed.), *Gays and Films,* rev. ed. (New York: Zoetrope, 1984).

Except for my treatment of soap operas, I offered little on the wasteland of daytime and game-show television. The fine critic Elayne Rapping has done that job in her book, *The Looking Glass World of Non-Fiction Television* (Boston: South End Press, 1987). For other aspects of cultural hegemony beyond just the electronic media, one should consider the dean of media critics, Herbert Schiller, specifically his *Culture, Inc.* (New York: Oxford University Press, 1989).

One can read further on the subjects treated herein by looking at the many worthwhile citations in previous chapters, especially earlier books by Schiller and the writings of critics like Terry Christensen, Hal

Himmelstein, Elayne Rapping, Todd Gitlin, Jeffrey Schrank, Jerry Mander, Nora Sayre, J. Fred MacDonald, George Gerbner, Erik Barnouw, Marie Winn, Prairie Miller, and others.

The reader might wish to view the movies that were given favorable mention in this book, ones that depict labor struggles and other such dissident issues. As already noted, most of them have suffered from very limited and brief distribution. They are what Prairie Miller calls the "disappeared" movies, difficult or impossible to find even when one is looking hard for them. Many are available as videocassettes, including *Matewan, The Molly Maguires, A World Apart, The Killing Floor, Salt of the Earth, Salvador, Latino, Under Fire, Rude Awakening, The Milagro Beanfield War, Reds, Burn!, Eight Men Out,* and *Missing.* But you may have to look hard for the video store that carries them or is willing to order them. It is like trying to find bookstores that carry dissident books.

Acknowledgments (continued from p. iv)

Excerpt from *Heroes* by John Pilger. © 1986 John Pilger. Reprinted by permission of Pan Books/Cape.

Excerpt from "In Prime Time, Everybody's Rich," by Benjamin J. Stein, from *The Washington Post*, October 17, 1984. © 1984 by The Washington Post. Reprinted by permission.

Excerpt from "The Goldbergs—Stereotypes Loved by Americans," by Francine Klagsbrun, from *The New York Times*, August 8, 1988. © 1988 by The New York Times Company. Reprinted by permission.

PHOTO CREDITS

Page 24, Catherine Millinaire/Sygma
Page 63, Culver Photos
Page 72, Bettmann Archives
Page 101, Photofest
Page 122, Photofest
Page 133, Culver Photos
Page 134, Museum of Modern Art/Film Stills Archive
Page 169, Photofest
Page 180, Photofest
Page 188, Photofest
Page 205, Photofest

Index